BRITISH LITERATURE UNLOCKED

Vol III: The Age of Milton, Restoration, and The Augustan Age.

A Complete Guide for UGC NET

ANKIT SHARMA

TO THE POINT NOTES BASED ON PREVIOUS YEARS QUESTION PAPERS

Table of Contents

Foreword

The journey through British Literature is one marked by profound ideas, artistic transformations, and socio-political upheavals, all of which have shaped the literary canon as we know it. In "British Literature Unlocked: A Complete Guide for UGC NET," this literary heritage is meticulously unpacked, volume by volume, to serve as an essential resource for UGC NET English aspirants. Spanning six volumes, this series guides readers from the ancient foundations of the Greco-Roman period all the way to the nuanced expressions of the Modern and Postmodern ages. With each era, readers will find to-the-point notes, questions from the last decade of UGC NET exams, mnemonic codes, and strategic insights designed to simplify and streamline the study process, making preparation not only thorough but also deeply engaging.

Volume by Volume Breakdown

Volume I: Greco-Roman to Chaucer

Dive into the roots of Western literary thought, tracing the influences of classical antiquity up through the Middle Ages and Chaucer's groundbreaking contributions. This volume introduces foundational concepts and sets the stage for the evolution of British literature.

Volume II: Elizabethan to Jacobean

Enter the vibrant Renaissance period, where the works of Shakespeare, Marlowe, and their contemporaries reflect the artistic flourishing and complex socio-political shifts of the time. Each page delves into the drama, poetry, and prose that defined these eras.

Volume III: The Age of Milton, Restoration, and The Augustan Age.

Explore an age marked by poetic grandeur, the restoration of the monarchy, and the Augustan pursuit of clarity and wit. This volume captures the transformations in language, form, and ideology as literature moved into a reflective phase of transition.

Volume IV: The Age of Transition and The Age of Romanticism

Witness the emotional and imaginative power of the Romantic movement, a response to the rigid rationality of the previous era. This volume celebrates the Romantic poets and novelists who embraced nature, individualism, and emotion in revolutionary ways.

Volume V: The Victorian Age

This volume covers the prolific Victorian era, an age of dramatic change and conflict that grappled with industrialization, social reform, and expanding empire. Here, readers can explore the complex morality, realism, and unique characters of Victorian prose and poetry.

Volume VI: Modern and Postmodern Literature

The journey concludes with an in-depth look at Modern and Postmodern literature, where literary form, narrative structure, and thematic depth are pushed to their limits. From the experimental techniques of Modernism to the playful and questioning nature of Postmodernism, this volume brings British literature into the contemporary era.

Why This Book is Essential?

Designed for aspiring NET scholars, "British Literature Unlocked" offers a unique blend of academic precision and strategic insight. With mnemonics that transform complex historical timelines and literary movements into memorable codes, this guide ensures that vital information is readily accessible. Each volume is filled with analysed questions from the last ten years of UGC NET exams, helping you understand not only what to study but also how to approach the exam strategically. This guide offers a structured pathway through the vast landscape of British literature, reducing overwhelm and empowering students to confidently tackle their preparation.

An effective study companion, "British Literature Unlocked" is the result of years of dedicated analysis, scholarly research, and an in-depth understanding of the UGC NET requirements. The goal is to provide readers with more than just a study guide—it is to offer them a roadmap that navigates through the richness of British literary history with ease and engagement. As you turn these pages, may you not only prepare but also find joy in the timeless world of British literature, its stories, and its legacy.

This series invites you on an enlightening journey, guiding you through the ages and unlocking the potential for both academic success and a deeper appreciation of the literary arts. Welcome to "British Literature Unlocked: A Complete Guide for UGC NET."

CHAPTER 1

THE AGE OF MILTON AND PERIOD OF THE CIVIL WAR (1642-60)

Historical Background

- **Civil War dominates** the entire period discussed.
- Earlier years were marked by **quarrels and alarms** (1642).
- The Caroline era is the period in English and Scottish history named for the 24-year reign of Charles I (1625–1649).
- The term is derived from Carolus, Latin for Charles.
- Middle period occupied by **spasmodic fighting** until **Charles I's execution** (1649).
- Final portion covers the Commonwealth **establishment** and **Cromwell's rise and fall** (1654-58).
- **Monarchy restored** after **Cromwell's death** and following confusion (1660).

Devoloment of Literature:

- **The Reaction:**

    - Decline from **high Elizabethan standard** is evident.
    - **Shorter poems** with focus on intellectual fancy.
    - **Prose increases** as poetry declines in fervor.

- **The Pressure of Historical Events:**

    - **Civil War** narrows the focus, intensifies bitterness.
    - **Divides people** and impacts literature's tone.
    - **Poetry declines**, prose becomes fierce and disputatious.

- **The Dominance of Milton:**

    - **Milton sustains literature's reputation** during this period.
    - Other poets were **uneven, uninspired**, or **shallow**.
    - Milton's work alone offers satisfying **quantity** and **quality**.

- ➤ **The Metaphysical Poets:**

    - o Coined by **Johnson**, applied to **Donne** and **Cowley**.
    - o Poetry known for **sudden leaps** of **fancy**.
    - o Popular before the **Civil War**, including **Herrick** and **Herbert**.

- ➤ **The Cavalier Poets:**

    - o Different from **Metaphysical poets**, more **military**.
    - o **Lovelace** and **Suckling** are key representatives.
    - o Known for **swashbuckling** and **cavalier** attitudes.

- ➤ **The Expansion of Prose:**

    - o **Prose develops** despite **civil strife's effects**.
    - o **Sermons**, pamphlets, history, politics saw growth.
    - o **Remarkable advance** in prose **style** and output.

- ➤ **The Collapse of the Drama:**

    - o **Civil disturbances** and Puritan opposition **oppressed drama**.
    - o The age was **not dramatic** in **temper**.
    - o **Theaters closed** in 1642, dramatic output diminished.

Development of Literary Forms

The Lyric:

- ➤ The period is **rich in lyrical poetry**.
- ➤ Themes mainly focus on **love** or **religion**.
- ➤ **Love poems** dedicated to literary figures like **Althea**.
- ➤ Characters resemble **stock figures** of pastoral poetry.
- ➤ Language lacks **deep passion**, more polite compliment.
- ➤ Lyric often involves **verbal quibbles** or **courtly jest**.
- ➤ Herrick, Lovelace, Carew represent this **poetic class**.
- ➤ **George Wither** writes with freshness and sweetness.
- ➤ **Andrew Marvell** sometimes reveals **genuine passion**.
- ➤ Anonymous songwriters created lyrics like **"Phillada flouts me."**
- ➤ **Religious lyrics** are often **passionately inspired** but vague.
- ➤ **Crashaw** and **Vaughan** exemplify this type of lyric.

- ➤ **Incongruity in style** sometimes disfigures religious lyrics.
- ➤ **Milton's lyrics** are superbly phrased but lack spontaneity.
- ➤ His sonnets are among the **noblest of their class**.
- ➤ **Milton's sonnets** show much more **depth of feeling**.

The Epic:

- ➤ The **true epic** deals with sublime subjects grandly.
- ➤ **Beowulf** is epic-like, but not a true epic.
- ➤ **Cowley's Davideis** and **Davenant's Gondibert** aspire to epics.
- ➤ Both fail, lacking the **inner spirit** of true epics.
- ➤ **Milton's Paradise Lost** has heat and inspiration.
- ➤ The **Fall of Man** is weak for heroic action.
- ➤ **King Arthur's story** would have been more appropriate.
- ➤ **Milton's style** triumphs in epical unity and character.
- ➤ **Paradise Regained** is shorter and weaker than **Paradise Lost**.
- ➤ **Milton's epics** adhere to orthodox epical structures.

The Ode:

- ➤ **Spenser's Epithalamion** and **Prothalamion** perfect irregular odes.
- ➤ The **Pindaric ode** appears in this transitional age.
- ➤ Pindaric odes are **stringently structured** despite appearing irregular.
- ➤ The language of these odes is **ornately artificial**.
- ➤ **Pindaric odes** suit the era's desire for artificiality.
- ➤ **Cowley's Pindarique Odes** are the first in English.
- ➤ These odes use **mannered, unreal diction**.
- ➤ They balance **artificiality** with a show of freedom.
- ➤ Popularity of **Pindaric odes** grew in succeeding generations.
- ➤ **Cowley** set the standard for English Pindaric odes.

Descriptive and Narrative Poetry:

- ➤ **Milton's L'Allegro** and **Il Penseroso** belong to this class.
- ➤ **Herrick's pastorals** and **Crashaw's religious poems** also fit.
- ➤ **Denham's Cooper Hill** (1641) praised as a descriptive poem.
- ➤ **William Chamberlayne's Pharonnida** is a romantic poem (1659).
- ➤ These poems avoid **wild nature**, seeking bookish landscapes.

- ➤ Influence of **artificial classical landscapes** is apparent.
- ➤ **New classicism** begins to emerge in these works.
- ➤ Focus shifts from real nature to **conventional imagery**.
- ➤ The poems reflect a growing trend toward **classicism**.
- ➤ Descriptive poetry of this period shows **increasing artificiality**.

Drama:

- ➤ **Massinger's plays** sustain the spirit of Elizabethan drama.
- ➤ **Ford** follows the tragic school of **Webster** and **Tourneur**.
- ➤ **James Shirley** wrote comedies like **The Lady of Pleasure** (1637).

Prose:

(a) The Sermon:

- ➤ The period is called the **"Golden Age of the English pulpit."**
- ➤ **Jeremy Taylor**, **Fuller**, and **Robert South** were notable sermon writers.
- ➤ **Richard Baxter's Saints' Everlasting Rest** (1649) remains significant.

(b) Philosophical Works:

- ➤ **Sir Thomas Browne** wrote on **moral philosophy**.
- ➤ **Hobbes** contributed significantly to **political philosophy**.
- ➤ **John Hales** focused on **religious philosophical** works.

(c) Historical Works:

- ➤ **Clarendon** and **Fuller** wrote important historical works.
- ➤ Clarendon's and Fuller's works represent **historical scholarship**.
- ➤ **Historical prose** advanced significantly during this period.

(d) Miscellaneous Prose:

- ➤ **Milton**, **Hobbes**, and **Fuller** wrote important pamphlets.
- ➤ **Isaac Walton's Compleat Angler** (1653) is a classic.
- ➤ **James Howell's Letters** (1645) introduced early **essay-journalism**.

JOHN MILTON (1608–74)

Life and Career:

- **John Milton** was born in **London in 1608**.
- He was educated at **St Paul's School** and **Cambridge**.
- Milton knew **at least ten languages** and was widely read.
- His knowledge spanned **literature**, **history**, **theology**, **philosophy**, and **natural sciences**.
- **Milton's Commonplace Book** contains notes from his extensive reading.
- The **British Library** now holds **Milton's Commonplace Book**.
- He lived through the **English Civil Wars** between **Royalists** and **Republicans**.
- Milton was both a **celebrated poet** and a **political controversialist**.
- Most of Milton's prose was written during the **middle period of his life (1640–60)**,
- He wrote on stamping out corruption among clergy (**Of Reformation**, 1641–42).
- Advocated for **freedom of the press** in **Areopagitica** (1644).
- **In 1643 he married a woman much younger than himself,** and almost immediately **his wife left him,** and did not return for two years.
- Supported **divorce on mutual incompatibility** in **The Doctrine and Discipline of Divorce** (1643).
- Argued for **Charles I's execution** in **Eikonoklastes** (1649).
- Milton wrote **many works** aimed at an **international audience**.
- After the **monarchy's restoration**, Milton faced threats of **arrest** and **execution**.
- His controversial writings made him a target after **1660**.
- **Paradise Lost** is Milton's most famous and greatest **epic poem**.
- **Paradise Lost, Paradise Regained**, and **Samson Agonistes** cement Milton's reputation.
- Milton advocated for the **abolition of the Church of England**.
- He supported the **execution of Charles I** in his prose works.
- Milton's political philosophy opposed **tyranny** and **state-sanctioned religion**.
- His influence extended to the **American** and **French revolutions**.

- ➢ Milton valued **liberty of conscience** and religious toleration in theology.
- ➢ He upheld the **paramount importance of Scripture** as a guide for faith.
- ➢ As a civil servant, Milton was the voice of the **English Commonwealth**.
- ➢ He defended the government against **polemical attacks** from abroad after 1649.
- ➢ **Macaulay wrote an "Essay on Milton" (1859).**
- ➢ **In "The Metaphysical Poets," T.S. Eliot contrasts the poetry of the French writers Jean Racine and Charles Baudelaire with that of John Milton and John Dryden.**
- ➢ **Arnold in his *Study of Poetry*** argues that this immortal poet lacks high seriousness. Chaucer does not have the **high seriousness that Homer, Shakespeare, Milton, and many others had.**

Extra Notes:

Miltonic verse, also known as Miltonic blank verse or Miltonic epic, is the poetic style of John Milton, which is characterized by English heroic verse without rhyme. Milton's use of blank verse in Paradise Lost (1667) restored the style to its former grandeur and made it more acceptable to readers and poets.

"An Essay on Man" is a poem published by Alexander Pope in 1733–1734. It was dedicated to Henry St John, 1st Viscount Bolingbroke (pronounced 'Bull-en-brook'), hence **the opening line: "Awake, my St John...".** It is an effort to rationalize or rather "**vindicate the ways of God to man**" (l.16), a variation of John Milton's claim in the opening lines of Paradise Lost, that he will "justifie the wayes of God to men" (1.26)

Poetry and drama

- ➢ The great bulk of Milton's poetry was written during two periods separated from each other **by twenty years:**
  - ○ **the period of his university career and his stay at Horton, from 1629 to 1640**; and
  - ○ **Most of Milton's prose was written during the middle period of his life (1640–60),**

- o **the last years of his life, from about 1660 to 1674.** The years between were filled by a few sonnets.

Code 1: Christ Shakepeare 23 Lane Castle of Comudas

Code 2: Blind Milton wrote Paradise lost and regained with Samson

- ➢ *1629: On the Morning of Christ's Nativity*
- ➢ *1630: On Shakespeare*
- ➢ *1631: On Arriving at the Age of Twenty-Three*
- ➢ *1632: L'Allegro*
- ➢ *1632: Il Penseroso*
- ➢ *1634: A Mask Presented at Ludlow Castle, 1634, commonly known as Comus (a masque)*
- ➢ *1637: Lycidas*
- ➢ *1645: Poems of Mr. John Milton, Both English and Latin*
- ➢ *1652: When I Consider How My Light is Spent (Commonly referred to as "On his blindness," though Milton did not use this title)*
- ➢ *1655: On the Late Massacre in Piedmont*
- ➢ *1667: Paradise Lost*
- ➢ *1671: Paradise Regained*
- ➢ *1671: Samson Agonistes*
- ➢ *1673: Poems, &c, Upon Several Occasions*
- ➢ *Arcades: a masque. (date is unknown).*
- ➢ *On his Deceased wife, To The Nightingale, On reaching the Age of twenty four.*

Prose:
Code 3: Reform Educational Books for the King

- ➢ ***Of Reformation (1641)***
- ➢ *Of Prelatical Episcopacy (1641)*
- ➢ *Animadversions (1641)*
- ➢ *The Reason of Church-Government Urged against Prelaty (1642)*
- ➢ *Apology for Smectymnuus (1642)*
- ➢ *Doctrine and Discipline of Divorce (1643)*
- ➢ *Judgment of Martin Bucer Concerning Divorce (1644)*
- ➢ ***Of Education (1644)***
- ➢ ***Areopagitica (1644)***
- ➢ *Tetrachordon (1645)*
- ➢ *Colasterion (1645)*
- ➢ *The Tenure of Kings and Magistrates (1649)*
- ➢ ***Eikonoklastes (1649)***
- ➢ *Defensio pro Populo Anglicano [First Defence] (1651)*
- ➢ *Defensio Secunda [Second Defence] (1654)*

> - *A Treatise of Civil Power (1659)*
> - *The Likeliest Means to Remove Hirelings from the Church (1659)*
> - *The Ready and Easy Way to Establish a Free Commonwealth (1660)*
> - *Brief Notes Upon a Late Sermon (1660)*
> - *Accedence Commenced Grammar (1669)*
> - *The History of Britain (1670)*
> - *Artis logicae plenior institutio [Art of Logic] (1672)*
> - *Of True Religion (1673)*
> - *Epistolae Familiaries (1674)*
> - *Prolusiones (1674)*
> - *A Brief History of Moscovia, and other less known Countries lying Eastward of Russia as far as Cathay, gathered from the writings of several Eye-witnesses (1682)*
> - *De Doctrina Christiana (1823)*

Early Poems:

- **Milton began composing mature poetry** during his undergraduate years.
- His early works include the **Ode on the Morning of Christ's Nativity** (1629).
- **On Shakespeare** (1630) and **On Arriving at the Age of Twenty-three** (1631) show his early promise.
- These poems demonstrate his **command of diction** and high literary ideals.
- At **Horton**, Milton wrote **L'Allegro** and **Il Penseroso** in 1634.
- These works reflect the experiences of the **gay** and **thoughtful man**.
- **Comus** (1637), a masque, contains **beautiful blank verse** and lyrical measures.
- **Lycidas** (1637), an elegy for his friend **Edward King**, is among Milton's highest achievements.
- **Lycidas** combines **pastoral form** with Milton's **majestic intensity** and passion.
- The elegy has a **haunting beauty** with an irregular **stanza and rhyme sequence**.

Mature Poetry (1660–74):

- This period showcases **Milton's matured poetry**, including a few sonnets.

- His **Italian sonnets** show impressive command and **sonorous sweep**.
- **On his Blindness** and **On the Late Massacre in Piedmont** are his finest sonnets.
- **Paradise Lost** was begun in 1658 and published in 1667.
- The poem, divided into **twelve books**, follows the **classical epic form**.
- It deals with the **fall of man, Lucifer's rebellion**, and **celestial warfare**.
- Milton's **rich imagination** is fed by **classical** and **Biblical lore**.
- The **blank verse** of **Paradise Lost** is innovative, commanding, and deeply musical.
- **Paradise Lost** established a tradition in **English blank verse**.
- Despite a few lapses, the poem is a **masterpiece** of **modulation** and **dignity**.

Later Works:

- Milton's last volume (1671) contained **Paradise Regained** and **Samson Agonistes**.
- **Paradise Regained** tells of **Christ's temptation**, complementing **Paradise Lost**.
- Despite Milton's hopes, **Paradise Regained** is **briefer** and **poorer** than its predecessor.
- The poem lacks the **imagination** and **ornate rhythms** of **Paradise Lost**.
- **Samson Agonistes** tells the story of **Samson's death** as a Philistine prisoner.
- Milton saw **resemblances** between himself and the Biblical hero **Samson**.
- **Samson Agonistes** follows the **Greek tragic form** with unity of time, place, and action.
- The poem's style is **bleak, bare**, and at times **harsh**.
- **Samson Agonistes** is marked by **pity** and **hope**, reflecting Milton's own soul.
- Though severe, the work has passages of **profound emotional depth** and **intensity**.

L'Allegro (1631)

- **L'Allegro** means **"the happy man"** in Italian.
- It is a **pastoral poem** published in Milton's **1645 Poems**.
- **L'Allegro** is often paired with its contrasting poem, **Il Penseroso**.
- The poem depicts a **joyful day** spent in **mirth and pleasure**.
- It is uncertain when **L'Allegro** was composed, likely after Milton left **Cambridge**.
- The poem was first published in **Poems of Mr. John Milton** (1645/1646).
- **L'Allegro** serves as a **balance** to Milton's **Latin poems** in the collection.
- The poem's **iambic tetrameter** couplets create a flowing, joyful rhythm.
- **L'Allegro** focuses on themes of **mirth**, **pastoral joy**, and **happiness**.
- It presents a **vision of poetic mirth**, embracing life's pleasures.

Il Penseroso (1645):

- **Il Penseroso** means **"the thinker"**, depicting a **melancholic man**.
- It was first published in **The Poems of Mr. John Milton** (1645/1646).
- **Il Penseroso** is a **companion piece** to **L'Allegro**.
- The speaker invokes **"divinest Melancholy"** to inspire contemplative verses.
- The poem rejects **"vain deluding Joys"**, favoring **deep reflection**.
- It explores the speaker's **allegorical journey** into **melancholic inspiration**.
- The poem is composed in **iambic tetrameter** couplets, like **L'Allegro**.
- **Melancholy** is presented as a **source of prophetic poetic inspiration**.
- **Il Penseroso** embodies a **contemplative paradigm** of the **poetic genre**.
- The poem's **ambiguous style** invites **interpretive exploration** from critics.

Comus (1634)

- **Comus** is a **masque** written by **John Milton** in 1634.

- ➢ It was performed at **Ludlow Castle** for **John Egerton**, Earl of Bridgewater.
- ➢ The masque was presented on **Michaelmas night**, 29 September 1634.
- ➢ **Milton's masque honors chastity**, contrasting revelry with virtue.
- ➢ The **Lady** character represents **private heroism** and **virtue**.
- ➢ **Comus**, the evil sorcerer, represents **hedonism** and **pleasure**.
- ➢ **Comus** is the son of **Bacchus** and **Circe**, figures from mythology.
- ➢ The Lady is imprisoned by **Comus's magic** in his palace.
- ➢ The Lady defends **temperance** and **chastity** in a debate with Comus.
- ➢ She is rescued by her brothers with the help of **Attendant Spirit** and **Sabrina**.
- ➢ **Comus** was printed anonymously in **1637** by **Humphrey Robinson**.
- ➢ Milton included **Comus** in his **Poems of 1645** and **1673**.
- ➢ **Thomas Arne** adapted **Comus** into a popular musical masque in 1738.
- ➢ **Comus** ran for more than **seventy years** in **London** theaters.
- ➢ The masque explores the **conflict between good and evil**, Milton's central theme.

Lycidas (1637)

- ➢ **Lycidas** is an **elegy** written by **Milton** in 1637.
- ➢ It was included in a **volume of elegies** published in **1638**.
- ➢ The elegy commemorates **Edward King**, Milton's friend from **Cambridge**.
- ➢ **King drowned** in a shipwreck in August **1637** on his way to Ireland.
- ➢ The poem follows the conventions of a **classical pastoral elegy**.
- ➢ **Lycidas**, a shepherd in **Virgil's Eclogues**, represents **King**.
- ➢ Milton muses on **fame**, the **meaning of existence**, and **divine judgment**.
- ➢ The speaker laments **the massive task** of memorializing his friend.
- ➢ The speaker asks mythological figures, **"Where were ye, Nymphs?"** when he drowned.
- ➢ **Apollo** (Phoebus) reminds the speaker that **true fame** exists in **Heaven**.
- ➢ **St. Peter** gives a speech on **unworthy clergy** who lead their flocks astray.

- The speaker apologizes for the poem's **digressions** and continues the elegy.
- The speaker asks the **valleys** to send flowers to adorn **Lycidas' coffin**.
- The poem ends with the belief that **Lycidas is reborn** in **Heaven**.
- The hopeful closing line reads, **"Tomorrow to fresh woods, and pastures new."**

Epitaphium Damonis (1639)

- **Epitaphium Damonis** is Milton's lament for his friend **Charles Diodati**.
- The poem is indebted to **Theocritus**, **Virgil**, and **Ovid**, as well as **Neo-Latin poets**.
- It combines **pastoral form** with a more intimate, **Renaissance tone**.
- Milton confides his plans for a future **Arthurian epic** to his deceased friend.
- The poem weds **Christian sensibility** to a **classical pastoral form**, reflecting Renaissance influence.

Of Education (1644)

- **Of Education** was published in **1644**, outlining Milton's views on **educational reform**.
- Written as a letter in response to **Samuel Hartlib**, a Puritan reformer.
- Milton emphasized education as a way to equip individuals for **public and private duties**.
- Education should also repair the **"ruins of our first parents"** by teaching the **knowledge of God**.
- The tractate outlines the **dual objectives** of education: **public** service and **private** moral improvement.

Milton's Divorce Tracts (1643–1645)

- Milton's **divorce tracts** argue for the legitimacy of divorce on grounds of **spousal incompatibility**.
- The tracts include **The Doctrine and Discipline of Divorce**, **Tetrachordon**, and **Colasterion**.

- These writings were **highly controversial**, drawing hostility from religious figures.
- Milton later regretted publishing them in English, but they are crucial for understanding **Paradise Lost**.
- The **Westminster Confession of Faith** eventually allowed for divorce in cases of **infidelity** and **abandonment**.

Areopagitica (1644)

- **Areopagitica** is a 1644 prose **polemic** by **John Milton** opposing censorship.
- The work advocates for **freedom of speech** and **expression**.
- Its principles have influenced modern justifications of **free speech**.
- The title is derived from **"Areopagus,"** a high court in **Athens**.
- **Milton's argument** is rooted in **Greek models** of intellectual liberty.
- He opposes **licensing**, comparing it to the **papacy's tyranny**.
- Milton believes **free circulation of ideas** is essential for **moral development**.
- He argues that **truth** will ultimately prevail over **falsehood**.
- Despite Areopagitica's efforts, licensing laws were not repealed for **50 years**.
- **Areopagitica** remains a cornerstone in the literature of **human rights**.
- Milton defends the right to **constructive criticism** over **false flattery**.
- He encourages **Parliament** to follow **"the voice of reason"** in policy decisions.
- Milton supported previous laws requiring **printer's names** on books.
- He argues that **libellous works** can be destroyed **after the fact**.
- **"The fire and the executioner** will be the timeliest remedy" for dangerous books.
- Milton seeks to hold **authors and publishers accountable** for harmful work.
- Despite advocating free speech, Milton has limits on **libel** and **blasphemy**.
- **"I mean not tolerated Popery"**, which Milton believes should be extirpated.
- He advocates for using **charitable means** to win back the misled before punishment.

> The interpretation of Milton's statement on **religious tolerance** remains debated.

Paradise Lost (1667)

> **The first version,** published in **1667,** consists of **ten books** with over **ten thousand lines** of verse.
> **A second edition followed in 1674,** arranged **into twelve books** (in the manner of **Virgil's Aeneid**) with minor revisions throughout.
> It is considered Milton's **masterpiece**.
> The poem concerns the biblical story **of the Fall of Ma**n: the temptation of Adam and Eve by the fallen angel Satan and their expulsion from the Garden of Eden.
> **The 12-book structure,** the technique of beginning in medias res (in the middle of the story), the invocation of the muse, and the use of the epic question are all classically inspired.
> The subject matter, however, is **distinctly Christian.**
> The main characters in the poem are **God, Lucifer (Satan), Adam, and Eve**.
> **William Blake and Percy Bysshe Shelley saw Satan as the real hero** of the poem and applauded his rebellion against the tyranny of Heaven.
> Many other works of art have been inspired by Paradise Lost, notably **Joseph Haydn's oratorio The Creation (1798)** and **John Keats's long poem Endymion.**
> Milton wrote a companion piece, **Paradise Regained, in 1671,** which dramatizes the temptation of Christ.
> **"Darkness Visible" is a novel by William Golding.** The title of the novel comes from a line in John **Milton's epic poem "Paradise Lost,"**

Plot Summary:
> The poem **begins in medias res,** with **Satan** and his fallen angels already banished to **Hell**.
> In **Pandæmonium,** the capital city of Hell, **Satan** organizes his followers using his rhetorical skills.
> **Mammon, Beelzebub, Belial,** and **Moloch** join Satan in a debate about their next move.
> **Satan volunteers** to corrupt **God's new creation,** Earth, and **Mankind,** embarking on a dangerous journey.

- Satan braves the **Abyss**, similar to **Odysseus** or **Aeneas**, and enters the newly created **World**.
- In the poem, the **Angelic War** over Heaven is recounted multiple times from various perspectives.
- **Satan's rebellion** mirrors an epic battle, with the war lasting three days between angels.
- **The Son of God** defeats the rebellious angels alone, banishing them from **Heaven**.
- After the rebellion, **God creates the World**, culminating in the creation of **Adam and Eve**.
- **Adam and Eve** are granted **total freedom** but are forbidden to eat from the **Tree of Knowledge**.
- The story of **Adam and Eve's temptation** presents a **domestic epic** focused on human relationships.
- **Satan**, disguised as a serpent, tempts **Eve** by preying on her **vanity** and using rhetoric.
- After **Eve eats the fruit**, **Adam** knowingly commits the same sin out of love for Eve.
- Milton portrays **Adam as a heroic figure** and a greater sinner than Eve, knowing the consequences.
- After eating the fruit, **Adam and Eve** experience **lust**, guilt, and shame for the first time.
- They realize their sin and engage in **mutual recrimination**, blaming each other.
- **Satan** returns to Hell triumphantly, believing they now have dominion over **Paradise**.
- However, **Satan** and his followers are punished, transforming into **snakes**, sharing their guilt.
- **Eve** appeals to **Adam** for reconciliation, and they seek **God's forgiveness** together.
- They **bow on the supplicant knee**, seeking **grace** and receiving God's forgiveness.
- **Adam**, in a vision by **Archangel Michael**, sees Mankind's future up to the **Great Flood**.
- Adam is troubled by the vision of **Mankind's suffering** and **fall from grace**.
- **Michael** offers hope, telling Adam about **Mankind's redemption** through **Jesus Christ**.

- Adam and Eve are **cast out of Eden**, beginning their new life outside the **Garden**.
- **Michael tells Adam**, "a paradise within thee, happier far," symbolizing inner peace.
- Adam and Eve now have a **distant relationship with God**, who is omnipresent but invisible.
- The poem portrays the **fall of Mankind** and the hope for redemption through **Jesus Christ**.
- **Satan's journey** from **Hell to Earth** mirrors classical epics, while **Adam and Eve's** story reflects personal conflict.
- Milton uses **grand themes** of temptation, sin, and redemption in **Paradise Lost**.
- The poem ends with **Adam and Eve's expulsion**, setting the stage for Mankind's future struggles.

Book-Wise Summary:

Book I

- **Milton introduces** his epic with the story of **Man's Fall** and Satan's rebellion.
- **Satan** and the fallen angels are seen **writhing in a burning lake** in Hell.
- **Satan rallies** his army with a powerful speech, encouraging them to corrupt **Mankind**.
- The **fallen angels**, presented as military figures, build the palace **Pandæmonium**.
- The book ends with preparations for the **council of Hell**, where strategies will be discussed.

> *OF Mans First Disobedience, and the Fruit*
> *Of that Forbidden Tree, whose mortal tast*
> *Brought Death into the World, and all our woe,*
> *With loss of Eden, till one greater Man*
> *Restore us, and regain the blissful Seat,*
> *Sing Heav'nly Muse, that on the secret top*
> *Of Oreb, or of Sinai, didst inspire*
> *That Shepherd, who first taught the chosen Seed,*
> *In the Beginning how the Heav'ns and Earth*

Rose out of Chaos: or if Sion Hill
Delight thee more, and Siloa's brook that flow'd
Fast by the Oracle of God; I thence
Invoke thy aid to my adventrous Song,
That with no middle flight intends to soar
Above th' Aonian Mount, while it pursues
Things unattempted yet in Prose or Rhime.

Book II

- **Satan, sitting on his throne**, calls a **council of devils** to decide their next move.
- **Moloch** advocates for open war, while **Belial** favors inaction out of fear of greater suffering.
- **Mammon** suggests they build their own kingdom in **Hell**, away from God's rule.
- **Beelzebub**, influenced by Satan, proposes they corrupt the newly created **Man**.
- Satan volunteers to explore this **New World**, passing through the **gates of Hell** guarded by **Sin** and **Death**.

Book III

- **God foresees** Satan's plan to provoke **the Fall of Mankind** but emphasizes **Man's free will**.
- The **Son of God** offers himself as a **ransom** for humanity's salvation.
- **Satan**, disguised as a lowly angel, tricks **Uriel** into giving him directions to **Paradise**.
- The book raises questions about **free will**, **predestination**, and the fall of both **angels** and **Man**.
- **Satan reaches the edge of Paradise**, setting the stage for the **temptation of Adam and Eve**.

Book IV

- **Satan stands on Mount Niphates**, reflecting on his fall and growing **despair**.
- He sees **Adam and Eve** in their innocence, provoking further **envy** and **hatred**.

- ➢ **Satan leaps into Paradise** and takes the form of a **cormorant**, observing the couple.
- ➢ **Uriel warns Gabriel** of Satan's presence, and the angels confront Satan, who eventually **flees**.
- ➢ **Adam and Eve** remain innocent, engaging in **unfallen love**, unaware of Satan's presence.

Book V

- ➢ **Eve wakes from a troubling dream**, stirred by Satan's whispered words of **disobedience**.
- ➢ **Adam tries to comfort her**, but both are disturbed by the presence of **evil**.
- ➢ **God sends Raphael** to warn Adam and Eve about **Satan's treachery** and lies.
- ➢ **Raphael tells the story** of the **rebel angels' fall**, starting with Satan's **jealousy** of the Son.
- ➢ **Abdiel**, the lone angel, refuses Satan's rhetoric, **denouncing the rebellion** and predicting the rebels' destruction.

Book VI

- ➢ **Raphael continues** the story of the war in Heaven and **Abdiel's return** to God's forces.
- ➢ The battle between **Satan's army** and the loyal angels continues for **three days**.
- ➢ **Satan's army invents artillery**, throwing the good angels to the ground.
- ➢ **God sends his Son**, who defeats Satan's forces and casts them into **Hell**.
- ➢ The Son returns to Heaven in a **victorious parade**, hailed by all the angels.

Book VII

- ➢ **Raphael** begins by reminding Adam of the **dangers of excessive knowledge**.
- ➢ He explains how **God created the World** through the Son after Satan's fall.

> - **Heaven rejoices** at the news of the creation of the new **material World**.
> - Raphael describes the **six days of Creation**, mirroring the **Genesis account**.
> - The **heavenly hosts** celebrate the creation of **Man**, God's final masterpiece.

Book VIII

> - **Adam asks Raphael** about the nature of the **universe** and planetary movements.
> - **Raphael advises** Adam to focus on the **Earth**, leaving **Heaven's secrets** alone.
> - Adam recounts his creation, his **first encounter with God**, and the creation of **Eve**.
> - A discussion on the **nature of love** between Adam and Eve follows.
> - **Raphael departs**, warning Adam once more to **resist temptation**.

Book IX

> - **Milton declares** that the poem now takes on a **tragic mode**.
> - **Satan enters Paradise** disguised as a serpent, plotting to tempt **Eve**.
> - **Eve suggests** she and Adam split up to work more efficiently, despite **Adam's warnings**.
> - **Satan tempts Eve**, convincing her to eat the **forbidden fruit** from the Tree of Knowledge.
> - **Eve shares the fruit** with Adam, and both realize their sin as they feel **guilt and shame**.
> - **Milton portrays a marital quarrel between Adam and Eve, where they argue about whether they should work together or separately in the garden.**
> - The speech rhythms of their argument reflect the emotional intensity of their disagreement.For instance, when Adam says,

> *"Why dost thou then suggest to me distrust,*
> *Knowing who I am, as I know who thou art?"*

The rhythm is slow and measured, reflecting his controlled anger. **In contrast, when Eve says,**

> *"But let us once be true to one another!*
> *Though the tempest rage outside, we'll weather it together,"*

The rhythm is faster and more urgent, reflecting her desperation to reconcile with Adam.

Book X

- > **God sends the Son** to confront **Adam and Eve** and deliver their sentences.
- > **Eve is condemned** to **pain in childbirth**, and Adam to **hard labor**.
- > In Hell, **Sin and Death** build a **bridge** to the mortal world, sensing Satan's victory.
- > **Satan returns triumphantly** to Hell, only for him and his followers to be **turned into snakes**.
- > **Adam and Eve begin to reconcile**, seeking **repentance** and hoping for redemption.

Book XI

- > **The Son defends** Adam and Eve's **remorse** before God, but they must still leave **Paradise**.
- > **God sends Michael** to remove them from Eden, which causes Adam and Eve great **grief**.
- > **Michael puts Eve to sleep** and shows Adam the **future sins and deaths** of mankind.
- > Adam sees the **exceptions of Enoch and Noah**, who are saved through their **virtue**.
- > Adam realizes the consequences of their sin but is shown the **promise of redemption**.
- > Milton does refer to "Agra and Lahore of Great Mogul" in Book XI of "Paradise Lost."
- > In lines 389-393 of Book XI, Milton writes:

> *"The great empires of the world,*
> *Built and established by the Persian, the Greek,*
> *The Roman, or whoever, Babylon of old,*
> *Egyptian Thebes, or yet the Persian's glory,*
> *Agra and Lahor of Great Mogul"*

Here, Milton is referring to the great cities of Agra and Lahore, which were part of the Mughal Empire in India. The Mughal Empire was one of the largest and most powerful empires in world history, and it ruled over much of the Indian subcontinent from the 16th to the 19th centuries.

Book XII

- **Michael reveals** the future, including the story of **Nimrod** and the **Tower of Babel**.
- He tells Adam about **Abraham**, whose lineage will fulfill **God's promise**.
- **Moses**, Isaac, and Jacob continue **God's covenant** with Abraham's descendants.
- Michael reassures Adam that **Jesus Christ** will overcome **Satan and Death** through his sacrifice.
- **Comforted by this prophecy**, Adam and Eve are led out of **Paradise**, beginning *their new life*.

> *They looking back, all the eastern side beheld*
> *Of Paradise, so late their happy seat,*
> *Waved over by that flaming brand, the gate*
> *With dreadful faces thronged and fiery arms:*
> *Some natural tears they dropped, but wiped them soon;*
> *The world was all before them, where to choose*
> *Their place of rest, and providence their guide:*
> *They hand in hand with wandering steps and slow,*
> *Through Eden took their solitary way.*
> *~XII.641-end.*

Paradise Ragained (1671)

- **First published in 1671.**
- The volume in which it appeared also contained the poet's **closet drama Samson Agonistes.**
- Milton composed at his cottage in Chalfont St Giles in Buckinghamshire.
- Four books long and comprises **2,065 lines.**

> In contrast, Paradise Lost is twelve books long and contains **10,565 lines.**
> **Barbara K. Lewalski has labeled the work a "brief epic."**

Summary:

Book 1

> **Jesus is baptized** by John, and **Satan plans** to tempt Him.
> **Jesus enters the wilderness** to fast for 40 days, pondering His mission.
> **Satan, disguised as an old man**, tempts Him to turn stones to bread, but Jesus rebukes him.

Book 2

> **Simon, Andrew, and Mary** worry about Jesus' whereabouts after His baptism.
> **Satan prepares his demons**, knowing this temptation will be more difficult than with Adam.
> **Jesus resists temptations** of hunger, power, and wealth, staying true to His divine purpose.

Book 3

> **Satan taunts Jesus** with lack of achievements, comparing Him to **Alexander the Great.**
> Jesus rejects **glory through violence**, emphasizing **suffering as His path.**
> **Satan shows Jesus the world's kingdoms**, but Christ leaves their fate to **Divine providence.**

Book 4

> **Satan offers Jesus** the world's kingdoms in exchange for worship, but **Jesus rebukes him.**
> **Jesus rejects the wisdom of Ancient Greece**, favoring the **Psalms and Prophets.**

> ➢ After enduring **Satan's final temptations, angels help Jesus,** celebrating His victory.

Samson Agonistes (1671)

> ➢ **Samson Agonistes** is a tragic **closet drama** by **John Milton.**
> ➢ Published alongside **Paradise Regained** in the year **1671.**
> ➢ The play focuses on **Samson's final phase of life.**
> ➢ **Samson** is portrayed as **blinded** and a prisoner of the **Philistines.**
> ➢ **Milton**, blind when writing, parallels **Samson's blindness.**
> ➢ **"Eyeless in Gaza at the mill with slaves"** describes Samson's despair.
> ➢ **Samson conquers self-pity** and regains his **old strength.**
> ➢ He pulls down the **pillars of Dagon's temple**, sacrificing himself.
> ➢ **Samson's death** results in the destruction of his **Philistine captors.**
> ➢ **Milton combines Greek tragedy** with **Hebrew Scripture.**
> ➢ He believed **the Bible's classical forms** were superior.
> ➢ **Greek tragedy influences** are drawn from **Aeschylus, Sophocles,** and **Euripides.**
> ➢ **Milton states**, "Of the style and uniformity... they only will best judge."
> ➢ The work blends **Greek tragic structure** with **biblical themes.**
> ➢ **Samson Agonistes** explores themes of **strength, redemption**, and **sacrifice.**

John Milton: When I Consider How My Light is Spent or On His Blindness:

> ➢ The last three lines, ***"They also serve who only stand and wait,"*** are often quoted.
> ➢ Express his frustration and wavering faith that his blindness brought on at first.
> ➢ He doesn't understand **why God would make him blind if writing his great talent** requires sight or what he is expected to do about it.
> ➢ By the end of the poem, he **has decided that his God is patient and forgiving.**
> ➢ He needs to keep trying **his best and bear his disability gracefully.**
> ➢ The poem is a traditional sonnet and employs figurative language to illustrate Milton's ideas.

> ➢ This poem is a traditional sonnet containing 14 lines and uses the Italian sonnet rhyme scheme **a b b a a b b a c d e c d e.**

When I consider how my light is spent,
Ere half my days, in this dark world and wide,
And that one Talent which is death to hide
Lodged with me useless, though my Soul more bent
To serve therewith my Maker, and present
My true account, lest he returning chide;
"Doth God exact day-labour, light denied?"
I fondly ask. But patience, to prevent
That murmur, soon replies, "God doth not need
Either man's work or his own gifts; who best
Bear his mild yoke, they serve him best. His state
Is Kingly. Thousands at his bidding speed
And post o'er Land and Ocean without rest:
They also serve who only stand and wait."

On Shakespeare

Milton's poem "On Shakespeare", published in the second folio edition of Shakespeare's plays in 1632. "On Shakespeare" is a poem by John Milton, published in the second folio edition of William Shakespeare's plays in 1632. In the poem, Milton praises Shakespeare as a great poet and dramatist and expresses his admiration for Shakespeare's works.

On Shakespeare
John Milton - 1608-1674

"What needs my Shakespeare for his honour'd Bones,
The labour of an age in pilèd Stones,
Or that his hallow'd reliques should be hid
Under a stary pointing Pyramid?
Dear son of Memory, great heir of Fame,
What need'st thou such weak witnes of thy name?
Thou in our wonder and astonishment
Hast built thy self a live-long Monument.
For whilst to th' shame of slow-endeavouring art,
Thy easie numbers flow, and that each heart

> *Hath from the leaves of thy unvalu'd Book*
> *Those Delphick lines with deep impression took,*
> *Then thou our fancy of it self bereaving,*
> *Dost make us Marble with too much conceaving;*
> *And so Sepulcher'd in such pomp dost lie,*
> *That Kings for such a Tomb would wish to die."*

London, 1802 by Wordsworth

> ***MILTON! thou shouldst be living at this hour:***
> *England hath need of thee: she is a fen*
> *Of stagnant waters: altar, sword, and pen,*
> *Fireside, the heroic wealth of hall and bower,*
> *Have forfeited their ancient English dower*
> *Of inward happiness. We are selfish men;*
> *Oh! Raise us up, return to us again,*
> *And give us manners, virtue, freedom, power!*
> *Thy soul was like a Star, and dwelt apart;*
> *Thou hadst a voice whose sound was like the sea:*
> *Pure as the naked heavens, majestic, free,*
> *So didst thou travel on life's common way,*
> *In cheerful godliness; and yet thy heart*
> *The lowliest duties on herself did lay*

Questions:

Question 1
What is the correct chronological order of the works of John Milton?

    A. Paradise Lost.
    B. Paradise Regained
    C. Lycidas
    D. Comus
    E. L'Allegro

Choose the correct answer from the options given below :

    (1) E, D, C, A, B

(2) C, D, B, A, E
(3) A, B, E, C, D
(4) C, E, A, B, D

Explanations:
Answer: (1) E, D, C, A, B

- *1632: L'Allegro*
- *1632: Il Penseroso*
- *1634: A Mask Presented at Ludlow Castle, 1634, commonly known as Comus (a masque)*
- *1637: Lycidas*
- *1652: When I Consider How My Light is Spent (Commonly referred to as "On his blindness," though Milton did not use this title)*
- *1667: Paradise Lost*
- *1671: Paradise Regained*
- *1671: Samson Agonistes*

Question 2

What is the correct chronological sequence of British poets in order of their birth ?

A. Andrew Marvell
B. John Milton
C. John Donne
D. Richard Lovelace
E. Thomas Carew

Choose the correct answer from the options given below :

(1) C, E, B, D, A
(2) D, B, C, A, E
(3) B, C, D, E, A
(4) A, D, E, C, B

Explanations:
Answer: (1) C, E, B, D, A

- **John Donne (1571-1631) (C)**

- Robert Herrick (1591-1674)
- **Thomas Carew (1595-1640) (E)**
- **JOHN MILTON (1608–74) (B)**
- **Richard Lovelace (1618-1657) (D)**
- Sir John Suckling (1609-1641)
- Edmund Waller (1606-1687)
- Henry Vaughan (1621-1695)
- **Andrew Marvell (1621-1678) (A)**
- John Cleveland (1613-1658)
- Abraham Cowley (1618-1667)
- George Herbert (1593-1633)
- Richard Crashaw (1613-1649)
- Sir John Denham (1615-1669)
- Thomas Traherne (1636-1674)

Question 3

Who said of the blank verse, quoting an unnamed critic, that it is -... verse only to the eye", adding further that it "has neither the easiness of prose nor the melody of numbers"?

1. Samuel Taylor Coleridge
2. Alexander Pope
3. Samuel Johnson
4. John Dryden

Explanations:
Ans: Samuel Johnson

ESSAY ON POETIC THEORY from Lives of the Poets BY SAMUEL JOHNSON

"LIFE OF MILTON"

Poetry may subsist without rhyme, but English poetry will not often please, nor can rhyme ever be safely spared but where the subject is able to support itself. **The blank verse makes some approach to that which is called the "lapidary style"; has neither the easiness of prose nor the melody of numbers, and therefore tires by long continuance.** Of the Italian writers without rhyme, whom Milton alleges as precedents, not one is popular; what reason could urge in its defense has been confuted by the ear.

The highest praise of genius is original invention. Milton cannot be said to have contrived the structure of an epic poem, and therefore owes reverence to that vigour and amplitude of mind to which all generations must be indebted for the art of poetical narration, for the texture of the fable, the variation of incidents, the interposition of dialogue, and all the stratagems that surprise and enchain attention. But of all the borrowers from Homer, Milton is perhaps the least indebted. **He was naturally a thinker for himself, confident of his own abilities and disdainful of help or hindrance;** he did not refuse admission to the thoughts or images of his predecessors, but he did not seek them. From his contemporaries he neither courted nor received support; there is in his writings nothing by which the pride of other authors might be gratified or favor gained, no exchange of praise nor solicitation of support. His great works were performed under discountenance and in blindness, but difficulties vanished at his touch; he was born for whatever is arduous; and his work is not the greatest of heroic poems, only because it is not the first.

Question 4:

Who among the following are the two great masters of the French language that T. S Eliot contrasts with Dryden and Milton in The Metaphysical Poets'?

- A. Francois Villon
- B. Jean Racine
- C. Charles Baudelaire
- D. Arthur Rimbaud

Choose the correct answer from the options given below:

1. A and C only
2. A and D only
3. B and C only
4. B and D only

Explanations:
Answer: 3. B and C only

In "The Metaphysical Poets," T.S. Eliot contrasts the poetry of the French writers Jean Racine and Charles Baudelaire with that of John Milton and John Dryden. Eliot praises Racine and Baudelaire for their use of language and their ability to express complex emotions and ideas with simplicity and precision. He contrasts them with Milton and Dryden, whom he sees as more concerned with the expression of moral or political values in their poetry.

Eliot's comparison can be found in the following excerpt from "The Metaphysical Poets":

*"The French writers, the great masters of the language, have been more concerned with the form of language than with its content. They have been occupied with devising rhetorical devices to convey states of mind, rather than with the exploration of states of mind. They have been concerned, not so much with expressing themselves as with expressing human nature. **The greatest of them, Racine and Baudelaire, have a much closer affinity with the metaphysical poets than has Dryden or Milton.**"*

Question 5
Which book of Paradise Lost incorporates the speech rhythms of Adam and Eve's marital quarrel?

1.   Book 4
2.   Book 6
3.   Book 7
4.   Book 9

Explanations:
Answer: 4. Book 9.

In Book 9 of Paradise Lost, John Milton portrays a marital quarrel between Adam and Eve, where they argue about whether they should work together or separately in the garden. The speech rhythms of their argument reflect the emotional intensity of their disagreement. For instance, when Adam says, **"Why dost thou then suggest to me distrust, / Knowing who I am, as I know who thou art?"** the rhythm is slow and measured, reflecting his controlled anger. In contrast, when Eve says, "But let us once be true to one another! / Though the tempest rage outside, we'll weather it together," the rhythm is faster and more urgent, reflecting her desperation to reconcile with Adam.

Extra Perk:

Book 1: Satan's rebellion, expulsion from Heaven.
Book 2: Satan's council of fallen angels.
Book 3: God's omniscience, creation of universe.
Book 4: Satan tempts Eve, Raphael's arrival.
Book 5: Gabriel's warning, Raphael's story of creation.
Book 6: War in Heaven, Satan seduces Eve.
Book 7: Raphael's teachings on universe, creation.

Book 8: Adam's request to Raphael for knowledge.
Book 9: Temptation and fall of man.
Book 10: God passes sentence, Adam and Eve's penance.
Book 11: Michael's vision of future events.
Book 12: Michael shows Adam and Eve visions of future.

Question 6
Who was Milton's model when he recast the fast edition (1667) of Paradise Lost in 10 books to 12 books of the second edition (1674)?

1. Lucan
2. Virgil
3. Ovid
4. Homer

Explanations:
Answer: 2. Virgil

When Milton recast the first edition of "Paradise Lost" (1667) into the second edition (1674), **he used Virgil as his model. In the second edition**, Milton divided the epic poem into twelve books, following the structure of Virgil's "Aeneid," which is also divided into twelve books. Milton admired Virgil and sought to emulate his epic style and organization in his own work. The influence of Virgil can be seen in the way Milton constructs the narrative and develops the characters and themes throughout "Paradise Lost."

Question 7:
In which book of Paradise Lost does Milton refer to "Agra and Lahore of Great Mogul"?
1. Book III
2. Book IV
3. Book VII
4. **Book XI**

Correct Explanations:
Yes, Milton does refer to "Agra and Lahore of Great Mogul" in Book XI of "Paradise Lost."

In Book XI, Milton describes the aftermath of Adam and Eve's fall from grace and their expulsion from the Garden of Eden. As he surveys the fallen world, he sees a vision of future events, including the rise and fall of empires and the coming of the Messiah.

In lines 389-393 of Book XI, Milton writes:

"The great empires of the world,
Built and established by the Persian, the Greek,
The Roman, or whoever, Babylon of old,
Egyptian Thebes, or yet the Persian's glory,
Agra and Lahor of Great Mogul"

Here, Milton is referring to the great cities of Agra and Lahore, which were part of the Mughal Empire in India. The Mughal Empire was one of the largest and most powerful empires in world history, and it ruled over much of the Indian subcontinent from the 16th to the 19th centuries.

Milton's reference to Agra and Lahore is part of his broader vision of history and the fate of human empires, which he presents in "Paradise Lost" as a series of rises and falls, ultimately leading to the coming of the Messiah and the redemption of humanity.

Question 8
Identify the poems termed as "pastoral elegies" :

- A. Lycidas
- B. In Memory of W.B. Yeats
- C. Adonais
- D. Thyrsis
- E. In Memoriam

Choose the most appropriate answer from the options given below :
1. C, D and E only
2. **A, C and D only**
3. B, C and E only
4. A, B and C only

Correct Explanations:
Lycidas, a poem by John Milton, written in 1637 for inclusion in a volume of elegies published in 1638 to commemorate the death of Edward King, Milton's contemporary at the University of Cambridge, who had drowned in a shipwreck in August 1637. The poem mourns the loss of a virtuous and

promising young man about to embark upon a career as a clergyman. Milton muses on fame, the meaning of existence, and heavenly judgment, adopting **the conventions of the classical pastoral elegy** (Lycidas was a shepherd in Virgil's Eclogues).

Adonais, a pastoral elegy by Percy Bysshe Shelley, was written and published in 1821 to commemorate the death of his friend and fellow poet John Keats earlier that year. Referring to Adonis, the handsome young man of Greek mythology who a wild boar killed, the title was probably taken from Bion's Lament for Adonis, which Shelley had translated into English. Written in 55 Spenserian stanzas, Adonais is ranked with John Milton's "Lycidas" for its purity of classical form.

Thyrsis, an elegiac poem by Matthew Arnold, was first published in Macmillan's Magazine in 1866. It was included in Arnold's New Poems in 1867. It is considered one of Arnold's finest poems. In Thyrsis, Arnold mastered an intricate 10-line stanza form. The 24-stanza poem eulogizes his friend, poet Arthur Hugh Clough, who died in 1861. Arnold portrays Clough as Thyrsis, a traditional Greek name for a shepherd-poet. **In rich pastoral imagery, Arnold recalls the Oxford countryside** the two explored as students in the 1840s and reviews the fate of their youthful ideals after they left the university.

Other Explanations:

In 'In Memory of W.B. Yeats, ' Auden taps into themes of life after death, the power of poetry, and the human condition. The powerful and wide-ranging themes are discussed within the context of Yeats' life and death. Auden uses an exacting tone and direct language to depict the events around Yeat's death. The mood is at times uplifting and others concerning and worrying. There are many dark images and many fewer hopeful ones.

In Memoriam, in full In Memoriam A.H.H., a poem by Alfred, Lord Tennyson, was written between 1833 and 1850 and published anonymously in 1850. Consisting of 131 sections, a prologue, and an epilogue, this chiefly elegiac work examines the different stages of Tennyson's mourning over the death of his close friend Arthur Henry Hallam. In Memoriam reflects the Victorian struggle to reconcile traditional religious faith with the emerging theories of evolution and modern geology. The verses show the development over three years of the poet's acceptance and understanding of his

Question 9
Match List I with List I:

List I	List II
(A) The Poetics of Prose	(I) Stanley Fish
(B) Problems of Dostoevsky's Poetics	(II) Tzvetan Todrov
(C) Surprised by Sin	(III) Mikhail Bakhtin
(D) The Way Women Write	(IV) Mary Hiatt

Choose the correct answer from the options given below:

1. (A)-(IV). (B)-(II). (C)-(I). (D)-(III)
2. (A)-(II). (B)-(IV), (C)-(III). (D)-(I)
3. **(A)-(II), (B)-(III), (C)-(I), (D)-(IV)**
4. (A)-(III), (B)-(IV). (C)-(II). (D)-(I)

Correct Explanations:
The Poetics of Prose, by Tzvetan Todorov: Tzvetan Todorov was a Bulgarian- French historian, philosopher, structuralist literary critic, sociologist and essayist.

Problems of Dostoevsky's Poetics is a book by the 20th-century Russian philosopher and literary theorist Mikhail Bakhtin. Problems of Dostoevsky's Poetics is considered a seminal work in Dostoevsky's studies and an important contribution to literary theory. Bakhtin introduces several key concepts, such as polyphony and carnivalization, to elucidate what he saw as unique in Dostoevsky's literary art.

Stanley Fish explains in his partly biographical essay, "Milton, Thou Shouldst be Living at this Hour" (published in There's No Such Thing as Free Speech . . . And It's a Good Thing, Too), that he came to Milton by accident. **The eventual result was Surprised by Sin: The Reader in Paradise Lost (1967; rpt. 1997).** Fish's 2001 book, How Milton Works, reflects five decades' worth of his scholarship on Milton.

The Way Women Write (1977) by Hiatt, Mary. This book maintains that because male critics have evaluated feminine writing according to the standards of masculine style, women have received biased criticism in the past.

Question 10
Who among the following refers to "high seriousness" as a quality of a great poet and quotes John Milton to prove the same?

   A.   T.S. Eliot
   B.   Ezra Pound
   C.   Matthew Arnold
   D.   I. A Richards:
   E.   G. M, Hopkins-

Choose the correct answer from the options given below;
   1.   A and B only
   2.   B and C only
   3.   D and E only
   4.   C only

Correct Explanation:
High Seriousness means the grand style or the serious treatment of the subject matter. A poet can achieve the quality of high seriousness when he treats a serious subject in a simple and intense matter.

"The Study of Poetry" is a milestone in the history of English literary criticism. In this critical essay, Matthew Arnold gives poetry a very high position. He is confident in the high of poetry. According to him, poetry attains the place of religion. It is able to make room in the heart of man. It is an application of ideas to human life. The best kind of poetry is a criticism of life. It is an interpretation of life. It has the power to console, sustain and form us. At the same time, it delights us too. Thus Arnold sets high standards for poetry. He proclaims that truth and high seriousness are two essential qualities of excellent poetry. He tries to represent them as a proper standard for the evaluation of poetry.

Arnold has a very high opinion of Chaucer. It is Chaucer who establishes romantic poetry in England. Chaucer is the father of splendid English poetry.

His poetry has largeness, freedom, and kindness. Arnold thus showers high praise on Chaucer. But surprisingly he also remarks that Chaucer is not a classic. **He argues that this immortal poet lacks high seriousness. Chaucer does not have the high seriousness that Homer, Shakespeare, Milton, and many others had.**

Question 11:
Choose the correct chronological sequence in which the following texts were written.

- A. Lycidas
- B. Hero and Leander
- C. Masque of Comus
- D. Paradise Lost
- E. The Waste Land

Choose the correct option from the following
1. A, B, D, E, C
2. B, C, A, D, E
3. B, A, E, C, D
4. B, E, D, C, A

Explanations:
Ans: B, C, A, D, E

Hero and Leander: It is a narrative poem written by Christopher Marlowe in 1593. The poem tells the story of the love affair between Hero, a priestess of Aphrodite, and Leander, a young man from Abydos. It is considered one of Marlowe's greatest works.

Masque of Comus: It is a masque (a form of festive courtly entertainment) written by John Milton in 1634. It tells the story of a virtuous lady who becomes lost in the woods and is tempted by the evil sorcerer Comus. The masque is notable for its use of music, dance, and elaborate stage effects.

Lycidas: It is a pastoral elegy written by John Milton in 1637. The poem mourns the death of Edward King, a fellow Cambridge student of Milton's, who drowned in the Irish Sea. It is considered one of Milton's greatest works.

Paradise Lost: It is an epic poem written by John Milton in 1667. The poem tells the story of Adam and Eve's fall from grace and their expulsion from the Garden of Eden. It is considered one of the greatest works of English literature.

The Waste Land: It is a modernist poem written by T.S. Eliot in 1922. The poem is a fragmented and highly allusive work that reflects the disillusionment and fragmentation of post-World War I Europe. It is considered one of the most important works of modernist literature.

Question 12

"What needs my Shakespeare for his honoured bones
The labour of an age in piled stones?
Or that his hallowed reliques should be hid
Under a star-ypointing pyramid?"

These lines are written by

1. Ben Jonson
2. **John Milton**
3. Robert Browning
4. William Wordsworth

Explanations:
The lines are from Milton's poem "On Shakespeare", published in the second folio edition of Shakespeare's plays in 1632. "On Shakespeare" is a poem by John Milton, published in the second folio edition of William Shakespeare's plays in 1632. In the poem, Milton praises Shakespeare as a great poet and dramatist and expresses his admiration for Shakespeare's works.

On Shakespeare
John Milton - 1608-1674

"What needs my Shakespeare for his honour'd Bones,
The labour of an age in pilèd Stones,
Or that his hallow'd reliques should be hid
Under a stary pointing Pyramid?

Dear son of Memory, great heir of Fame,
What need'st thou such weak witnes of thy name?
Thou in our wonder and astonishment
Hast built thy self a live-long Monument.
For whilst to th' shame of slow-endeavouring art,
Thy easie numbers flow, and that each heart
Hath from the leaves of thy unvalu'd Book
Those Delphick lines with deep impression took,
Then thou our fancy of it self bereaving,
Dost make us Marble with too much conceaving;
And so Sepulcher'd in such pomp dost lie,
That Kings for such a Tomb would wish to die."

Question 13
Arrange the correct chronological sequence of the publication of the following texts:

A. *September 1, 1939*
B. *The Collar*
C. *Beppo*
D. *Paradise Lost*
E. *Seeing Things*

Choose the correct answer from the options given below:

1. B, D. C, A. E
2. B. A, E, C, D
3. A, E, B. C, D
4. C, B. A, D, E

Explanations
Answer: 1. B, D. C, A. E

"The Collar" is a poem written by the Welsh poet George Herbert and was published in 1633 as part of his collection of poems titled The Temple. This poem explores the struggles of a man who has lost his faith and is filled with anger over the commitments he made to God. He believes that his devotion to his faith has been in vain and begins to imagine a life free from religious constraints. He renounces his commitments and declares himself liberated. The central themes of the poem revolve around the conflict between one's beliefs and the desire for personal autonomy in defiance of religious restrictions. The speaker attempts to set his own boundaries and guide his own path rather than following the guidance of God. He tries to convince himself that a life of freedom will provide the satisfaction that his faith failed to deliver.

Paradise Lost is a renowned epic poem composed in blank verse by the English poet John Milton (1608–1674) during the 17th century. The initial version was **published in 1667** and consisted of ten books comprising over ten thousand lines of verse. A revised edition was released in 1674, featuring twelve books organised in a similar manner to Virgil's Aeneid, with minor revisions throughout.

Beppo: A Venetian Story is an extensive poem written by Lord Byron in 1817 while he was in Venice. Beppo represents Byron's initial venture into composing using the Italian ottava rima metre, which accentuates satirical digression. This work serves as a precursor to Byron's most renowned and often regarded as his best poem, Don Juan. The poem encompasses 760 verses, divided into 95 stanzas.

"September 1, 1939" is a poem by W. H. Auden, composed shortly after the German invasion of Poland that marked the commencement of World War II. It was initially published in The New Republic on October 18, 1939, and later included in Auden's collection titled Another Time (1940). The poem intentionally echoes the stanzaic structure of W. B. Yeats's "Easter, 1916," another poem that explores a significant historical event. Similar to Yeats's piece, Auden's poem transitions from a depiction of historical failures and frustrations to a glimpse of potential transformation in the present or future.

Seeing Things is the eighth collection of poetry by Seamus Heaney, the recipient of the 1995 Nobel Prize in Literature. It was published in 1991 and draws inspiration from the visions of the afterlife depicted in the works of Virgil and Dante Alighieri. Heaney employs these inspirations to come to terms with the death of his father, Patrick, in 1986.

Question 14

Which of the following works of Milton seeks to adapt the form of Greek tragedy?

1. Samson Agonistes
2. Paradise Regained
3. Lycidas
4. Comus

Explanations
Answer: 1. Samson Agonistes

***Samson Agonistes* is a tragedy by John Milton, published in 1671 along with his epic *Paradise Regained*. It is considered one of the greatest English dramas following the Greek model and is known as a closet tragedy**, more suitable for reading than performance. The play portrays the final phase of Samson's life as recounted in the biblical Book of Judges. Despite being blind when he wrote it, Milton depicts Samson, once a mighty warrior, now blinded and imprisoned by the Philistines. Overcoming self-pity and despair, Samson regains his strength and brings down the temple of the Philistine god Dagon, sacrificing himself along with his captors.

Other Explanations

***Lycidas* is a poem by John Milton, composed in 1637 as part of a volume of elegies published in 1638 to commemorate the death of his contemporary at the University of Cambridge, Edward King,** who drowned in a shipwreck. The poem mourns the loss of a virtuous and promising young man who was about to begin a career as a clergyman. Following the conventions of the classical pastoral elegy, Milton contemplates themes of fame, the meaning of life, and divine judgement.

***Comus* is a masque by John Milton, performed on September 29, 1634,** at Ludlow Castle in Shropshire before John Egerton, the Earl of Bridgewater, and later published anonymously in 1637. Milton wrote the masque to honour the earl's appointment as lord president of Wales and the Marches. It serves as an allegory against excessive revelry and celebrates private heroism in chastity and virtue. **The story revolves around a virtuous Lady who gets lost in the woods and encounters the evil sorcerer Comus.** Despite his attempts to imprison her, the Lady defends temperance and chastity in a debate with

Comus and is eventually freed by her two brothers, aided by the Attendant Spirit and the river nymph Sabrina.

Question 15
Match List I with List II

List I	List II
A. Christopher Hill	I. Milton
B. Catherine Belsey	II. Milton's Language
C. E.M.W. Tillyard	III. John Milton: Language, Gender, Power
D. Thomas N Corns	IV. Milton and the English Revolution

Choose the correct answer from the options given below:

       1. A-IV, B-III, C- I, D-II
       2. A-II, B-III, C-IV, D-I
       3. A-II, B-IV, C-I, D-III
       4. A-III, B- I, C-II, D-IV

Explanations:
Answer: 1. A-IV, B-III, C- I, D-II

A. "Milton and the English Revolution" by Christopher Hill: This book examines the relationship between John Milton's writings and the English Revolution, exploring Milton's involvement in the political and social changes of the time.

B. "*John Milton: Language, Gender, Power* (1988)" by Catherine Belsey: This work explores the intersections of language, gender, and power in John Milton's writings, analysing how Milton's use of language reflects and shapes social and gender dynamics.

C. "*Milton* (1946) " by E. M. W. Tillyard: This book provides a comprehensive study of John Milton's life, works, and literary achievements, offering insights into his poetry, prose, and his role in the cultural and intellectual landscape of his time.

D. "Milton's Language" (1990) by Thomas N. Corns: This work focuses specifically on the language used by John Milton in his writings, exploring his innovative linguistic techniques and their significance in his poetry and prose.

Question 16
Find the chronological sequence of John Milton's publications:

> A. "Paradise Lost"
> B. "Lycidas"
> C. "On the Morning of Christ's Nativity"
> D. "On Shakespeare"
> E. "Paradise Regained"

Choose the correct answer from the options given below:

> 1. A, B.C, D, E
> 2. B, D, E, C. A
> 3. C. D, E. B. A
> 4. C, D. B, A, E

Explanations:
Answer: 4. C, D. B, A, E

Poetry and drama
- **1629: On the Morning of Christ's Nativity**
- **1630: On Shakespeare**
- 1631: On Arriving at the Age of Twenty-Three
- 1632: L'Allegro
- 1632: Il Penseroso
- 1634: A Mask Presented at Ludlow Castle, 1634, commonly known as Comus (a masque)
- **1637: Lycidas**
- 1645: Poems of Mr John Milton, Both English and Latin
- 1652: When I Consider How My Light is Spent (Commonly referred to as "On his blindness", though Milton did not use this title)[a]
- 1655: On the Late Massacre in Piedmont
- **1667: Paradise Lost**
- **1671: Paradise Regained**
- **1671: Samson Agonistes**

- ➢ 1673: Poems, &c, Upon Several Occasions
- ➢ Arcades: a masque. (date is unknown).
- ➢ On his Deceased wife, To The Nightingale, On reaching the Age of twenty four.

Prose

- ➢ **Of Reformation (1641)**
- ➢ Of Prelatical Episcopacy (1641)
- ➢ Animadversions (1641)
- ➢ The Reason of Church-Government Urged against Prelaty (1642)
- ➢ Apology for Smectymnuus (1642)
- ➢ **Doctrine and Discipline of Divorce (1643)**
- ➢ Judgement of Martin Bucer Concerning Divorce (1644)
- ➢ **Of Education (1644)**
- ➢ **Areopagitica (1644)**
- ➢ Tetrachordon (1645)
- ➢ Colasterion (1645)
- ➢ The Tenure of Kings and Magistrates (1649)
- ➢ **Eikonoklastes (1649)**
- ➢ Defensio pro Populo Anglicano [First Defence] (1651)
- ➢ Defensio Secunda [Second Defence] (1654)
- ➢ A Treatise of Civil Power (1659)
- ➢ The Likeliest Means to Remove Hirelings from the Church (1659)
- ➢ The Ready and Easy Way to Establish a Free Commonwealth (1660)
- ➢ Brief Notes Upon a Late Sermon (1660)
- ➢ Accedence Commenced Grammar (1669)
- ➢ **The History of Britain (1670)**
- ➢ Artis logicae plenior institutio [Art of Logic] (1672)
- ➢ Of True Religion (1673)
- ➢ Epistolae Familiaries (1674)
- ➢ Prolusiones (1674)
- ➢ A brief History of Moscovia, and other less known Countries lying Eastward of Russia as far as Cathay, gathered from the writings of several Eye-witnesses (1682)
- ➢ **De Doctrina Christiana (1823)**

Charles I, the Civil War and The Eikon Basilik

- **Eikon Basilike is an autobiography by Charles I.**
- **The penultimate chapter is a farewell to his eldest son.**
- Charles I wrote, 'Farewell, till We meet in Heaven.'
- The book portrays Charles I as a **just and pious King.**
- **Thirty-five editions were printed in the first year.**
- The **small format allowed readers to conceal** the book.

Roundheads and The Cavalier poets.

Roundheads:

- **The supporters of the Parliament of England** during the English Civil War (1642–1651).
- Also known **as Parliamentarians, they fought against King Charles I** of England and his supporters, known as the **Cavaliers or Royalists.**
- Cavaliers claimed to rule by absolute monarchy and the principle of the divine right of kings.
    - **Leviathan** by **Hobbes** argues for **absolute monarchy** and **social contract.**
    - **Hobbes was aligned with Royalists**, not a true **Cavalier or Roundhead.**
- The goal of the Roundhead party was to give the Parliament supreme control over the executive administration of the country/kingdom.
- From 1641 Milton gave up poetry for prose polemics for the sake of Puritan causes.
- He was a Protestant and from his childhood he disliked the religious policy of King Charles.
- **John Milton might be called a Roundhead.**
- The Cavaliers, or Royalists, supported the king and tended toward Catholicism.
- **John Milton** was aligned with the **Roundheads**, supporting the **Parliamentary cause** against the monarchy during the English Civil War.
- He was a **staunch republican** and a vocal critic of King Charles I.
- **Andrew Marvell** supported Parliament and worked with **Milton.**
- **George Wither** was a Puritan poet and **satirist.**

> ➤ **John Bunyan** supported Parliament and served in its **army**.

The Cavalier poets:
> ➤ It was a school of **English poets of the 17th century** that came from the classes that supported **King Charles I during the English Civil War (1642–1651)**.
> ➤ Charles, a connoisseur of the fine arts, supported poets who created the art he craved.
> ➤ These poets, in turn, grouped themselves with the **King and his service**, thus becoming Cavalier Poets.

List of the Cavalier Poets:
Code: (Loyal Cavalier Care well for love sick)

The best-known cavalier poets are

> ➤ Robert Herrick
> ➤ Richard Lovelace
> ➤ Thomas Carew
> ➤ Sir John Suckling
> ➤ Edmund Waller

Robert Herrick (1591-1674)

(**Code**: Herrick Whisper to the Noble Virgins, Anthea and Julia: "Gather Rosebuds and Cherry)

> ➤ English cleric and poet, the most original of the "sons of Ben [Jonson].
> ➤ His two volumes of poems are ***Noble Numbers (1647)*** and ***Hesperides (1648).***
> ➤ He is best known for Hesperides, a book of poems.
>> o Contained about **1,400 poems**, primarily concise, with many **brief epigrams.**
>> o This includes the carpe diem poem "***To the Virgins, to Make Much of Time,***" with the first line "***Gather ye rosebuds while ye may.***"
>> o Among the best known of his shorter pieces are **To Anthea, To Julia, and Cherry Ripe.**
> ➤ He wrote **elegies, satires**, and **love songs**.

- ➢ **Herrick's poetry** reflects truth in **human sentiments**.
- ➢ His style is **light, worldly, and hedonistic**.
- ➢ Themes include **rural life** and **fleeting beauty**.
- ➢ Known for **technical mastery**, rhythm, and imagery.
- ➢ He belonged to the **Cavalier poets**, supporting Charles I.
- ➢ Influenced by **classical tradition** and **English folklore**.
- ➢ **Jonson** and **Burton** were major influences on Herrick.

Gather ye Rose-buds while ye may,
Old Time is still a-flying:
And this same flower that smiles to day,
To morrow will be dying.
The glorious Lamp of Heaven, the Sun,
The higher he's a getting;
The sooner will his Race be run,
And neerer he's to Setting.
That Age is best, which is the first,
When Youth and Blood are warmer;
But being spent, the worse, and worst
Times, still succeed the former.
Then be not coy, but use your time;
And while ye may, go marry:
For having lost but once your prime,
You may forever tarry.

Thomas Carew (1595-1640)

(**Code**: *Cruel Reptiles*)

- ➢ He was an English poet among the **'Cavalier' group of Caroline poets**.
- ➢ In 1630 Carew received a court appointment and became a server at the table to the king.
- ➢ The Earl of Clarendon considered him "*a person of pleasant and facetious wit*" among a **brilliant circle of friends, including Ben Jonson**.
- ➢ His longest poem was the sensuous ***Rapture***.
- ➢ He greatly admired the poems of John Donne, whom he called the king of ***"the universal monarchy of wit"*** *in his elegy on Donne*.

Richard Lovelace (1618-1657)

(**Code**: *Love story of Althea and Lucast in the prison*)

- ➢ He was a **cavalier poet** who fought on behalf of the king during the Civil War.
- ➢ His best-known works are "***To Althea, from Prison" and "To Lucasta, Going to the Warres."***
- ➢ Started writing while a student at Oxford, he wrote almost 200 poems.
- ➢ His first work was a drama, **The Scholars,** never published but performed at college and then in London.
- ➢ In 1640, he wrote a tragedy, **The Soldier**, based on his military experience.
- ➢ When serving in the Bishops' Wars, he wrote the **sonnet "To Generall Goring.**
- ➢ **"To Lucasta, Going to the Warres,"** written in 1640, concerning his first political action.
- ➢ **"To Althea, From Prison"** was written during his first imprisonment in 1642.
- ➢ Later that year, during his travels to Holland with General Goring, he wrote *The Rose,* followed *by The Scrutiny.*
- ➢ On 14 May 1649, **Lucasta** was published.
- ➢ He also wrote **poems on animal life: (Note: The same kind of Ted Hughes animal poems like-The Thought-Fox, Hawk Roosting, Jaguar, Crow, An Otter, The Hawk in the Rain, Thrushes**)

  - o **The Ant**
  - o **The Grasse-hopper**
  - o **The Snayl**
  - o **The Falcon**
  - o **The Toad**
  - o **Spyder.**

- ➢ In 1660, after Lovelace died, *Lucasta: Postume Poems* was published;
  - o It contains **A Mock-Song**, which has a darker tone than his previous works.

William Winstanley thought highly of Lovelace's work and compared him to an idol: ***"I can compare no Man so like this Colonel Lovelace as Sir Philip Sidney**,"* of which it is in an Epitaph made of him;

- "Nor is it fit that more I should aquaint
- Lest Men adore in one
- A Scholar, Souldier, Lover, and a Saint"

His most quoted excerpts are from the beginning of the last stanza of "To Althea, From Prison":

- *"Stone walls do not a prison make,*
- *Nor iron bars a cage;*
- *Minds innocent and quiet take*
- *That for an hermitage."*
- *And the end of "To Lucasta. Going to the Warres":*
- *"I could not love thee, dear, so much,*
- *Lov'd I not Honour more."*

Sir John Suckling (1609-1641)

(Code: *Sir Suckle Why so pale and wan on your wedding*)

- English poet, prominent among those renowned for careless gaiety and wit.
- The accomplishments of a **Cavalier poet**.
- He also invented the **card game cribbage.**
- He is best known for his poem **"Ballade upon a Wedding."**
- He was a gentleman of the privy **chamber to Charles I and a friend of the poets Thomas Carew, Richard Lovelace, and Sir William Davenant**.
- In 1641 Suckling took an active **part in the plot to rescue the Earl of Strafford** from the Tower.
- When the plot was discovered, Suckling fled to France and is believed to have **committed suicide.**
- The author of four plays, the most ambitious of which is the tragedy *Aglaura* (1637)
- Comedy *The Goblins (1638)*.

- o They all contain echoes of Shakespeare and Beaumont, and Fletcher.
- ➤ His reputation as a poet rests on his lyrics, the best of which justifies his description as *"natural, easy Suckling."*
- ➤ He inherited from Donne the tradition of the "anti-platonic" deflation of high-flown love sentiment.
- ➤ He can even be cynically chiding in such songs as this:
  - o *"Why so pale and wan, fond lover*?
- ➤ *A Session of the Poets* (1637; published 1646) is an amusing skit.
- ➤ His masterpiece street ballad is undoubted "*A Ballad Upon a Wedding,*".

Edmund Waller (1606-1687)

(**Code**: *Wall of Divine Rose*)
- ➤ **Waller** helped establish the **heroic couplet** in English poetry.
- ➤ **John Dryden** credited him with reforming poetic **numbers**.
- ➤ He entered **Parliament** in 1624, supporting the **Royalists**.
- ➤ Waller was accused of plotting for **Charles I** in 1643.
- ➤ He lived in exile until **Cromwell** allowed his return in 1651.
- ➤ **Waller retired** from politics after his second wife's death.
- ➤ Several of Waller's poems, including:
  - o *"Go, lovely Rose!"*
  - o *"To the King, upon his Majesties happy return."*
  - o *Divine Poems (1685).*
  - o *The Second Part of Mr. Waller's Poems* was published in 1690.

Metaphysical Poets:

- ➤ In the *Life of Cowley*, **Dr. Samuel Johnson** has made a critical assessment of the works of the **metaphysical poets**, especially of Cowley.
- ➤ According to Johnson, **Metaphysical poets** were led by **John Donne**.
- ➤ Their poetry explores **philosophical conceptions** of the universe.
- ➤ They primarily wrote **love** and **religious poems**.
- ➤ **Ontology**, a central branch of **metaphysics, investigates the nature of being and existence**, categorizing entities and probing the fundamental structures that underpin reality.

- ➤ English poets whose work was characterized by the **inventive use of conceits**.
  - ○ **Extended metaphors** or **unusual comparisons used in poetry to connect two seemingly unrelated ideas or objects.**
  - ○ Often found in Metaphysical poetry, conceits are known for **their intellectual complexity and imaginative leaps**, making abstract concepts relatable.
  - ○ **For example, in John Donne's poems,** he might compare **love to a compass or the soul to a spider's web.**
- ➤ A greater emphasis on the spoken rather than the lyrical quality of their verse.
- ➤ John Donne's poetry, the chief of the Metaphysicals.
- ➤ **Others include:**
  - ○ **(Code:** Marvelous COW Crush The HERB in CleVonland**)**
  - ○ Henry Vaughan
  - ○ Andrew Marvell
  - ○ John Cleveland
  - ○ Abraham Cowley
  - ○ George Herbert
  - ○ Richard Crashaw.
- ➤ **John Dryden censured Donne for affecting "the metaphysics" and for perplexing "the minds of the fair sex with nice speculations of philosophy when he should engage their hearts . . . with the softnesses of love." Samuel Johnson, in referring to the learning that their poetry displays, also dubbed them "the metaphysical poets," and the term has continued in use ever since.**

Henry Vaughan (1621-1695)

(Code:Thaliva Retreat)

- ➤ **Welsh metaphysical poet**, author and translator and a medical physician.
- ➤ His religious poetry appeared in *Silex Scintillans* in 1650, with the 2nd part in 1655.
- ➤ In 1646 his Poems, with the *Tenth Satire of Juvenal Englished,* were published.
- ➤ Meanwhile, he was persuaded by reading the **religious poet George Herbert to renounce "idle verse."**

- ➢ The prose *Mount of Olives and Solitary Devotions* (1652) shows his authenticity and depth of convictions.
- ➢ His books include *Poems (1646), Olor Iscanus (1647), Silex Scintillans (1650), and Thalia Rediviva (1678)*.
- ➢ His regard for nature, moreover, has a closeness and penetration that sometimes (for example, in *The Retreat*) suggests Wordsworth.

Andrew Marvell (1621-1678)

(Code: *Marvell picks up Apple from the garden after returning from Ireland on his anniversary to meet his coy mirstrss and define love*)

- ➢ English **metaphysical poet,** satirist, and politician who sat in the **House of Commons** between 1659 and 1678.
- ➢ During the Commonwealth period, he was a **colleague and friend of John Milton.**
- ➢ Marvell was educated at Hull grammar school and **Trinity College, Cambridge,** taking a B.A. in 1639.
- ➢ His father's death in **1641 may have ended Marvell's promising academic career.** He was abroad for at least five years (1642–46), presumably as a tutor.
- ➢ In 1651–52 he was tutor to **Mary, daughter of Lord Fairfax,** the Parliamentary general, at Nun **Appleton**, Yorkshire.
- ➢ He probably wrote his notable poems "*Upon Appleton House*" and "*The Garden*" and **his series of Mower poems.**

Poems:
- ➢ **Upon Appleton House (1651)**
  - o Written for **Thomas Fairfax,** 3rd Lord Fairfax of Cameron.
  - o Written in **1651**, when Marvell worked as a tutor for **Fairfax's daughter, Mary.**
  - o An example of a country house poem.
  - o It describes **Fairfax's Nunappleton estate.**
  - o It also reflects upon the political and religious concerns of the time.
- ➢ **The Garden:**
  - o A romantic poem.
  - o The poet's **emotions and feelings are told through the words of nature.**

- o The poet explains the value of **nature and illustrates** it through the poem.
- ➢ **The Mower's Song (1681)**
  - o Pastoral poem published posthumously in **1681**.
  - o The work is the **last of four poems** by Marvell, known as the Mower poems.
  - o Though the mower in this poem is not named, scholars have stated that all the Mower poems are in the **voice of Damon the Mower**.
- ➢ **A Horatian Ode upon Cromwell's Return from Ireland (1650)**
  - o Although he **earlier opposed** Oliver Cromwell's Commonwealth government.
  - o He was a tutor to Cromwell's ward **William Dutton**.
  - o In 1657 he became assistant to John Milton as Latin secretary in the foreign office.
- ➢ **"The First Anniversary" (1655) and "On the Death of O.C." (1659)**
- ➢ **The Definition of Love**

My love is of a birth as rare
As 'tis for object strange and high;
It was begotten by Despair
Upon Impossibility.

Magnanimous Despair alone
Could show me so divine a thing
Where feeble Hope could ne'er have flown,
But vainly flapp'd its tinsel wing.

And yet I quickly might arrive
Where my extended soul is fixt,
But Fate does iron wedges drive,
And always crowds itself betwixt.

For Fate with jealous eye does see
Two perfect loves, nor lets them close;
Their union would her ruin be,
And her tyrannic pow'r depose.

And therefore her decrees of steel
Us as the distant poles have plac'd,

(Though love's whole world on us doth wheel)
Not by themselves to be embrac'd;

Unless the giddy heaven fall,
And earth some new convulsion tear;
And, us to join, the world should all
Be cramp'd into a planisphere.

As lines, so loves oblique may well
Themselves in every angle greet;
But ours so truly parallel,
Though infinite, can never meet.

Therefore the love which us doth bind,
But Fate so enviously debars,
Is the conjunction of the mind,
And opposition of the stars.

To His Coy Mistress (1681)

- ➤ Poem of **46 lines**, published in 1681.
- ➤ The poem explores the **conflict between love and time.**
- ➤ The poet tells his **mistress** they have **all the time.**
- ➤ He'd spend **hundreds of years praising** her beauty.
- ➤ She could **spend years** refusing his **romantic advances.**
- ➤ He gently reminds her **time is limited** for **mortals.**
- ➤ The poet urges her to **embrace love** before **beauty fades.**
- ➤ The argument is **ingeniously constructed** and **cleverly presented.**
- ➤ The reader sees an **impatient lover** and life's fleeting nature.
- ➤ The poem is written in **iambic tetrameter (consisting of four iambic feet)** and rhymes in couplets.
    - o The first verse paragraph ("Had we...") is ten couplets long,
    - o The second ("But...") six, and
    - o The third ("Now, therefore...") seven.
    - o The logical form of the poem runs: if... but... therefore....
- ➤ **First stanza** describes love without **time's constraints.**
- ➤ He could **spend centuries admiring** her beauty.
- ➤ Her **coyness wouldn't discourage** his persistent admiration.
- ➤ **Second stanza** laments **how short human life is.**
- ➤ Once life ends, the **opportunity is gone.**

- The speaker states, **no one embraces death**.
- **Last stanza** urges her to **accept his love**.
- He argues they should **love with passion**.
- **Loving fully** makes the most of **limited time**.
- Their passion defies the **brevity of life**.

> *Had we but world enough and time,*
> *This coyness, lady, were no crime.*
> *We would sit down, and think which way*
> *To walk, and pass our long love's day.*
> *Thou by the Indian Ganges' side*
> *Shouldst rubies find; I by the tide*
> *Of Humber would complain. I would*
> *Love you ten years before the flood,*
> *And you should, if you please, refuse*
> *Till the conversion of the Jews.*
> *My vegetable love should grow*
> *Vaster than empires and more slow;*
> *An hundred years should go to praise*
> *Thine eyes, and on thy forehead gaze;*
> *Two hundred to adore each breast,*
> *But thirty thousand to the rest;*
> *An age at least to every part,*
> *And the last age should show your heart.*
> *For, lady, you deserve this state,*
> *Nor would I love at lower rate.*
> *But at my back I always hear*
> *Time's wingèd chariot hurrying near;*
> *And yonder all before us lie*
> *Deserts of vast eternity.*
> *Thy beauty shall no more be found;*
> *Nor, in thy marble vault, shall sound*
> *My echoing song; then worms shall try*
> *That long-preserved virginity,*
> *And your quaint honour turn to dust,*
> *And into ashes all my lust;*
> *The grave's a fine and private place,*
> *But none, I think, do there embrace.*
> *Now therefore, while the youthful hue*

Sits on thy skin like morning dew,
And while thy willing soul transpires
At every pore with instant fires,
Now let us sport us while we may,
And now, like amorous birds of prey,
Rather at once our time devour
Than languish in his slow-chapped power.
Let us roll all our strength and all
Our sweetness up into one ball,
And tear our pleasures with rough strife
Through the iron gates of life:
Thus, though we cannot make our sun
Stand still, yet we will make him run.

John Cleveland (1613-1658)

(**Code**: Cleveland [*The Character of a London Diurnal (1647)*])

- ➢ English poet, the most popular of his time and then,
- ➢ And later times, the most commonly abused metaphysical poet.
- ➢ **Cleveland** attacked **Charles I's enemies** in his satire **"The Rebel Scot"**.
- ➢ He was **imprisoned for delinquency** in **1655**.
- ➢ **Released by Cromwell**, he still upheld his **royalist beliefs**.
- ➢ Cleveland's poems first appeared in *The Character of a London Diurnal (1647)* and then in some 20 collections in the next quarter-century.
- ➢ Cleveland's political satires **influenced** his friend **Samuel Butler (in Hudibras)**, and his use of **heroic couplets foreshadowed that of Dryden**.

Abraham Cowley (1618-1667)

(**Code**: *Owl of Thisbe Constantly referred as demi goddess*)

- ➢ **Cowley** was born in London in **1618**.
- ➢ He studied at **Westminster** and **Cambridge**, excelling as a scholar.
- ➢ Cowley supported the **King** during the **Civil War**.
- ➢ After **the Restoration**, he lived in **retirement** writing books.
- ➢ **Cowley was an infant prodigy**, writing from a young age.
- ➢ At ten, he wrote the epic *Piramus and Thisbe*.

- ➢ Produced an even longer poem called *Constantia and Philetus* (1630).
- ➢ He produced many works, including **poems, plays, and essays**.
- ➢ His best-known poem is *The Davideis* (1637).
- ➢ His stage comedy *The Guardian (1641, revised 1661*) introduced the **fop Puny,** who became a staple of Restoration comedy.
- ➢ He also wrote *The Mistress* and *Pindarique Odes*.
- ➢ His prose works include **Essays** and a discourse on **Cromwell**.
- ➢ In the *Life of Cowley*, **Dr. Samuel Johnson** has made a critical assessment of the works of the **metaphysical poets**, especially of Cowley.
- ➢ He promoted the Royal Society, publishing *A Proposition for the Advancement of Experimental Philosophy* (1661).
- ➢ In his retirement, he wrote sober, reflective essays reminiscent of Montaigne.
- ➢ His prose works included his *Essays and Discourse concerning Oliver Cromwell (1661)*.
- ➢ In 1737 Alexander Pope said: "*Who now reads Cowley?*".
- ➢ Perhaps his most effective poem is the **elegy on the death of his friend and fellow poet Richard Crashaw.**

George Herbert (1593-1633)

(**Code**: *Herbert Alter the East Wings in the Temple*)
- ➢ **Welsh poet,** orator, and priest of the Church of England.
- ➢ Good education that led to his admission to **Trinity College, Cambridge,** in 1609.
- ➢ **None of his poems was published during his lifetime**.
- ➢ On his death-bed he gave to a friend the manuscript of *The Temple*,
    - o A collection of religious poems in various meters.
    - o **Full Title: *The Temple: Sacred Poems and Private Ejaculations*.**
    - o **Some of his poems, such as "The Altar" and "Easter Wings,"**
    - o They are called **"pattern" poems**.
    - o Joseph Addison in the 18th century called **"false wit."**
- ➢ **Coleridge** wrote of Herbert's diction, *"Nothing can be more pure, manly, and unaffected."*

> ➤ Herbert also wrote at Bemerton *A Priest to the Temple: Or The Country Parson, his Character and Rule of Life (1652)*.

Richard Crashaw (1613-1649)

(**Code**: *Crash on the Steps of the Temple while praying to our Lord*)

> ➤ English poet, teacher, High Church Anglican cleric, and Roman Catholic convert.
> ➤ One of the significant metaphysical poets.
> ➤ Crashaw was educated at Charterhouse School and Pembroke College, Cambridge.
> ➤ Crashaw's English religious poems were republished in Paris in 1652 under the title **Carmen Deo Nostro ("Hymn to Our Lord")**. Some of his most delicate lines are those appended to *"The Flaming Heart,"* a poem on St. Teresa of Avila.

Sir John Denham (1615-1669)

> ➤ Established a leisurely meditative poem as a new English genre describing a particular landscape.
> ➤ Wrote a tragedy, *The Sophy (1641)*, but his poem, *Cooper's Hill (1642)*.

Thomas Traherne (1636-1674)

> ➤ English poet, Anglican cleric, theologian, and religious writer.
> ➤ Traherne is best known today is the *Centuries of Meditations*.
> ➤ His prose works include:
>   - *Roman Forgeries (1673),*
>   - *Christian Ethics (1675),*
>   - *A Serious and Patheticall Contemplation of the Mercies of God* (1699).

Questions:

Question 17

Arrange the following groups of poets in their chronological sequence in relation to English literary history:

    A.   The Imagist poets
    B.   The Cavalier poets
    C.   The Movement poets
    D.   The Lake poets

Choose the correct answer from the options given below
1. B, D, C, A
2. D, A, B, C
3. D, B, A, C
4. **B, D, A, C**

Correct Explanations:
The cavalier poets was a school of English poets of the 17th century, that came from the classes that supported King Charles I during the English Civil War (1642–1651). The best-known cavalier poets are Robert Herrick, Richard Lovelace, Thomas Carew, and Sir John Suckling.

The Lake Poets were a group of English poets who all lived in the Lake District of England, United Kingdom, in the first half of the nineteenth century. As a group, they followed no single "school" of thought or literary practice then known. The three main figures of what has become known as the Lakes School were William Wordsworth, Samuel Taylor Coleridge, and Robert Southey. They were associated with several other poets and writers, including Dorothy Wordsworth, Charles Lamb, Mary Lamb, Charles Lloyd, Hartley Coleridge, John Wilson, and Thomas De Quincey.

Imagism was a movement in early-20th-century Anglo-American poetry that favored precision of imagery and clear, sharp language. It is considered to be the first organized modernist literary movement in the English language. Imagist publications appearing between 1914 and 1917 featured works by many of the most prominent modernist figures in poetry and other fields, including Pound, H.D. (Hilda Doolittle), Amy Lowell, Ford Madox Ford, William Carlos Williams, F. S. Flint, and T. E. Hulme.

The Movement was a term coined in 1954 by J. D. Scott, literary editor of The Spectator, to describe a group of writers, including Philip Larkin, Kingsley Amis, Donald Davie, D. J. Enright, John Wain, Elizabeth Jennings, Thom Gunn, and Robert Conquest.

What is the correct chronological sequence of British poets in order of their birth ?

A. Andrew Marvell
B. John Milton
C. John Donne
D. Richard Lovelace
E. Thomas Carew

Choose the correct answer from the options given below :

(1) C, E, B, D, A
(2) D, B, C, A, E
(3) B, C, D, E, A
(4) A, D, E, C, B

Explanations:
Answer: (1) C, E, B, D, A

- **John Donne (1571-1631) (C)**
- Robert Herrick (1591-1674)
- **Thomas Carew (1595-1640) (E)**
- **JOHN MILTON (1608–74) (B)**
- **Richard Lovelace (1618-1657) (D)**
- Sir John Suckling (1609-1641)
- Edmund Waller (1606-1687)
- Henry Vaughan (1621-1695)
- **Andrew Marvell (1621-1678) (A)**
- John Cleveland (1613-1658)
- Abraham Cowley (1618-1667)
- George Herbert (1593-1633)
- Richard Crashaw (1613-1649)
- Sir John Denham (1615-1669)
- Thomas Traherne (1636-1674)

Who composed Lucasta: Postume Poems, published posthumously?

1. George Herbert
2. Thomas Carew
3. Richard Lovelace
4. Sir John Suckling

Explanations:
Answer: 3. Richard Lovelace

Richard Lovelace (9 December 1617 – 1657) was an English poet in the seventeenth century. He was a cavalier poet who fought on behalf of Charles I during the English Civil War. His best known works are "To Althea, from Prison", and **"To Lucasta, Going to the Warres"**. "To Lucasta, Going to the Warres" in 1649 was published in the collection Lucasta by Lovelace of that year. The initial poems were addressed to Lucasta, not clearly identified with any real-life woman, under the titles "Going beyond the Seas" and "Going to the Warres", on a chivalrous note.

Other Explanations:
George Herbert was an English poet and Anglican priest who lived from 1593 to 1633. He is known for his religious poetry characterised by its deep spirituality and intricate use of metaphysical conceits. Some of his notable poems include: **The Temple: Sacred Poems and Private Ejaculations"** by George Herbert is a collection of religious poems. Here are some of the notable poems included in the collection:

- The Church Porch
- The Altar
- The Sacrifice
- Love (III)
- Redemption
- The Collar
- The Pulley
- The Windows
- The Elixir
- The Bag

Thomas Carew was an English poet associated with the Cavalier poets during the 17th century. His poems often reflect the themes of courtly love, beauty, and sensuality. Some of his famous works include:

> ➤ *An Elegie upon the death of the Deane of Pauls, Dr. John Donne*
> ➤ *To Saxham*
> ➤ *To my worthy Friend, M. D'Avenant, upon his Excellent Play, The Iust Italian*
> ➤ *On the Marriage of T. K. and C. C. the Morning Stormie*
> ➤ *Various love poems and songs dedicated to "Celia"*
> ➤ *A Rapture*
> ➤ *Loves Courtship*
> ➤ *Poems addressing the nature of poetry itself*
> ➤ *Elegy on John Donne*

Sir John Suckling (10 February 1609 – after May 1641) was an English poet, prominent among those renowned for careless gaiety and wit – **the accomplishments of a cavalier poet.** He also invented the card game cribbage. He is best known for his poem "Ballade upon a Wedding".

> ➤ *"Why So Pale and Wan, Fond Lover?"*
> ➤ *"Song: Ballad upon a Wedding"*
> ➤ *"I Pr'ythee Send Me Back My Heart"*
> ➤ *"The Constant Lover"*
> ➤ *"Out upon It! I Have Loved"*
> ➤ *"Love's Offence"*
> ➤ *"Song: Love Will Find out the Way"*
> ➤ *"A Doubt of Martyrdom"*
> ➤ *"The Soldier's Song"*
> ➤ *"The Unfortunate Lover"*

Question 20

Which one of the following is a set of Metaphysical Poets?

1. John Donne, Henry Vaughan, and Andrew Marvell.
2. John Dryden, George Herbert, and Alexander Pope.
3. Samuel Johnson, T. S. Eliot and Herbert Grierson.
4. Henry Vaughan, John Dryden, and John Donne.

Explanations:
Ans: John Donne, Henry Vaughan, and Andrew Marvell.

Metaphysical poet, is any of the poets in 17th-century England who were inclined to the personal and intellectual complexity and concentration that is displayed in the poetry of **John Donne, the chief of the Metaphysicals. Others include Henry Vaughan, Andrew Marvell, John Cleveland, and Abraham Cowley, as well as, to a lesser extent, George Herbert and Richard Crashaw.**

Their work is a blend of emotion and intellectual ingenuity, characterized by **conceit or "wit"**—that is, by the sometimes violent yoking together of apparently unconnected ideas and things so that the reader is startled out of his complacency and forced to think through the argument of the poem. Metaphysical poetry is less concerned with expressing feeling than with analyzing it, with the poet exploring the recesses of his consciousness. The boldness of the literary devices used—especially **obliquity, irony, and paradox** —are often reinforced by a dramatic directness of language and by rhythms derived from that of living speech.

Esteem for Metaphysical poetry never stood higher than in the 1930s and '40s, largely because of **T.S. Eliot's influential essay "The Metaphysical Poets" (1921), a review of Herbert J.C. Grierson's anthology Metaphysical Lyrics & Poems of the Seventeenth Century.** In this essay, Eliot argued that the works of these men embody a fusion of thought and feeling that later poets were unable to achieve because of a **"dissociation of sensibility,"** which resulted in works that were either intellectual or emotional but not both at once. In their own time, however, the epithet **"metaphysical" was used pejoratively: in 1630 the Scottish poet William Drummond of Hawthornden** objected to those of his contemporaries who attempted to "abstract poetry to metaphysical ideas and scholastic quiddities." At the end of the century, **John Dryden censured Donne for affecting "the metaphysics" and for perplexing "the minds of the fair sex with nice speculations of philosophy when he should engage their hearts . . . with the softnesses of love." Samuel Johnson, in referring to the learning that their poetry displays, also dubbed them "the metaphysical poets," and the term has continued in use ever since.** Eliot's adoption of the label as a term of praise is arguably a better guide to his personal aspirations about his own poetry than to the Metaphysical poets themselves; his use of metaphysical underestimates these poets' debt to lyrical and socially engaged verse. Nonetheless, the term is useful for identifying the often intellectual character of their writing.

Question 21

Who among the following are the two great masters of the French language that T. S Eliot contrasts with Dryden and Milton in The Metaphysical Poets'?

A. Francois Villon
B. Jean Racine
C. Charles Baudelaire
D. Arthur Rimbaud

Choose the correct answer from the options given below:

1. A and C only
2. A and D only
3. B and C only
4. B and D only

Explanations:
Answer: 3. B and C only

In "The Metaphysical Poets," T.S. Eliot contrasts the poetry of the French writers Jean Racine and Charles Baudelaire with that of John Milton and John Dryden. Eliot praises Racine and Baudelaire for their use of language and their ability to express complex emotions and ideas with simplicity and precision. He contrasts them with Milton and Dryden, whom he sees as more concerned with the expression of moral or political values in their poetry.

Eliot's comparison can be found in the following excerpt from "The Metaphysical Poets":

*"The French writers, the great masters of the language, have been more concerned with the form of language than with its content. They have been occupied with devising rhetorical devices to convey states of mind, rather than with the exploration of states of mind. They have been concerned, not so much with expressing themselves as with expressing human nature. **The greatest of them, Racine and Baudelaire, have a much closer affinity with the metaphysical poets than has Dryden or Milton.**"*

Question 22

Which two of the following are Samuel Johnson's statements about metaphysical poets?

(A) they were singular in their thoughts
(B) they were careful in their diction

(C) they affected combination of dissimilar images
(D) they avoided occult resemblances

Choose the most appropriate answer from the options given below:

1. (B) and (C) Only
2. (C) and (D) Only
3. (B) and (A) Only
4. (A) and (C) Only

Explanations:
Answer: 4. (A) and (C) Only

Samuel Johnson made two statements about metaphysical poets:

(A) they were singular in their thoughts: Johnson praised the metaphysical poets for their unique and original thinking. He admired their ability to explore unconventional ideas and delve into complex intellectual realms.

(C) they effected a combination of dissimilar images: Johnson recognized the metaphysical poets' skill in creating surprising and imaginative connections between seemingly unrelated images or concepts. He appreciated their ability to merge disparate elements in their poetry, resulting in striking and thought-provoking metaphors.

Johnson's statements highlight the distinctiveness and innovative nature of metaphysical poetry, emphasizing its intellectual depth and unconventional style.

Question 23

In "The Life of Cowley", which two of the following criticisms were made by Samuel Johnson against a group of writers he termed the 'metaphysical poets'?

A. They made an inappropriate combination of wit and imagination.
B. Instead of writing poetry, they only wrote verses.
C. They neither copied nature nor life.
D. They never tried to be singular in their thoughts.

Choose the correct answer from the options given below:
1. **A and B only**
2. B and C only

3. B and D only
4. C and D only

Correct Explanations:

Samuel Johnson in his essay "The Life of Cowley" was critical of the group of poets known as the metaphysical poets, whom he accused of being too focused on using wit and elaborate language at the expense of genuine emotion and meaningful content. Johnson felt that they were more interested in creating clever verses than in writing real poetry and that their work lacked the beauty and grace that characterized the great poets of earlier eras.

"The metaphysical poets were men of learning, and, to show their learning was their whole endeavour; but, unluckily resolving to show it in rhyme, instead of writing poetry, they only wrote verses, and, very often, such verses as stood the trial of the finger better than of the ear; for the modulation was so imperfect, that they were only found to be verses by counting the syllables."

Question 24

How does T.S. Eliot sum up the peculiar quality of Marvell's " Horatian Ode"?

1. Description
2. **'telescoping of images and multiplied associations (UGC Key)**
3. 'a tough reasonableness beneath a slight lyric grace
4. 'a contrast of ideas, different in degree but the same in principle

Correct Explanations:

T.S. Eliot sums up the peculiar quality of Marvell's "Horatian Ode" as "a tough reasonableness beneath a slight lyric grace". The description "telescoping of images and multiplied associations" is actually how Eliot characterises the metaphysical poets in general, not specifically Marvell's "Horatian Ode". The third option, "a contrast of ideas, different in degree but the same in principle", is a description of the method of the metaphysical poets as well.

T.S. Eliot indeed wrote about Marvell's "Horatian Ode." Still, he did not describe its peculiar quality as a "telescoping of images and multiplied associations." Rather, Eliot referred to the poem as having "a unity of sensibility, a profound and delicate sensibility." Here is the full quote:

"Marvell's Horatian Ode has a unity of sensibility, a profound and delicate sensibility, which is nowhere else to be found in the literature. It is a quality which cannot be explained in the abstract, which is dependent upon a particular sensitive apprehension of life. It is this quality which makes the poem a classic."

Question 25

Which of the following two poems are linked with each other in terms of form?

A. "The Last Ride Together"
B. "Ulysses"
C. "Upon Appleton House: To My Lord Fairfax"
D. "To Penshurst"
E. "The Waste Land"

Choose the correct answer from the options given below:

1. A and E only.
2. A and B only.
3. A and D only.
4. **C and D only.**

Explanations:
"Upon Appleton House: To My Lord Fairfax" and "To Penshurst" are linked with each other in terms of form. Both poems are examples of **country-house poems, which were popular in the seventeenth century.** These poems describe the beauty and tranquility of country estates and the noble families who lived there. They often use a descriptive and contemplative style, praising the virtues of country life and rural landscapes. Additionally, both poems were written by poets associated with the metaphysical school of poetry: Andrew Marvell wrote "Upon Appleton House," and Ben Jonson wrote "To Penshurst."

Other Explanations:
"The Last Ride Together" is a poem by Robert Browning that explores the theme of unrequited love. The speaker is addressing his beloved, who is about to marry someone else. He asks for one last ride together before he lets her go. The poem is structured as a dramatic monologue, with the speaker trying to persuade his beloved to spend one last moment with him. The poem is notable

for its use of dramatic irony, as the reader knows that the beloved will not accept the speaker's offer.

"Ulysses" is a poem by Alfred, Lord Tennyson that explores the theme of the search for meaning and purpose in life. The poem is written in the voice of the legendary hero Ulysses, who is now an old man, looking back on his life. He expresses his desire to set out on one final adventure, to seek new experiences and regain his former glory. The poem is notable for its use of blank verse and its complex syntax, which reflects Ulysses' restless, searching spirit.

"Upon Appleton House: To My Lord Fairfax" is a poem by Andrew Marvell that celebrates the beauty and harmony of nature. The poem is written in the voice of the speaker, who is visiting his friend's country estate. The poem is structured as a series of descriptions of the landscape, the animals, and the people who inhabit the estate. The poem is notable for its use of vivid imagery and its celebration of the natural world.

"To Penshurst" is a poem by Ben Jonson that celebrates the beauty and harmony of country life. The poem is written in the voice of the speaker, who is visiting the country estate of his patron. The poem is structured as a series of descriptions of the landscape, the animals, and the people who inhabit the estate. The poem is notable for its use of vivid imagery and its celebration of the natural world.

"The Waste Land" is a poem by T.S. Eliot that is widely regarded as one of the most important works of modernist poetry. The poem is structured as a series of fragmented scenes and voices, which reflect the dislocation and fragmentation of modern life. The poem is notable for its use of allusions and quotations from a wide range of literary and cultural sources, including Shakespeare, Dante, and Hindu mythology.

Question 26

Who composed Lucasta: Postume Poems, published posthumously?

1. George Herbert
2. Thomas Carew
3. Richard Lovelace
4. Sir John Suckling

Explanations:
Answer: 3. Richard Lovelace

Richard Lovelace (9 December 1617 – 1657) was an English poet in the seventeenth century. He was a cavalier poet who fought on behalf of Charles I during the English Civil War. His best known works are "To Althea, from Prison", and **"To Lucasta, Going to the Warres"**. "To Lucasta, Going to the Warres" in 1649 was published in the collection Lucasta by Lovelace of that year. The initial poems were addressed to Lucasta, not clearly identified with any real-life woman, under the titles "Going beyond the Seas" and "Going to the Warres", on a chivalrous note.

Question 27

Which among the following was not recognised as a major dialogue of Plato?

1. Crito
2. Phaedo
3. Symposium
4. Metaphysics

Explanations:
Answer: 4. Metaphysics

Metaphysics: Aristotle's principle work in which he explores First Philosophy, discussing abstract topics such as substance theory, causation, form and matter, the existence of mathematical objects, and the cosmos, laying the foundation for metaphysics as a branch of philosophy.

Question 28

"My love is of a birth as rare
As, tis, for object, striage and high;
It was forgotten by despair
Upon impossibility." (Andrew Marvell)

Name the poem from which these lines have been taken.

1. "The Garden"

2. "The Horatian Ode"
3. "The Definition of Love"
4. "To His Coy Mistress"

Explanations:
Answer: 3. "The Definition of Love"

Question 29

Chronologically arrange the following works on literary criticism in order of their publication:

A. An Apologie for Poetrie
B. The Art of Rhetorique
C. Preface to Lyrical Ballads
D. An Essays in Criticism
E. The Metaphysical Poets

Choose the correct answer from the options given below:

1.   E,A,B,C,D
2.   B,A,C,D,E
3.   C,D,B,A, E
4.   ACE D.B

Explanations:
Answer: 2. B,A,C,D,E **Corrected (B,A,D,C,E)**

Thomas Wilson (1524–1581), an esteemed English diplomat and judge, notably served as a privy councillor and Secretary of State to Queen Elizabeth I from 1577 to 1581. Renowned for his contributions to **English literature, his works "The Art of Logique" (1551) and "The Arte of Rhetorique" (1553)** stand as pioneering comprehensive studies on logic and rhetoric in English. Additionally, Wilson authored "A Discourse upon Usury" (1572) and became the first to translate Demosthenes into English, marking significant literary achievements of his time.

Sir Philip Sidney began his journey as a poet in 1578, with a relatively brief but impactful literary career spanning 7 to 8 years. His seminal work, **"The Defence of Poesy," also known under the titles "The Defence of**

Poesie" and "An Apologie for Poetrie," stands as a powerful testament to the value of poetry, penned by someone deeply versed in both the practice and the classical understanding of the art.

***An Essay on Criticism* is one of the first major poems written by the English writer Alexander Pope (1688–1744), published in 1711**. It is the source of the famous quotations "To err is human; to forgive, divine", "A little learning is a dang'rous thing" (frequently misquoted as "A little knowledge is a dang'rous thing"), and "Fools rush in where angels fear to tread".

***The Preface to Lyrical Ballads* is an essay, composed by William Wordsworth, for the second edition published in __1800__ of the poetry collection Lyrical Ballads, and then greatly expanded in the third edition of 1802

***The Metaphysical Poets* by T.S. Eliot First published in the Times Literary Supplement, 20 October 1921**. By collecting these poems from the work of a generation more often named than read, and more often read than profitably studied, Professor Grierson has rendered a service of some importance.

Question 30

Match List I with List II

List I (Poet)	List II (Poem)
A. John Donne	(i) "The Retreat"
B. Andrew Marvell	(ii) "A Valediction of Weeping"
C. George Herbert	(iii) "The Garden"
D. Henry Vaugham	(iv) "The Collar"

Choose the correct answer from the options given below:

1. (a)-(iv), (b)-(iii), (c)-(ii), (d)-(i)
2. (a)-(ii), (b)-(iv), (c)- i), (d)-(iii)
3. (a)-(iv), (b)-(i), (c)-(ii), d)-(iii)
4. (a)-(ii), (b)-(iii), (c)-(iv), (d)-(i)

Explanations:
Answer: 4. (a)-(ii), (b)-(iii), (c)-(iv), (d)-(i)

(a) - (ii) John Donne's poem "A Valediction of Weeping"

(b) - (iii) Andrew Marvell's poem "The Garden"
(c) - (iv) George Herbert's poem "The Collar"
(d) - (i) Henry Vaughan's poem "The Retreat"

John Donne's poem "A Valediction of Weeping" explores the theme of farewell and separation, expressing the speaker's emotions as they bid farewell to a loved one with tears.

Andrew Marvell's poem "The Garden" depicts a garden as a symbol of nature's beauty and purity, contrasting it with the corruption of the city and emphasizing the need for contemplation and connection with nature.

George Herbert's poem "The Collar" delves into themes of spiritual struggle and surrender, as the speaker wrestles with his desires and ultimately finds solace and freedom in submission to God.

Henry Vaughan's poem "The Retreat" reflects on the transitory nature of life and the search for inner peace, drawing on the imagery of nature and the contemplative retreat of the soul.

Question 31

Which two rivers are mentioned by Andrew Marvell at the beginning of 'To His Coy Mistress'?

    A. The Ganges
    B. Thames
    C. Humber
    D. The Jhelum

Choose the correct answer from the options given below:

    1. A and D only
    2. A and B only
    3. A and C only
    4. B and C only

Explanations:
Answer: 3. A and C only

In the poem "To His Coy Mistress," Andrew Marvell mentions the rivers Ganges and Humber in order to emphasize the transience of human life and the urgency of his love for his mistress.

The lines from the poem where the rivers are mentioned are:

> *Had we but World enough, and Time,*
> *This coyness, Lady, were no crime.*
> *We would sit down, and think which way*
> *To walk, and pass our long Loves Day.*
> ***Thou by the Indian Ganges side***
> ***Should'st Rubies find: I by the Tide***
> ***Of Humber would complain.*** *I would*
> *Love you ten years before the Flood:*
> *And you should if you please refuse*
> *Till the Conversion of the Jews.*

In the first stanza, Marvell mentions the Ganges, which is a river in India associated with life and eternity, and the Humber, which is a river in England associated with death and transience. By juxtaposing these two rivers, Marvell is highlighting the fleeting nature of human life and the urgency of his love for his mistress. He is saying that while he would like to spend centuries admiring her beauty, the reality of mortality and the inevitability of death mean that they must seize the moment and enjoy each other while they can.

Extra Perk:

- The Ganges: "To His Coy Mistress" by Andrew Marvell
- Thames: "The Waste Land" by T.S. Eliot
- Humber: "Humber Bridge" by Sean O'Brien
- The Jhelum: "The Call of the East" by Laurence Hope

Question 32

Which two poems in the following list are *Odes Written in the Horatian manner*?

(A) Ben Jonson, "To the Immortal Memory and Friendship of that Noble Pair, Sir Lucius Cary and Sir H. Morison"
(B) Andrew Marwell, "Upon Cromwell's Return from Ireland"
(C) Alexander Pope, "Ode on Solitude"
(D) Alfred Tennyson, "Ode on the Death of the Duke of Wellington"

Choose the correct answer from the options given below:

1. (A) and (B) Only
2. (B) and (D) Only
3. (B) and (C) Only
4. (A) and (D) Only

Explanations:
Answer: 3. (B) and (C) Only

The two poems in the given list that are Odes written in the Horatian manner are option (B) Andrew Marvell's "Upon Cromwell's Return from Ireland" and option (C) Alexander Pope's "Ode on Solitude."

The reason for this categorization is that Odes written in the Horatian manner follow the style and structure of the Roman poet Horace. They typically contain a measured and balanced form, focusing on subjects like nature, morality, or philosophical contemplation.

Marvell's poem "Upon Cromwell's Return from Ireland" and Pope's poem "Ode on Solitude" both conform to this style, utilizing Horatian elements in their composition. nBen Jonson's poem "To the Immortal Memory and Friendship of that Noble Pair, Sir Lucius Cary and Sir H. Morison" is not categorized as an Ode in the Horatian manner, and Alfred Tennyson's "Ode on the Death of the Duke of Wellington" is not included in the list as an option.

Question 33

Match List I with List II

List I (Book)	List II (Poet)
A. Anniversaries	I. Abraham Cowley
B. The Temple	II. John Donne
C. The Rehearsal Transpros'd	III. George Herbert
D. Pindarique Odes	IV. Andrew Marvell

Choose the correct answer from the options given below:

1. A-I; B-IV; C-II; D-III
2. **A-II; B-III; C-IV; D-I**
3. A-III; B-I; C-IV; D-II
4. A-IV; B-II; C-I; D-III

Correct Explanations:
The correct match between List I (Book) and List II (Poet) is:

The Rehearsal Transpros'd (1672–3), Marvell deploys Menippean satire to parry Samuel Parker's bullying intolerance and lobby Parliament to extend the royal indulgence for Dissenters.

Abraham Cowley, who published fifteen *Pindarique Odes* in 1656, was the poet most identified with the form though many others had composed irregular verses.

Donne's poems, the *Anniversaries*, were written to commemorate the death of Elizabeth Drury, the 14-year-old daughter of his patron, Sir Robert Drury.

The Temple is written by George Herbert.

Question 34

Arrange the following critical works in their chronological order of publication:

- A. "Preface to Lyrical Ballads"
- B. "A Defence of Rhyme"
- C. "Life of Cowley"
- D. "The Frontiers of Criticism"

Choose the correct answer from the options given below:

1. A, C, B and D
2. B, A, C and D
3. B, C, A and D
4. C, A, D and B

Explanations:
Answer: 3. B, C, A and D

"Life of Cowley": This is a biography of the English poet Abraham Cowley, written by Samuel Johnson and first published in 1779. The biography was part of a larger project by Johnson to write biographies of English poets from the time of William Shakespeare to his own time. The "Life of Cowley" is notable for its detailed analysis of Cowley's poetry and its place in English literary history.

"Preface to Lyrical Ballads": This is a critical essay written by William Wordsworth and originally published in 1798 as the preface to the first edition of "Lyrical Ballads," a collection of poems co-authored by Wordsworth and Samuel Taylor Coleridge. The preface is considered a landmark in the development of English Romanticism and contains Wordsworth's famous declaration that "poetry is the spontaneous overflow of powerful feelings."

"A Defence of Rhyme": This is an essay by Percy Bysshe Shelley that was published in 1821. In the essay, Shelley argues against the idea that poetry must adhere to strict rules of rhyme and meter, and defends the use of irregular or free verse. Shelley also argues that rhyme can be limiting to the poet's creativity and that the true purpose of poetry is to express the poet's thoughts and emotions.

"The Frontiers of Criticism": This is a collection of essays by Matthew Arnold, published in 1961. The essays explore various aspects of literary criticism, including the relationship between literature and society, the role of the critic, and the challenges facing literary criticism in the modern age. The title essay, "The Frontiers of Criticism," argues that literary criticism should be concerned with evaluating literature in relation to the larger cultural and social context in which it is produced.

Question 35

"Discordia Concors" a phrase used by Johnson in his Life of Cowley, implies:

A. A term used to refer to ironic inversion of residual ideology in a text
B. A combination of two philosophically similar discourses
C. A term used to refer to diminishing metaphor
D. A combination of dissimilar images
E. A combination of contradictory ideas and concepts

Choose the most appropriate answer from the options given below:

1. D and E only
2. C and D only
3. A and E only
4. B and D only

Explanations:
Answer: 1. D and E only

Enantiosis, synoeciosis or discordia concors is a rhetorical device in which opposites are juxtaposed so that the contrast between them is striking. Dr. Johnson in his Lives of the Poets (1779) defined discordia concors as

*"But wit, abstracted from its effects upon the hearer, may be more rigorously and philosophically considered as a kind of **"discordia concors;" a combination of dissimilar images,** or discovery of occult resemblances in things apparently unlike. Of wit, thus defined, they have more than enough. The most heterogeneous ideas are yoked by violence together; nature and art are ransacked for illustrations, comparisons, and allusions; their learning instructs, and their subtilty surprises; but the reader commonly thinks his improvement dearly bought, and, though he sometimes admires, is seldom pleased."*

Question 36

Arrange the following poets in accordance with their years of birth.

A. George Herbert
B. Edmund Spenser
C. Philip Sidney
D. John Donne
E. Oliver Goldsmith

Choose the correct answer from the options given below:

1. ABDCE
2. **BCDAE**
3. EBADC
4. ADEBC

Explanations:
- Edmund Spenser (1552/1553 – 1599)
- Philip Sidney (1554 – 1586)
- George Herbert (1593 – 1633)
- John Donne (1572 – 1631)
- Oliver Goldsmith (c. 1730 – 1774)

Question 37

Arrange the correct chronological sequence of the publication of the following texts:

A. September 1, 1939
B. The Collar
C. Beppo

D. Paradise Lost
E. Seeing Things

Choose the correct answer from the options given below:

1. B, D. C, A. E
2. B. A, E, C, D
3. A, E, B. C, D
4. C, B. A, D, E

Explanations
Answer: 1. B, D. C, A. E

"The Collar" is a poem written by the Welsh poet George Herbert and was published in 1633 as part of his collection of poems titled The Temple. This poem explores the struggles of a man who has lost his faith and is filled with anger over the commitments he made to God. He believes that his devotion to his faith has been in vain and begins to imagine a life free from religious constraints. He renounces his commitments and declares himself liberated. The central themes of the poem revolve around the conflict between one's beliefs and the desire for personal autonomy in defiance of religious restrictions. The speaker attempts to set his own boundaries and guide his own path rather than following the guidance of God. He tries to convince himself that a life of freedom will provide the satisfaction that his faith failed to deliver.

Paradise Lost is a renowned epic poem composed in blank verse by the English poet John Milton (1608–1674) during the 17th century. The initial version was **published in 1667** and consisted of ten books comprising over ten thousand lines of verse. A revised edition was released in 1674, featuring twelve books organised in a similar manner to Virgil's Aeneid, with minor revisions throughout.

Beppo: A Venetian Story is an extensive poem written by Lord Byron in 1817 while he was in Venice. Beppo represents Byron's initial venture into composing using the Italian ottava rima metre, which accentuates satirical digression. This work serves as a precursor to Byron's most renowned and often regarded as his best poem, Don Juan. The poem encompasses 760 verses, divided into 95 stanzas.

"September 1, 1939" is a poem by W. H. Auden, composed shortly after the German invasion of Poland that marked the commencement of World War II. It was initially published in The New Republic on October 18, 1939, and later included in Auden's collection titled Another Time (1940). The poem intentionally echoes the stanzaic structure of W. B. Yeats's "Easter, 1916," another poem that explores a significant historical event. Similar to Yeats's piece, Auden's poem transitions from a depiction of historical failures and frustrations to a glimpse of potential transformation in the present or future.

Seeing Things is the eighth collection of poetry by Seamus Heaney, the recipient of the 1995 Nobel Prize in Literature. It was published in 1991 and draws inspiration from the visions of the afterlife depicted in the works of Virgil and Dante Alighieri. Heaney employs these inspirations to come to terms with the death of his father, Patrick, in 1986.

PROSE WRITERS OF THE CIVIL WAR

SIR THOMAS BROWNE (1605–82)

(**Code**: Doctor Brown Burn Religio Medici)

> ➢ He may be taken as representative of the best prose-writers of the period.
> ➢ He was born in London, educated at Winchester and Oxford, and studied medicine.
> ➢ ***Pseudodoxia Epidemica, Enquiries into Very many received Tenets, and commonly presumed truths*** (1646), often known as Browne's ***Vulgar Errors***.
> ➢ ***Hydriotaphia, Urne-Burial, or, A Discourse of the Sepulchral Urnes lately found in Norfolk Garden of Cyrus, or the Quincuncial Lozenge, or Net-Work Plantations of the Ancients***.
> ➢ ***In the Garden***, in which he traces the history of horticulture from the Garden of Eden to the Persian gardens in the reign of Cyrus.
> ➢ ***Thomas Browne's The Anatomy of Melancholy (1621):*** The Anatomy of Melancholy is a medical treatise on melancholy, now known as depression, written by Thomas Browne. It was first published in 1621.
> ➢ ***The Anatomy of Melancholy*** is also the book by Robert Burton.

> - ***A Letter to a Friend, Upon Occasion of the Death of his Intimate Friend*** (1690).
> - Religio Medici (1643)
> - **Religio Medici (The Religion of a Doctor)** is a spiritual testament and early psychological self-portrait.
>   - Structured upon the **Christian virtues of Faith and Hope (part 1)** and **Charity (part 2)**.
>   - Browne expresses his beliefs in the doctrine of sola fide, the existence of hell, the **Last Judgment, the resurrection**, and other tenets of Christianity.

"Pious spirits who passed their days in raptures of futurity, made little more of this world, than the world that was before it, while they lay obscure in the chaos of preordination, and night of their fore-beings. And if any have been so happy as truly to understand Christian annihilation, ecstasies, exolution, liquefaction, transformation, the kiss of the spouse, gustation of God, and ingression into the divine shadow, they have already had an handsome anticipation of heaven; the glory of the world is surely over, and the earth in ashes unto them.

To subsist in lasting monuments, to live in their productions, to exist in their names and predicament of chimeras, was large satisfaction unto old expectations, and made one part of their Elysiums. But all this is nothing in the metaphysics of true belief. To live, indeed, is to be again ourselves, which being not only an hope, but an evidence in noble believers, 'tis all one to lie in St Innocent's churchyard, as in the sands of Egypt. Ready to be anything, in the ecstasy of being ever, and as content with six foot as the moles of Adrianus"
Hydriotaphia or Urne-Burial

Thomas Fuller (1608-1661)

(Code: *Full of Holy War of Church of England*)
> - Born in Northamptonshire, his father being a **clergyman**.
> - He was educated at Cambridge, and took holy orders.
> - He received various appointments, and by his witty sermons attracted the notice of Charles I.
> - During the Civil War he was a chaplain to the Royalist forces;
> - But when his side was defeated he made his peace with the Parliamentary party and was permitted to carry on his literary labors.

- ➤ He died the year after the Restoration.
- ➤ His serious historical books include *The History of the Holy War (1639),* dealing with the Crusades.
- ➤ *The Church-History of Britain (1655).*
- ➤ Among his pamphlets are
  - o *Good Thoughts in Bad Times (1645),*
  - o *An Alarum to the Counties of England and Wales (1660).*
- ➤ The work that has given him his reputation is his *Worthies of England*, published by his son in 1662.

Jeremy Taylor (1613–67)

(**Code**: Tale of Loly Living and Holy Dying)

- ➤ The son of a barber, he was born and educated at Cambridge
- ➤ He is sometimes known as the "Shakespeare of Divines" for his poetic style of expression.
- ➤ He is frequently cited as one of the greatest prose writers in the English language.
- ➤ His prose works, which consisted of tracts, sermons, and theological books.
- ➤ His collections of sermons were:
  - o *The Liberty of Prophesying (1647),*
  - o *Holy Living (1650),*
  - o *Holy Dying (1651).*

Izaak Walton (1593-1683)

- ➤ English biographer and author of *The Compleat Angler or or The Contemplative Man's Recreation (1653).*
  - o A pastoral discourse on the joys and stratagems of fishing.
- ➤ He also wrote several short **biographies**, including one of his friends **John Donne.**
- ➤ Donne died in 1631, Walton composed **"An Elegie"** for the volume.
- ➤ In 1640 he wrote *The Life and Death of Dr. Donne* to accompany a collection of Donne's sermons.
- ➤ Other Biographies:
  - o *The Life of Sir Henry Wotton (1651)*
  - o *The Life of Mr. Richard Hooker*
  - o *The Life of Mr. George Herbert*

Thomas Hobbes (1588-1679)

- ➤ English philosopher, scientist, and historian, is best known for his political philosophy.
- ➤ He is best remembered for **Leviathan (1651)**.
  - o Full: *Leviathan or The Matter, Forme and Power of a Commonwealth Ecclesiasticall and Civil,*
  - o Government primarily as a device for ensuring collective security.
  - o **Sovereign person or entity the responsibility** for the safety and well-being of all.
  - o The name derives from the biblical Leviathan.
  - o Most influential examples of **social contract theory**.
  - o Rule by an **absolute sovereign**.
  - o Written during the English Civil War (1642–1651)
  - o Civil war and the brute situation of a state of nature ("*the war of all against all*") could be avoided only by a strong, undivided government.

Edward Hyde, Earl of Clarendon (1609–74)

- ➤ Born in Wiltshire, educated at Oxford, and **studied law**.
- ➤ A man of excellent address, he was a successful lawyer, and became a member of the House of Commons.
- ➤ His great work, *The History of the Great Rebellion,* was begun as early as 1646 and finished during the years of his last exile.

Questions:

Question 38

Arrange the works in chronological sequence:

- A.   Matthew Arnold's Culture and Anarchy
- B.   Thomas Browne's The Anatomy of Melancholy
- C.   Thomas Hobbes' Leviathan
- D.   Walter Pater's Studies in the History of the Renaissance
- E.   PB Shelley's Defense of Poesie

Choose the correct answer from the options given below:

1. B, C, E, A, D
2. A, B, C, D, E
3. C, D, E, A, B
4. D, C, B, A, E

Explanations:
Ans: B, C, E, A, D

Thomas Browne's The Anatomy of Melancholy (1621): The Anatomy of Melancholy is a medical treatise on melancholy, now known as depression, written by Thomas Browne. It was first published in 1621.

Thomas Hobbes' Leviathan (1651): Leviathan is a political treatise written by Thomas Hobbes, published in 1651. The book concerns the structure of society and legitimate government, and is considered one of the earliest and most influential examples of social contract theory.

Matthew Arnold's Culture and Anarchy (1869): Culture and Anarchy is a series of essays by Matthew Arnold, published in 1869. It critiques the contemporary culture of Victorian England, and advocates for a "sweetness and light" approach to life and culture.

Walter Pater's Studies in the History of the Renaissance (1873): Studies in the History of the Renaissance is a collection of essays by Walter Pater, published in 1873. It discusses the art, literature, and culture of the Italian Renaissance, and is considered a key text in the development of aestheticism.

PB Shelley's Defense of Poesie (written in 1821, published in 1840): A Defence of Poetry is an essay by the English poet Percy Bysshe Shelley, written in 1821 and first published posthumously in 1840. It argues that poets are the unacknowledged legislators of the world, and that poetry has the power to inspire revolution and social change.

Question 39

Who wrote the popular instruction manual for fishermen titled The Compleat Angler, or The Contemplative Man's Recreation?

1. Isaac Walton

2. Jeremy Taylor
3. Richard Baxter
4. Thomas Hobbes

Explanations:
Ans: Isaac Walton.

The Compleat Angler, or The Contemplative Man's Recreation is a popular instruction manual for fishermen that was written by **Izaak Walton in 1653.** The book is considered a classic work of English literature and has been in print continuously since its first publication. **The Compleat Angler is a celebration of the joys of fishing and of the natural world,** and it provides practical advice for anglers of all levels of experience.

Extra Perk:

Jeremy Taylor, Richard Baxter, and Thomas Hobbes were all influential English writers and thinkers in the 17th century.

Jeremy Taylor was a bishop and theologian known for his devotional writings and his defense of Anglicanism. **He is best known for his book "Holy Living and Holy Dying,"** which provides guidance on how to live a virtuous and pious life and prepare for a peaceful death.

Richard Baxter was a Puritan theologian and preacher known for his prolific writing and his efforts to unify the Church of England. He is best known for **his book "The Reformed Pastor,"** which provides guidance for clergy on how to care for their congregations and lead a righteous life.

Thomas Hobbes was a philosopher and political theorist who is best known for his book **"Leviathan,"** which argues for the **necessity of a strong central government to prevent the chaos and violence of the state of nature.** He was also an influential thinker on questions of morality and human nature, and his ideas have had a lasting impact on modern political theory.

Question 40

Which according to Thomas Hobbes is the only 'science' God has bestowed on mankind, that informs the structure of his monumental work, Leviathan?

1. Astronomy
2. Architecture
3. Occult sciences
4. Geometry

Explanations:
Answer: 4. Geometry

Thomas Hobbes, a philosopher of the 17th century, believed that geometry was the only true science that could provide certainty and knowledge. In his magnum opus "Leviathan," Hobbes uses geometry as a metaphor to explain the structure of his philosophical system and the nature of political authority.

According to Hobbes, geometry is a deductive science that begins with axioms or definitions and then logically derives conclusions from them. Geometry provides a model of reasoning that is certain, unambiguous, and applicable to all areas of human knowledge. Hobbes saw this method as a powerful tool for discovering truth and achieving certainty, especially in the realm of political theory.

Question 41

Arrange the following in the chronological order of their publication:

A. Past and Present
B. Leviathan
C. Unto This Last
D. The Life of Samuel Johnson

Choose the correct answer from the options given below:

1. (B) (D) (A) (C)
2. (B) (A) (D) (C)
3. (C) (D) (A) (B)
4. (C) (A) (D) (B)

Explanations:
Answer: 1. (B) (D) (A) (C)

➤ Leviathan
➤ The Life of Samuel Johnson
➤ Past and Present
➤ Unto This Last

Leviathan by Thomas Hobbes was published in 1651 and is a significant work of political philosophy.

The Life of Samuel Johnson by James Boswell was published in 1791 and is a renowned biography of the prominent English writer and lexicographer.

Past and Present by Thomas Carlyle was published in 1843 and explores social and political issues of the time.

Unto This Last by John Ruskin was published in 1860 and presents his views on political economy and social justice.

Question 42

Find the chronological order of publication of the given works:

- A. Boswell's Life of Johnson
- B. Hobbes's Leviathan
- C. Pepys's Diary
- D. Bunyan's Pilgrim's Progress
- E. Locke's Human Understanding

Choose the correct answer from the options given below:

1. **BCDEA**
2. ACDEB
3. CDABE
4. DEACB

Explanations:
- ➤ Bunyan's Pilgrim's Progress, published in 1678
- ➤ Hobbes's Leviathan, published in 1651
- ➤ Locke's Human Understanding, published in 1689
- ➤ Pepys's Diary, published in 1825 (though written in the 1660s and 1670s)
- ➤ Boswell's Life of Johnson, published in 1791.

Question 43

Thomas Hobbes's philosophical tract Leviathan was first published in

1. 1631
2. 1641
3. 1651
4. 1661

Explanations:
Answer: 3. 1651

Leviathan is the magnum opus of Thomas Hobbes, a prominent early-modern English philosopher, scientist, and ethicist. This significant work, **first published in 1651,** is titled **Leviathan, or, The Matter, Form, and Power of a Commonwealth, Ecclesiastical and Civil.** Hobbes developed his political philosophy in this book, building upon ideas presented in his earlier work, De Cive (1642).

Hobbes's political theory revolves around the **concept of collective security, viewing government as a means to ensure the safety and well-being of society.** He proposes that political authority is justified through a hypothetical social contract among the people, granting power to a sovereign (whether a monarch, legislature or other form of political authority). **This sovereign becomes responsible for the protection and welfare of all citizens.**

Leviathan had a profound impact on subsequent philosophers who embraced the social-contract framework, including **renowned thinkers like John Locke, Jean-Jacques Rousseau, and Immanuel Kant.** Moreover, Hobbes's influence extended to those who explored the connection between moral and political decision-making in rational individuals, considering self-interest in a broader sense.

Key Points:

- **Hobbes rejects Aristotle's thesis**
- Human nature unsuited to politics
- Passions magnify self-interest
- War comes naturally to humans
- Political order requires delegation
- Social contract for safety
- **Sovereign's absolute authority**
- **Subjects' obligation to obey**

- ➢ Prudential and moral reasons
- ➢ Seek peace, avoid war
- ➢ Life outside the state: poor, nasty, brutish, short
- ➢ Laws of nature bound by peace
- ➢ **Sovereign receives obedience as a gift**
- ➢ **Sovereign retains total liberty**
- ➢ **Sovereign not bound by law**
- ➢ Safety and well-being decisions
- ➢ No real historical event
- ➢ Delegation for collective security
- ➢ Transfer of governing right
- ➢ Subjects endure the sovereign's rule.

CHAPTER 2

The Age of Restoration or The Age of Dryden (1660–1700)

Historical Background

- ➢ **Three historical events** deeply influenced the literary movements of the time:
    - o The Restoration of the year **1660**;
    - o The **Roman Catholic controversy** that raged during the latter half of Charles II's reign;
    - o **The Revolution of the year 1688.**
- ➢ **Charles I** (1600-1649) King of England, Scotland, and Ireland from 27 March 1625 until his **execution in 1649.**
- ➢ The Interregnum was the period between the **execution of Charles I on 30 January 1649 and the arrival of his son Charles II in London on 29 May 1660,** which marked the start of the Restoration.
- ➢ **The Restoration of the monarchy:** Pepys witnessed the return of Charles II to England in 1660 and the restoration of the monarchy after the Puritan Commonwealth period.
- ➢ **Restoration** describes years after a **new political settlement**.
- ➢ Often refers to **King Charles II's reign** (1660–1685).
- ➢ Sometimes includes **King James II's brief reign** (1685–1688).
- ➢ Can cover **later Stuart monarchs** until **Queen Anne's death**.
- ➢ **Restoration comedy** includes works up to **1710**.
- ➢ **Restoration of Charles II** revolutionized **English literature**.
- ➢ Collapse of Puritanism led to **excessive freedoms**.
- ➢ **Commonwealth** promoted decorum; **Restoration** encouraged levity.
- ➢ Immoral tendencies were **prominent in comedies** of the time.
- ➢ Religious-political passions strongly influenced **contemporary literature**.
- ➢ **James**, the heir-apparent, was **openly Papist**.
- ➢ Suspicion of **Catholics colored writings** of the period.
- ➢ **Titus Oates' lies** fueled the public's **anti-Catholic frenzy**.
- ➢ **Charles II** worked to **save his brother James**.
- ➢ **Dryden's Absalom and Achitophel** reflects these turbulent years.
- ➢ **James II's Catholicism** led to rejection after **three years**.
- ➢ **Protestant sovereigns** replaced **James II** in **1688 Revolution**.

- ➢ Religious passions declined; **political issues** became **literary focus**.
- ➢ Charles Lamb's "On the Artificial Comedy of the Last Century" is a critical essay from the 19th century in which Lamb discusses the differences between comedy in his own time and the Restoration period.
- ➢ L.C. Knights is known for his essay "Restoration Comedy: The Reality and the Myth."
- ➢ Edward Bond wrote **Restoration (1981)**

THE NEW CLASSICISM

- ➢ **Elizabethan writers lacked genius**; turned to **classical Latin writers**.
- ➢ Imitation of **ancients deepened** during **Pope's era**.
  - ○ *Learn hence for ancient rules a just esteem;*
  - ○ *To copy nature is to copy them.* —Pope's rule for excellence.
- ➢ **Charles II admired French literature**, especially **comedy**.
- ➢ **Molière** greatly influenced **Restoration comedy**.
- ➢ **French and classical models** combined in **heroic plays**.
- ➢ **Dryden's Tyrannic Love** exemplifies the **heroic play**.
- ➢ The **new school imitated** the ancients **coldly and rigidly**.
- ➢ **Pope's age** focused on strict adherence to **classical rules**.
  - ○ *Those Rules of old, discovered, not devised,*
  - ○ *Are Nature still, but Nature methodised.* —Pope.
- ➢ **Correctness** demanded **restraint, care, and imitation** of the classics.
- ➢ **Dryden's work** was considered **"copious"** by later writers.
- ➢ **Johnson called Dryden "Augustan"**, comparing him to **Augustus of Rome**.
  - ○ which he *"found of brick and left of marble."*
- ➢ **Dryden's ideas** dominated English literature **through the 18th century**.

RESTORATION POETRY

- ➢ The lyric, ariel, historical, and epic poems were being developed throughout the period.
- ➢ **English poets** lacked a **national epic** like other countries.
- ➢ **Spenser's Faerie Queene** was well known but not enough.
- ➢ **Sir William Davenant** attempted the epic with **Gondibert**.

- **Critics condemned** Gondibert's rhyme as **unheroic** (Dryden Epic).
- **Milton's Paradise Lost** aimed to be the **English epic.**
- **Milton rejected** English nationalism for **Christianity** in **Paradise Lost.**
- **Milton initially attempted** an epic on **King Arthur.**
- **Richard Blackmore** wrote **Prince Arthur** and **King Arthur**, both failures.
- The **Restoration period** ended without a recognized **English epic.**
- **Beowulf** is now considered an **English epic**, but was unknown then.
- **Restoration poetry** favored **rhyming couplets in iambic pentameter**.
- **Dryden** praised the couplet's **restraint and dignity** (Dryden Epic).
- **Heroic couplets** were used for **heroic subjects** with **minimal enjambment**.
- **Mock-heroic couplets** became popular after **Hudibras** by **Samuel Butler.**
- **Hudibrastic verse** parodied heroic poems, used for satire.
- **Swift** used the **Hudibrastic form** for much of his poetry.
- **Dryden, Rochester, Buckingham**, and **Dorset** were **court poets.**
- **Aphra Behn, Matthew Prior**, and **Robert Gould** were **outsider royalists.**
- **Court poets** relied on **wit, satire**, and **sexual awareness.**
- **Behn, Dryden, Rochester**, and **Gould** wrote for **both stage and page.**

Samuel Butler (1612–80)

- Besides Dryden and the tragedy-writers the only considerable poet of the period is Samuel Butler.
- His fame rests on one work, **Hudibras.**
- **In 1663 he published Hudibras**, which was at once a success. Two other parts followed in 1664 and 1678 respectively.
- Hudibras was reprinted many times in the centuries following Butler's death.
- Two of the more special editions are those edited by Zachery Grey (1744) and Treadway Russell Nash (1793).
- The standard edition of the work was edited by John Wilders (1967).
- **Hudibras** is a **satire on the Puritans.**
- The poem is **modeled on Don Quixote and Sancho Panza's adventures.**

- ➢ **Sir Hudibras**, a Puritan knight, has **absurd adventures**.
- ➢ The poem lacks **pathos** and **genuine insight**.
- ➢ **Hudibras** is **wholly satirical**, almost **spiteful**.
- ➢ Adventures chosen to **ridicule** the **maladroit hero**.
- ➢ **Humor** is keen and **caustic**, yet restrained.
- ➢ Features **mock-scholarly learning** and **playful tropes**.
- ➢ Written in **jigging octosyllabic couplets** for unique style.
- ➢ The meter is **varied, uniform**, and **relished** by readers.
- ➢ Sometimes **near-doggerel**, but retains a **distinct style**.
- ➢ Each couplet ends with **ingenious and amusing rhyme**.

Question 44

Hudibras of Samuel Butler reflects on the revolt against

1. **Puritanism**
2. Hellenism
3. Humanism
4. Anglicanism

Correct Explanations:
"Hudibras" by Samuel Butler is a satirical poem that reflects on the English Civil War and the Puritan Revolution, which took place in the mid-17th century. The poem presents the title character, Sir Hudibras, as a satirical representation of the Puritan movement, and mocks the religious and political conflicts of the time.

Sir William D'Avenant (1606-1668)

- ➢ D'Avenant, was an English poet and playwright. Along with Thomas Killigrew.
- ➢ He was made poet laureate on the strength of such successes as *The Witts* (licensed 1634), a comedy.
- ➢ **George Herbert** wrote *To my worthy Friend, M. D'Avenant*, upon his Excellent Play, The Iust Italian
- ➢ The masques
    - o *The Temple of Love,*
    - o *Britannia Triumphans,*
    - o *Luminalia;*
- ➢ A volume of poems, *Madagascar* (published 1638).

- ➢ Shakespeare was D'Avenant's godfather,
- ➢ Gossip held that the famous playwright may even have been his father.
- ➢ Works:
- ➢ ***Gondibert (1651)***:
    - o A tale of chivalry in 1,700 quatrains.
    - o After the execution of Charles I, his queen sent Davenant to aid the Royalist cause in America as lieutenant governor of Maryland.
    - o However, Davenant's ship was captured on the English Channel,
    - o He was imprisoned in the Tower of London until 1654.
- ➢ ***The first day's Entertainment*** (produced 1656)
    - o A work disguised under Declamations and Musick.
    - o This work led to his creation of the first public opera in England.
- ➢ ***The Siege of Rhodes Made a Representation by the Art of Prospective in Scenes And the Story sung in Recitative Musick*** (1656).

Thomas Kiligrew (1612-1683)

- ➢ He was an English dramatist and playhouse manager.
- ➢ He was better known for his wit than for his plays.
- ➢ However, the playwright **William Congreve appropriated some of the jokes in The *Parson's Wedding* (acted c. 1640).**
- ➢ **In 1641 Killigrew published two tragicomedies, The Prisoners and Claracilla, both probably produced before 1636.**

Nahum Tate (1652-1715)

- ➢ Irish poet, hymnist, and lyricist who became **Poet Laureate in 1692.**
- ➢ Tate is best known for **The History of King Lear**, his 1681 adaptation of Shakespeare's King Lear.
- ➢ His libretto for Henry Purcell's opera, Dido and Aeneas.

Thomas Shadwell (16542-1692)

- ➢ English dramatist and **poet laureate.**
- ➢ Known for his broad comedies of manners **and as the butt of John Dryden's satire.**
- ➢ He translated **Juvenal's *The Tenth Satyr (1687)*** and composed **bitter attacks upon John Dryden.**
- ➢ He satirized both **Howards in *The Sullen Lovers (1668)*,** an adaptation of Molière's Les Fâcheux.

Shadwell wrote 18 plays, including
- *The Royal Shepherdess (1669)*
- *The Enchanted Island (1674; adapted from Shakespeare's The Tempest)*
- *Psyche (1674–75)*
- *The Libertine (1675).*

John Dryden (1631-1700)

Life

- **Dryden's life** was long and exceedingly fruitful.
- He produced **poems, plays, and prose** for forty years.
- His work consistently maintained **high quality** throughout.
- **Dryden's poetry** remained fresh even in old age.
- He was born in **Northamptonshire** on **August 9, 1631**.
- Dryden came from a **landowning family** with political connections.
- He studied as a **King's Scholar** at **Westminster School**.
- **Rhetorical argument** influenced his **writing and critical thought**.
- He published his **first poem** in **1649**.
- He enrolled at **Trinity College**, Cambridge in **1650**.
- **Dryden graduated first** in his class in **1654**.
- His father died the same year he **earned his BA**.
- His **earliest important work** praised **Oliver Cromwell**.
- At the Restoration, he **supported Charles II** and the **Church of England**.
- His loyalty earned him **honors and pensions**.
- On **James II's accession**, Dryden became a **Roman Catholic**.
- He stayed loyal to **Catholicism** despite **1688 Revolution** hardships.
- Dryden lost his **Poet Laureate** title to **Shadwell**, his foe.
- In his final years, he produced **translations and narrative poems**.
- **Dryden** received a grand **funeral** at **Westminster Abbey** in **1700**.

Career

(Code: Heroic Extra Mira)
- Dryden was present at **Cromwell's funeral in 1658** and one year later published his first important poem, ***Heroic Stanzas (1659)***, eulogizing the leader.
  - It consists of ***thirty-seven quatrains*** of no particular merit.

- ➢ **In 1660**, Dryden celebrated the regime of King Charles II with **Astraea Redux (1660)**
  - o Samuel Johnson excused Dryden for this, writing in his *Lives of the Poets (1779)* **that "*if he changed, he changed with the nation*,"** he also notes that the earlier work was **"*not totally forgotten*"** and, in fact, **"*raised him, enemies.*"**
    - ▪ *"Methinks I see those crowds on Dover's strand,*
    - ▪ *Who in their haste to welcome you to land*
    - ▪ *Choked up the beach with their still growing store,*
    - ▪ *And made a wilder torrent on the shore."*
- ➢ He published *To His Sacred Majesty: A Panegyric on his Coronation* (1662), and *To My Lord Chancellor (1662)*, possibly to court aristocratic patrons.
- ➢ That year, Dryden was proposed for membership in the Royal Society.
- ➢ He was elected an early fellow.
- ➢ In 1663, he married **Lady Elizabeth**, the royalist sister of Sir Robert Howard.
- ➢ In 1664, **Pepys** records in his diary that he met *"Mr. Dryden, the poet"*; and he remained *"Mr. Dryden, the poet,"* till the day of his death.
- ➢ It is therefore as a poet that Dryden is chiefly to be judged.
- ➢ For more than **fifteen years succeeding** this Dryden devoted himself almost entirely to the writing of plays.

(**Code**: *The Wild Rival Indian Queen and Emperor Fall in Tyrannick love and God Married with Aureng-Zebe, That all for love*)

- ➢ *The Wild Gallant, a Comedy (1663/1669):* As Dryden stated in his Preface, it was "the first attempt I made in Dramatique Poetry."
- ➢ *The Rival Ladies, a Tragi-Comedy (1663/1664):* Dryden dedicated the published version to the Irish politician and playwright, the Earl of Orrery.
- ➢ *The Indian Queen, a Tragedy (1664/1665)*
- ➢ **Sir Robert Howard**, written in collaboration with John Dryden
- ➢ *The Indian Emperor, or the Conquest of Mexico by the Spaniards (1665/):* The Sequel of The Indian Queen
  > *"But of my crown thou too much care dost take;*
  > *That which I value more, my love's at stake."*
- ➢ *Secret Love, or the Maiden Queen (1667/)*

- *Sir Martin Mar-all, or the Feigned Innocence, a Comedy (1667/1668)*
- **The Tempest, or The Enchanted Island, a Comedy (1667/1670),** *an adaptation with William D'Avenant of Shakespeare's The Tempest*
- *An Evening's Love, or the Mock Astrology, a Comedy (1668/1668)*
- **Tyrannick Love, or the Royal Martyr, a Tragedy** *(1668 or 1669/1670)*
  - A retelling of the story of Saint Catherine of Alexandria
  - And her martyrdom by the Roman Emperor Maximinus,
  - The "tyrant" of the title, who is enraged at Catherine's refusal to submit to his violent sexual passion.
- *Almanzor and Almahide, or the Conquest of Granada by the Spaniards, a Tragedy, Part I & Part II (1669 or 1670/1672)*
- **Marriage-a-la-Mode, a Comedy** *(1673/1673)*
- *The Assignation, or Love in a Nunnery, a Comedy (1672/1673)*
- *Amboyna; or the Cruelties of the Dutch to the English Merchants, a Tragedy (1673/1673)*
- *The Mistaken Husband (comedy) (1674/1675)*
- *The State of Innocence, and Fall of Man, an Opera (/1674)*
- **Aureng-Zebe, a Tragedy** *(1676/1676)*
  - It is based loosely on the figures of Aurangzeb (Aureng-zebe)
  - The then-reigning Mughal Emperor of India;
  - His brother, Murad Baksh (Morat);
  - Their father, Shah Jahan (Emperor).
- **All for Love, or the World Well Lost, a Tragedy** *(1678/1678)*
- *Limberham, or the Kind Keeper, a Comedy (/1678)*
- *Oedipus, a Tragedy (1678 or 1679/1679), an adaptation with Nathaniel Lee of Sophocles' Oedipus*
- *Troilus and Cressida, or Truth found too late, a Tragedy (/1679)*
- *The Spanish Friar, or the Double Discovery (1681 or 1682/)*
- *The Duke of Guise, a Tragedy (1682/1683) with Nathaniel Lee*
- *Albion and Albanius, an Opera (1685/1685)*
- *Don Sebastian, a Tragedy (1690/1690)*
- *Amphitryon, or the Two Sosias, a Comedy (1690/1690)*
- *King Arthur, or the British Worthy, a Dramatic Opera (1691/1691)*
- *Cleomenes, the Spartan Hero, a Tragedy (1692/1692)*
- **Love Triumphant, or Nature will prevail, a Tragedy** *(1693 or 1694/1693 or 1694)*
- *The Secular Masque (1700/1700)*
- **When the bubonic plague swept through London in 1665**.
- Dryden moved to Wiltshire, where he wrote **Of Dramatick Poesie (1668)**

- **The Great Fire of London was in 1666**.
- **Annus Mirabilis** a poem published in 1667.
- It commemorated 1665–1666, the "year of miracles" of London.
- Despite the poem's name, the year had been one of great tragedy, including **the Great Fire of London**.
- Following the death of William Davenant in **April 1668, Dryden became the first official Poet Laureate of England**.
- Then, **about 1680,** events both political and personal drove him back to the poetical medium, with results both splendid and astonishing.
  - *Absalom and Achitophel, 1681*
  - *Mac Flecknoe, 1682*
  - *The Medal, 1682*
  - *Religio Laici, 1682*
    - To the Memory of Mr. Oldham, 1684
    - Threnodia Augustalis, 1685
- *The Hind and the Panther, 1687*
- *A Song for St. Cecilia's Day, 1687:* Britannia Rediviva, 1688, was written to mark the birth of James, Prince of Wales.
  - Epigram on Milton, 1688
  - Creator Spirit, by whose aid, 1690. Translation of Rabanus Maurus' Veni Creator Spiritus
  - The Works of Virgil, 1697
  - *Alexander's Feast, 1697*
  - *Fables, Ancient and Modern, 1700*
  - **Palamon and Arcite**
  - The Art of Satire

Absalom and Achitophel (1681)

- It is a **celebrated satirical poem** written in heroic couplets and published in **1681**.
- The verse tells the Biblical tale of the rebellion of **Absalom against King David**.
- In this context, it **is an allegory** used to represent a story contemporary to Dryden concerning **King Charles II and the Exclusion Crisis (1679–1681)**.
- The poem also references the **Popish Plot (1678) and the Monmouth Rebellion (1685)**.
- Absalom is the Duke of Monmouth, the unfortunate aspirant to the succession;

- ➤ Achitophel is his daring but injudicious counselor Shaftesbury.
- ➤ These two are surrounded by a cluster of lesser politicians.
- ➤ Each of whom Dryden bestows a Biblical name of deadly aptness and transparency.
- ➤ Dryden himself says not unfairly, *"It is not bloody, but it is ridiculous enough. I avoided the mention of great crimes, and applied myself to the representing of blind sides and little extravagances."* The hitting is hard, but not foul.
- ➤ **Monmouth into Absalom,**
- ➤ The beloved boy, **Charles into David** (who also had done some philandering),
- ➤ **Shaftesbury into Achitophel.**
- ➤ It paints **Buckingham**, an old enemy of **Dryden's, into Zimri,** the unfaithful servant.
- ➤ The poem places most of the blame for **the rebellion on Shaftesbury and makes Charles a very reluctant and loving man who has to be king before his father.**
- ➤ The poem also refers to some of the **Popish Plot** furore.
- ➤ **Plot:**
  - o **King David** represents **Charles II**, reigning over a divided nation.
  - o **Absalom** is **Monmouth**, David's illegitimate son, seeking the throne.
  - o **Achitophel** represents **Shaftesbury**, plotting rebellion against the king.
  - o **Achitophel** persuades **Absalom** to lead a rebellion for power.
  - o **Absalom** is initially hesitant but ultimately joins the plot.
  - o **Achitophel gathers support** from various factions opposing **David's rule.**
  - o **David learns** of the rebellion but chooses a peaceful response.
  - o **David's speech** highlights loyalty and condemns rebellion's consequences.
  - o **Absalom abandons** the plot, leading to **Achitophel's downfall.**
  - o **Achitophel's death** symbolizes the end of **the rebellion**

Mac Flecknoe (1682)

- ➤ *Mac Flecknoe; or, A satyr upon the True-Blue-Protestant Poet, T.S.*
- ➤ Verse mock-heroic satire and a direct **attack on Thomas Shadwell.**
- ➤ It opens with the lines:
  "All humane things are subject to decay,

> ***And, when Fate summons, Monarchs must obey":*** — lines 1-2
- ➤ Disagreements between Thomas Shadwell and Dryden.
- ➤ **Their quarrel blossomed from the following disputes:**
  - o "Their different estimates of the genius of Ben Jonson"
  - o "The preference of Dryden for comedy of wit and repartee and Shadwell, the chief disciple of Jonson, for humor's comedy."
  - o "A sharp disagreement over the true purpose of comedy"
  - o "Contention over the value of rhymed plays."
  - o "Plagiarism."

Religio Laici (1682)

- ➤ Religio Laici Or A Layman's Faith (1682)
- ➤ In response to the publication of an English translation of the ***Histoire critique due vieux testament*** by the French cleric **Father Richard Simon**.
- ➤ Simon's book applied detailed criticism to the textual history of the Bible.
- ➤ It consists of **462 lines** of consecutive rhyming couplets.
- ➤ Dryden added notes in the margins to indicate the topics and issues
  - o Opinions of the several sects of Philosophers concerning the Summum Bonum
  - o System of Deism
  - o Of Reveal'd Religion
  - o Objection of the Deist
  - o The Objection answered
  - o Digression to the Translator of Father Simon's Critical History of the Old Testament
  - o Of the infallibility of Tradition, in General
  - o Objection on behalf of Tradition; urged by Father Simon
  - o The Second Objection
  - o Answer to the Objection

The Hind and the Panther (1687)

- ➤ ***The Hind and the Panther: A Poem, in Three Parts (1687)***:
- ➤ In allegory in heroic couplets..
- ➤ At some 2600 lines, it is much the longest of Dryden's poems, translations

- ➢ The most controversial.
- ➢ The critic **Margaret Doody has called i**t "*the great, the undeniable, sui generis poem of the Restoration era...It is its own kind of poem, it cannot be repeated (and no one has repeated it).*"
- ➢ Dryden converted to Catholicism.
- ➢ Falls into **three parts:**
- ➢ **The first is a description of the different religious denominations**
  - Roman Catholic Church appears as "A milk-white Hind, immortal and unchanged,"
  - The Church of England as a panther,
  - The Independents as a bear,
  - The Presbyterians as a wolf,
  - The Quakers as a hare,
  - The Socinians as a fox,
  - The Freethinkers as an ape,
  - The Anabaptists as a boar;
- ➢ **The second part deals with the controversial topics of church authority and transubstantiation.**
- ➢ **The third part argues that the Crown and the Anglican and Catholic Churches should form a united front against the Nonconformist churches and the Whigs.**

All for Love, or the World Well Lost, a Tragedy (1678/1678)

- ➢ *All for Love, or the World Well Lost,* is a **1677 heroic** drama.
- ➢ **Tragedy written in blank verse.**
- ➢ Deals with the same topic as Shakespeare's Antony and Cleopatra.
- ➢ Dryden confines the action to Alexandria and focuses on the end of their doomed relationship.

Act One

- ➢ **Serapion** foresees Egypt's doom through ominous **omens.**
- ➢ **Alexas** is concerned about Cleopatra's relationship with **Antony.**
- ➢ Serapion hosts a festival to honor **Antony's achievements.**
- ➢ **Ventidius** arrives in Alexandria to help **Antony.**
- ➢ **Ventidius urges Antony** to leave Cleopatra for more troops.

Act Two

- **Cleopatra mourns** Antony's absence and sends **gifts** to win him back.
- **Alexas suggests** Cleopatra tie a bracelet on Antony's **wrist.**
- **Ventidius accuses Cleopatra** of being unfaithful to **Antony.**
- **Cleopatra proves her loyalty** by showing a letter rejecting **Octavius.**
- Antony proclaims his love for **Cleopatra**, overjoyed by her decision.

Act Three

- **Antony**, returning from battle, is overwhelmed with **love.**
- **Ventidius brings Dolabella**, who tries to negotiate **peace.**
- **Octavia appears** with Antony's children to stop the **war.**
- **Antony reunites** with **Octavia**, torn between love and duty.
- **Cleopatra and Octavia** argue over **Antony's loyalty** and rightful place.

Act Four

- **Octavia convinces Antony** to return to Rome with **her.**
- **Antony asks Dolabella** to say goodbye to **Cleopatra.**
- **Ventidius suspects** Cleopatra and Dolabella of **betrayal.**
- **Antony is enraged** by rumors of **Cleopatra's affair** with Dolabella.
- **Octavia leaves Antony**, hurt by his belief in **Cleopatra's innocence.**

Act Five

- **Antony's fleet betrays him**, turning against **Alexandria.**
- **Cleopatra flees**, advised by Alexas, who plans to **betray her.**
- **Alexas lies**, telling Antony that **Cleopatra is dead.**
- **Antony asks Ventidius** to end his life, but **Ventidius refuses.**
- **Antony dies**, followed by **Cleopatra's suicide** with **snake bites.**

An Essay of Dramatick Poesie (1668)

An Essay of Dramatic Poesy (1668)

- ➢ According to Dryden, **drama is a legitimate form of "poetry"** comparable to the epic.
- ➢ Defends the English drama against the drama of the ancients and the French.
- ➢ Written during the **plague of 1666** and was first published in 1668.
- ➢ Dryden refers to **Philip Sidney's *Defence of Poesie* in 1580.**
- ➢ The treatise is a dialogue between four speakers:
    - o **Eugenius**: Charles Sackville's (then Lord Buckhurst's (modern drama) modern plots are more "lively."
    - o **Crites**: Sir Robert Howard (classical drama)
    - o **Lisideius**: Sir Charles Sedley (French drama), plots of classical drama are more "just,". According to him, French plots carefully preserve Aristotle's unities of action, place, and time.
    - o **Neander**: "new man" and implies that Dryden himself (Elizabethan Drama). English dramatists **such as Ben Jonson kept the unities** when they wanted to, but they preferred to develop character and motive.
- ➢ In the days following the encounter between the Dutch fleet and the English fleet near the mouth of the Thames, they take a barge downriver towards the noise from the battle.
- ➢ Self-pride in being English.
- ➢ The four friends debate a series of three topics:
  - i. The relative merits of classical drama (upheld by Crites) and modern drama (pioneered by Eugenius);
  - ii. According to Lisideius, French drama is superior to English drama (a view shared by Neander, who famously called Shakespeare "the greatest soul, ancient or modern");
  - iii. While Neander had previously defended the Elizabethans, he now advances a proposition against the skeptic Crites, arguing that plays in rhyme are an improvement over blank verse drama. (also switching from his original position and defending the blank verse tradition of Elizabethan drama).
- Invoking all the unities from Aristotle's *Poetics* (as interpreted and refined by Italian and French scholars over the past century), these four

speakers discuss what defines a play as "a just and lively imitation" of human nature in action.

● He compared Shakespeare to Homer.
● He compared Ben Jonson to Virgil.

"It was that memorable day, in the first Summer of the late War, when our Navy engaged the Dutch: a day wherein the two most mighty and best appointed Fleets which any age had ever seen, disputed the command of the greater half of the Globe, the commerce of Nations, and the riches of the Universe. While these vast floating bodies, on either side, moved against each other in parallel lines, and our Country men, under the happy conduct of his Royal Highness, went breaking, by little and little, into the line of the Enemies; the noise of the Cannon from both Navies reached our ears about the City: so that all men, being alarmed with it, and in a dreadful suspense of the event, which we knew was then deciding, every one went following the sound as his fancy led him; and leaving the Town almost empty, some took towards the Park, some cross the River, others down it; all seeking the noise in the depth of silence."

"To begin, then, with Shakespeare. He was the man who, of all modern and perhaps ancient poets, had the largest and most comprehensive soul. All the images of nature were still present to him, and he drew them not laboriously, but luckily; when he describes anything, you more than see it, you feel it too. Those who accuse him to have wanted learning, give him the greater commendation. He was naturally learned; he needed not the spectacles of books to read nature; he looked inwards and found her there. I cannot say he is everywhere alike; were he so, I should do him injury to compare him with the greatest of mankind. He is many times flat, insipid; his comic wit degenerating into clenches, his serious swelling into bombast. But he is always great when some great occasion is presented to him; no man can say he ever had a fit subject for his wit, and did not then raise himself as high above the rest of poets,"

Complete Texts Summary:

➢ **Serapion** describes naval battle between **English and Dutch** fleets.
➢ **Eugenius, Crites, Lisideius, and Neander** take a boat ride.
➢ **Crites criticizes bad poets** writing about the battle.
➢ Group jokes about poets writing **victory or elegy poems**.
➢ **Crites mocks poets** for weak wit and forced wordplay.
➢ **Eugenius argues** poets should still be **appreciated**.
➢ They discuss **specific bad poets** with shallow humor.

- **Eugenius admits** some bad poets are still **popular**.
- **Crites compares poets' wit** to swallows on **the Thames**.
- Group laments the **decline of good poetry** in their age.
- **Eugenius defends modern poets**, claiming they rival the **Ancients**.
- He references **Horace** to support his view on **new vs. old** poetry.
- **Crites agrees** to debate **Dramatic Poesy**, focusing on **Ancients vs. Moderns**.
- **Eugenius admits** modern plays fall short of **older English dramas**.
- He praises modern poets like **Suckling, Waller, Denham, and Cowley**.
- **Eugenius claims** the **English Drama** surpasses Italian, French, and Spanish plays.
- They agree that **English verse** has improved in **expression and rhyme**.
- **Lisideius suggests** they define what makes a **good play** before debating further.
- The group requests **Lisideius** to offer a definition of a **play**.
- **Lisideius defines** a play as a **"lively image of human nature"**.
- **Crites objects** to Lisideius' definition as too broad and general.
- The group **turns the barge** and prepares for the evening return.
- **Crites defends the Ancients**, starting with **confidence in their superiority**.
- He argues modern poets **build on the foundations** of Ancient **models**.
- **Dramatic Poesy** reached **maturity** from **Thespis to Aristophanes**.
- Crites notes that **Arts and Sciences** often achieve perfection in one **century**.
- He compares recent advancements in **Philosophy** to Ancient **discoveries**.
- **Poesy** was more esteemed in Ancient times, with **greater honors** awarded.
- **Rivalries among poets** led to higher quality and innovation.
- **Emulation** and **envy** spurred **Ancient poets** to write better.
- **Crites criticizes** modern writers for their **laziness and malice**.
- He claims **Ancient poets** were **faithful imitators of nature**.
- **Aristotle's and Horace's works** laid the foundation for **drama rules**.
- The **Three Unities** (Time, Place, Action) were derived from **Ancient works**.
- **Unity of Time** means action should occur within **24 hours**.

- **Ancient plays** respected this rule, focusing on the **story's main action**.
- **Unity of Place** requires the scene to remain in **one location**.
- Crites acknowledges **painted scenes** but favors **single location for truth**.
- The **French** are praised for adhering to the **unity of place**.
- **Corneille's Liaison des Scenes** keeps the stage **continuously occupied**.
- **Crites explains the Unity of Action**, stating it must focus on **one complete action**.
- **Subplots** should be **subservient to the main action**, not competing with it.
- **Modern plays often violate the unities**, covering too many **actions and locations**.
- Crites praises **Ancient writers** for their **well-constructed plays**.
- **Meander's and Roman playwrights' lost works** would settle the **Ancients vs. Moderns debate**.
- **Admiration of Ancient plays** increases Crites' disappointment in **modern ones**.
- **Cultural and linguistic differences** hinder full appreciation of **Ancient works**.
- **Ben Jonson**, a great modern poet, imitated the **Ancients** and **admired their work**.
- Jonson was a **"plagiary"** of **Horace, Seneca, and others**, wearing their literary "clothes."
- **Crites uses Jonson's example** to convince Eugenius to **esteem the Ancients**.
- **Eugenius begins** by acknowledging the **value of Ancient rules**.
- He argues the **Moderns have added** to the Ancients' **foundation**.
- **Modern poets follow Nature** and create new **ideas and features**.
- He claims that **Arts can improve** over time, as seen in **Philosophy**.
- **Eugenius criticizes Greek Poesy**, saying **they lacked structure in Acts**.
- He explains that **Greek plays** were guided by the **singing of the Chorus**.
- **Aristotle's division** of plays into **Protasis, Epitasis, Catastasis, and Catastrophe** is highlighted.
- **Acts were not fully developed** in Greek plays, but Aristotle's ideas helped.

- **Horace later established** the rule of five acts in **Comedy**.
- **Eugenius argues** that the **Ancients did not perfect** the structure of a play.
- **Eugenius critiques the Ancients** for lacking a consistent number of Acts.
- He compares **Spanish and Italian plays**, which use **three Acts**.
- **Ancient tragedies** often used overdone **plots from Thebes or Troy**.
- The audience already knew **Oedipus' story**, diminishing the surprise.
- **Repeated stories** dulled the novelty and **destroyed audience delight**.
- **Roman comedies** borrowed plots from **Greek poets**, often repetitive.
- **Plot formulas** involved stolen girls, deception, and **happy reunions**.
- **Characters** in Roman comedies were stereotypical, like **debauched sons** or **braggart captains**.
- **Female leads** were often silent, present to be **married off in the final Act**.
- **Italian-style plots** were **transparent** and imitated only narrow aspects of **nature**.
- Eugenius questions the **Unity of Place** as an Ancient rule.
- He argues **Unity of Time** wasn't strictly observed either.
- **Terence's plays** take more than one day to unfold.
- **Euripides' plays** commit timing errors, like impossible journeys.
- **Terence's Eunuch** also shows illogical timing in character exits.
- Ancient plays often had **single character scenes** disrupting flow.
- **Scenes changed** whenever a new character entered the stage.
- Terence's **monologues** directly addressed the audience unnaturally.
- Ancient plays sometimes showed **prosperous wickedness and unhappy virtue**.
- **Medea's escape with dragons** shows **unpunished evil**, violating morality.
- **Ancient poets specialized** in either comedy or tragedy, not both.
- **Language changes** make judging ancient wit difficult today.
- Some **Proverbs or customs** may not translate effectively.
- **Plautus often** used bold metaphors and coined new words.
- **Horace criticized Plautus** for overly indulgent wordplay.
- **Cleveland's style** was marked by forced and unnatural expressions.
- **Virgil and Ovid** sometimes used bold metaphors sparingly.
- **Cleveland's wit** was delivered in complex, hard-to-read language.

- **Dr. Donne's wit** was deep and conveyed in simpler terms.
- Cleveland's best wit is independent of **complex wordplay**.
- **Seneca's genius for drama** is surpassed by Ovid's writing style.
- Ovid stirs **admiration and emotion** in his epic, unlike Seneca.
- **Medea's gravity** lacks emotional impact compared to Ovid's stories.
- Seneca's best scene in *Troades* shows **motherly tenderness**.
- **Ancient tragedy** often avoided love, focusing on horror.
- **Plautus' comedies** show brief moments of tenderness and passion.
- **Love in ancient plays** expressed simply with sighs and words.
- **Modern lovers** explore jealousy and complaints in detailed dialogues.
- **Crites argues** moderns changed the style, not improved it.
- **Ancient heroes were bold** about their virtues, unlike moderns.
- **Crites' moderation** pleased everyone, ending the previous dispute.
- **Lisideius asks Eugenius** why English plays surpass French ones.
- **Eugenius defends** England, claiming they equal French plays.
- **Lisideius argues** French plays have surpassed English ones recently.
- **French plays excel** in unity of time, place, and action.
- **English plays suffer** from under-plots, diverting audience attention.
- **Tragicomedy in England** is viewed as absurd and inconsistent.
- **French plays ground** their tragedies on known historical stories.
- **French surpass the Ancients** by mixing history and fiction effectively.
- **English tragicomedy's structure** undermines the emotional impact of plays.
- French **plays** skillfully mix **truth** with **fiction** for effect.
- They modify **fate** to reward **virtue**, unlike strict history.
- Poets use **historical events** for freedom in **plot outcomes**.
- English **historical plays** condense decades into **two-hour acts**.
- This results in **miniature**, less perfect portrayals of **nature**.
- French **plays** avoid excessive **plots** and unnecessary **turns**.
- Their focus on one **story** allows more **emotional depth**.
- French plays grant **freedom** for poetic **expression** and **passions**.
- English plays often **mix** comedy and tragedy inappropriately.
- In **Corneille's** tragedies, each **character** drives the **plot forward**.
- **French plays** avoid using **prosaic characters** for unnecessary **narrations**.
- **Narrations** should relate to **characters** involved in the main **plot**.

- **English plays** often rely on unnecessary **narrations**, losing audience **attention**.
- **French plays** avoid showing **battles** or **duels** on stage, using **narration** instead.
- **Death scenes** on stage in **English tragedies** often become **comic**.
- **Descriptions** of death in **words** leave a deeper **impression** than acting.
- **Relating** events offstage maintains audience **belief** and emotional **engagement**.
- **Corneille** argues that only the most **beautiful** or **passionate** moments should be shown.
- **Poets** should focus on the **characters' emotions**, not just **physical action**.
- **Horace** advises against showing overly **gruesome** or unrealistic **events onstage**.
- **Cruel actions** causing **aversion** or **impossibility** should be **avoided** or narrated.
- **Narrations** can reduce **tumult** or fit the **plot** into a **reasonable time**.
- **Ben Jonson** used narration in **The Magnetic Lady** to avoid **disorder** on stage.
- **Fletcher** used narration in **The King and No King** to unravel the **plot** effectively.
- French plays **avoid sudden character changes** without a **powerful reason**.
- **French poets** ensure that each **character's purpose** is clear with every entrance.
- **Rhyme** in French plays is preferred over **blank verse** for its **beauty**.
- **Neander** acknowledges French **plots** are more **regular** but not superior.
- **Imitation of nature** is essential to a play's **success; humor and passion** are vital.
- **Corneille's** comedy **The Liar** was better received in **France** than **England**.
- **French playwrights** like **Molière** now imitate the **English Stage**'s style.
- French plays have **mixed serious plots with mirth** post-Richelieu.
- **English playwrights** like **Ben Jonson** offer more **variety of humor** than the French.

- French have **regularized** the **Spanish plays**, but **plots** are often **too similar**.
- **Tragicomedy** is an **English invention**, balancing **passion and mirth** effectively.
- **English plots** often have **under-plots** with **intrigues**, adding **variety and complexity**.
- French focus on **one single plot**, but **English variety** can offer **greater pleasure**.
- French **declamations** are **long speeches** that **lack passion** and **concernment**.
- **Short speeches** and **quick replies** better **express emotion** and move the **audience**.
- **Fletcher's plays** excel in **wit and repartee**, surpassing the **French Poets**.
- **French plays** focus on making **one character central**, but **English plays** can have **multiple shining characters**.
- **Variety of characters** and **actions** creates a **labyrinth of design**, pleasing the audience.
- **Lisideius** praises the **French** for narrating actions instead of staging them, avoiding **tumult**.
- **English audiences prefer combats** and **horror** on stage, while French hide them.
- **Ben Jonson** avoided showing **death on stage**, but criticized **Shakespeare** for doing the same.
- **French stick to rigid rules**, but this limits **plot variety** and **imagination**.
- **Strict unities of time and place** create **absurdities** in **French plays**, limiting creative freedom.
- **English plays** like **Shakespeare's and Fletcher's** are **irregular** but offer more **variety and complexity**.
- **Corneille** admits the **French are constrained** by their own rules, limiting **stage beauty**.
- **English plays** explore **multiple plots** and **locations**, offering more **entertainment**.
- **French plays** often have **flat, predictable plots**, lacking complexity.
- **English plays** are more **varied and lively**, with **quicker writing**.
- **English plots** are not **borrowed from the French**, but crafted locally.

- **Shakespeare** and **Fletcher** are **models of character diversity** and **varied plots**.
- **Ben Jonson** followed **dramatic rules closely**, yet embraced both **rhyme and blank verse**.
- **Shakespeare** is praised for his **natural genius** and ability to depict **nature and emotions**.
- **Shakespeare** had a **comprehensive soul**, capturing both **nature** and **human experience**.
- **Shakespeare's greatness** is evident when he has a **fit subject for his wit**.
- **Mr. Hales of Eaton** believed **Shakespeare** excelled at any subject compared to other poets.
- **Shakespeare was more esteemed** than **Jonson** by his **contemporaries** and later critics.
- **Beaumont and Fletcher** improved on **Shakespeare's wit** with natural gifts.
- **Ben Jonson** valued **Beaumont's judgment**, even submitting his work for critique.
- **Philaster** brought **Fletcher and Beaumont** early success after prior failures.
- **Beaumont and Fletcher's plots** were more **regular** and depicted **gentlemen's conversations** better than Shakespeare's.
- Their plays had a **gayety in comedies** and **pathos in serious works**, making them popular.
- **Shakespeare's language** was considered somewhat **obsolete**, while Jonson's wit lacked the energy of Beaumont and Fletcher.
- **Jonson was the most learned writer** on the stage, but his focus was on **humor** and **mechanic people**, avoiding love and passion.
- He borrowed freely from the **Ancients**, especially in **Sejanus** and **Catiline**, openly using their works.
- **Shakespeare** was seen as the more **creative genius**, while **Jonson** was the more **precise and correct** poet.
- Jonson's **Discoveries** provided many **useful precepts** for perfecting stagecraft, similar to the French rules.
- **In Epicine, or The Silent Woman by Ben Jonson:**
- **Action's Length**: The entire play happens within three and a half hours.
- **Setting**: The play is set in **London**, mainly within two houses.

- ➤ **Continuity of Scenes**: The scenes remain largely unbroken, maintaining a smooth flow.
- ➤ **Plot**: The central plot revolves around settling **Morose's estate on Dauphine**.
- ➤ **Intrigue**: The intrigue is intricate, with various delightful characters and humors.
- ➤ **Character of Morose**: Morose is humorously sensitive to noise, a trait **based on real-life** observations.
- ➤ **Humor in the Play**: Jonson's use of humor in **Epicine** is defined by **odd and extravagant characters**, specific to certain individuals.
- ➤ **Multiple Characters and Subplots**: The play features multiple characters, each with their own role, contributing to the main plot.
- ➤ **Wit and Fancy**: This play is filled with **more wit and acuteness** than Jonson's other works, especially in representing **gentlemen's conversations**.
- ➤ **Well-Constructed Plot**: The **plot's resolution** is cleverly concealed until the last scene, making the audience believe it was inevitable once revealed.
- ➤ Rhyme in plays is unnatural for spontaneous dialogue.
- ➤ Dialogue should imitate natural, unpremeditated conversation.
- ➤ Blank verse is closer to real speech than rhyme.
- ➤ Rhyme makes characters seem unnaturally quick-witted poets.
- ➤ Overuse of rhyme reveals too much artificiality on stage.
- ➤ Plays should conceal art, not display it openly.
- ➤ Suspension of disbelief requires dialogue resembling natural speech.
- ➤ Audiences expect a realistic portrayal, even in fiction.
- ➤ Rhyme can't express high or low thoughts naturally.
- ➤ Verse constrains imagination; limits freedom in expression.
- ➤ Ovid's example shows verse can be excessive.
- ➤ Blank verse avoids rhyme's forced constraints.
- ➤ Rhyme doesn't make thoughts more natural.
- ➤ Good poets avoid errors in both rhyme and blank verse.
- ➤ Care and variety in verse prevent monotony.
- ➤ Confined sense in couplets can become tedious.
- ➤ Varied cadences enhance audience engagement.
- ➤ Verse can be made natural in itself.
- ➤ Rhyme and blank verse are both far from ordinary speech.
- ➤ Rhyme can be as natural as blank verse with correct word placement.
- ➤ Rhyme adds sweetness and advantage over blank verse.

- Aristotle's preference for prose-like verse applies to blank verse.
- Modern verse relies on rhyme and accent, unlike ancient verse.
- Rhyme is universal in French, Italian, and Spanish tragedies.
- Rhyme can be practical and not forced in all instances.
- Poets need not constrain themselves to perfect rhyme all the time.
- No genre of writing remains unchanged; our age may exceed past poets in verse.
- There's no need to compete with greats like Shakespeare, Jonson, and Fletcher.
- Verse writing has evolved; past masters may not have reached today's proficiency.
- The audience's preference is shifting toward accepting verse in serious plays.
- Recent plays written in verse, like *The Siege of Rhodes* and *The Indian Queen*, were well-received.
- **Rhyme and Blank Verse**: Rhyme can feel natural with well-chosen words.
- **Serious Plays**: Rhyme fits serious plays with elevated characters.
- **Nature Representation**: Plays reflect heightened emotions, not everyday speech.
- **Rhyme Elevates Drama**: Heroic rhyme elevates tragedy's noble portrayals.
- **Epic and Drama**: Rhyme suits both epic poetry and drama.
- **Sudden Thoughts**: Sudden thoughts can appear elevated through rhyme.
- **Repartees in Verse**: Coordinated rhyme in repartees enhances harmony.
- **Confederacy of Rhyme**: Rhyme completion in dialogue mirrors artistic coordination.
- **Art of Rhyme**: Rhyme adds skill and enhances dialogue's appeal.
- **Poet's Satisfaction**: Poets feel satisfied when rhyme completes dialogue.
- **Rhyme in Verse**: Rhyme can sound natural with poetic care.
- **Blank Verse Easier**: Blank verse risks making the poet too luxuriant.
- **Judgment in Writing**: Judgment controls imagination, verse adds structure.
- **Rhyme Aids Fancy**: Rhyme helps restrain an overly imaginative poet.
- **Verse Helps Judgment**: Verse serves as a rule to organize thoughts.

- ➤ **Ben Jonson's Exact Writing**: Jonson wrote well without relying on rhyme.
- ➤ **Ovid's Luxuriance**: Ovid may have been worse without verse structure.
- ➤ **Verse Refined Over Time**: Modern verse is more refined than earlier periods.
- ➤ **Poetic Tools**: Judgment, geography, and philosophy aid in writing correctly.

Questions:

Question 45

What is the correct sequence of various periods of Englah Literature

A. Caroline Age
C. Restoration Age
B, Jacobean, Age
D. Commonwealth Period
E. Augustan Age

Choose the correct answer from the options given below :

(1) D, B, A, E, C
(2) A, B, B, C, D
(3) B, A, D, C, B
(4) B, C, A, D, B

Explanations:
Answer: (3) B, A, D, C, A

B. (1603-1625) The Jacobean era was a period in English history that lasted from 1603 to 1625, during the reign of King James I

A. (1625 to 1649) The Caroline era is the period in English and Scottish history that corresponds to the reign of King Charles I, which lasted from 1625 to 1649. The term comes from the Latin word Carolus, which means Charles.

D. (1649-1660) The Commonwealth was the political structure during the period from 1649 to 1660 when England and Wales, later along with Ireland and Scotland, were governed as a republic after the end of the Second English Civil War and the trial and execution of Charles I.

C. (1660 to 1688) Restoration literature refers to English literature written during the period of the English Restoration, which lasted from roughly 1660 to 1688. This period was marked by the return of Charles II to the throne after the rule of republican governments following the execution of Charles I.

E. (1700–1745) The Augustan Age in English literature was a period from roughly 1700 to 1750, named after the Roman Emperor Augustus. It was a time when English writers were influenced by the Latin poets of Augustus's reign, and their work was characterized by order, balance, and clarity.

Question 46

What is the correct chronological sequence of famous dramatists in order of their birth ?

A. William Congreve
B. John Dryden
C. William Wycherley
D. George Barnard Shaw
E. John Millington Synge

Choose the correct answer from the options given below :

(1) B, C, A, D, E
(2) A, C, B, E, D
(3) C, B, A, D, E
(4) E, B, C, A, D

Explanations:
Answer: (1) B, C, A, D, E

B. John Dryden (1631-1700)
C. William Wycherley (1641-1716)
A. William Congreve (1670-1729)
D. George Bernard Shaw (1856-1950)

E. Edmund John Millington Synge (1871-1909)

Question 47

Match List I and List II List I

List I **Critics**	List II **Text**
A. Horace	I. A Defence of Rhyme
B. John Dryden	II. Timber: or, Discoveries
C. Samuel Daniel	III. Ars Poetica
D. Ben Jonson	IV. Of Dramatic Poesy

Choose the correct answer from the options given below:

1. A – II, B – I, C – IV, D – III
2. A – III, B – IV, C – II, D – I
3. A – III, B – IV, C – I, D – II
4. A – II, B – IV, C – I, D – III

Explanations:

Answer 3: A – III, B – IV, C – I, D – II

A. Horace's "Ars Poetica" is a treatise on the art of poetry. It was written in ancient Rome around 18 BCE and provides guidelines for writing poetry, including the importance of unity, clarity, and avoiding clichés.

B. John Dryden's "Of Dramatic Poesy" is a critical essay written in 1668. It is a conversation between four characters discussing the relative merits of ancient versus modern drama. The essay also explores the idea of the "rules" of drama and whether they should be followed or broken.

C. Samuel Daniel's "A Defence of Rhyme" is a 16th-century treatise defending the use of rhyme in poetry. At the time, there was a debate about whether rhyme was an appropriate technique for serious poetry. Daniel argues that rhyme can be used effectively to enhance the beauty and musicality of poetry.

D. Ben Jonson's "Timber: or, Discoveries" is a collection of notes and observations on literature and language. It was written in the early 17th century and covers a wide range of topics, including poetry, drama, and the use of language. The work is notable for its insights into Jonson's own creative process and his thoughts on other writers of his time.

Question 48

Who among the following are the two great masters of the French language that T. S Eliot contrasts with Dryden and Milton in The Metaphysical Poets'?

    A. Francois Villon
    B. Jean Racine
    C. Charles Baudelaire
    D. Arthur Rimbaud

Choose the correct answer from the options given below:

    1. A and C only
    2. A and D only
    3. B and C only
    4. B and D only

Explanations:
Answer: 3. B and C only

In "The Metaphysical Poets," T.S. Eliot contrasts the poetry of the French writers Jean Racine and Charles Baudelaire with that of John Milton and John Dryden. Eliot praises Racine and Baudelaire for their use of language and their ability to express complex emotions and ideas with simplicity and precision. He contrasts them with Milton and Dryden, whom he sees as more concerned with the expression of moral or political values in their poetry.

Eliot's comparison can be found in the following excerpt from "The Metaphysical Poets":

*"The French writers, the great masters of the language, have been more concerned with the form of language than with its content. They have been occupied with devising rhetorical devices to convey states of mind, rather than with the exploration of states of mind. They have been concerned, not so much with expressing themselves as with expressing human nature. **The greatest of them, Racine and Baudelaire, have a much closer affinity with the metaphysical poets than has Dryden or Milton.**"*

Question 49

Arrange the following plays in the chronological order of publication:

    A. All for Love
    B. Venice Preserved
    C. The School for Scandal

    D. The Country Wife

Choose the correct answer from the options given below
1. B, C, A, D
2. D, A, B, C
3. C, 8, D, A
4. A, D, C, B

Explanations:
Answer: 2. D, A, B, C

The chronological order of publication for the given plays is:

- *The Country Wife (1675)* **by William Wycherley**
- *All for Love (1677)* **by John Dryden**
- *Venice Preserved (1682)* **by Thomas Otway**
- *The School for Scandal (1777)* **by Richard Brinsley Sheridan**

Extra Perk:

"All for Love" is a tragedy play by John Dryden, first performed in 1677. It is a retelling of the story of Antony and Cleopatra, focusing on the relationship between the two lovers and their tragic endings.

"Venice Preserved" is a tragedy play by Thomas Otway, first performed in 1682. The play revolves around a group of conspirators who plot to overthrow the ruling council of Venice, but their plan is ultimately foiled and they are punished.

"The School for Scandal" is a comedy play by Richard Brinsley Sheridan, first performed in 1777. The play satirizes the manners and morals of the upper classes in 18th-century England, particularly their love of gossip and scandal.

"The Country Wife" is a comedy play by William Wycherley, first performed in 1675. The play follows the exploits of a young man named Horner who pretends to be impotent in order to gain access to the wives of the wealthy men of London, leading to a series of comic misunderstandings and mistaken identities.

Question 50

Arrange the following authors in the chronological order of their birth:

A. Oscar Wilde

B. William Langland
C. Geoffrey Chaucer
D. John Dryden
E. Alexander Pope

Choose the correct answer from the options given below:

1. B, C, D, E, A
2. A, B, C, E, D
3. B, C, D, A, E
4. C, B, A, D, E

Explanations:
Answer: 1. B, C, D, E, A

Oscar Wilde (1854- 1900)
- *The Picture of Dorian Gray*
- *The Importance of Being Earnest*
- *Lady Windermere's Fan*
- *An Ideal Husband*

William Langland (1332- 1386)
- *Piers Plowman*

Geoffrey Chaucer (1343- 1400)
- *The Canterbury Tales*
- *Troilus and Criseyde*

John Dryden (1631- 1700)
- *Absalom and Achitophel*
- *Mac Flecknoe*
- *All for Love*
- *The Conquest of Granada*

Alexander Pope (1688-1744)
- *The Rape of the Lock*
- *An Essay on Criticism*
- *An Essay on Man*
- *The Dunciad*
- *I hope this helps!*

Question 51
Arrange the following plays in their chronological order:

(A) The Tempest
(B) All For Love
(C) Volpone
(D) The School for Scandal

Choose the correct answer from the options given below :

1. (A), (C), (B), (D)
2. (C), (B), (A), (D)
3. (C), (A), (B), (D)
4. (A), (D), (B), (C)

Explanations:
Answer: 3. (C), (A), (B), (D

(C) Volpone - Written by Ben Jonson, it was first performed in **1605** and is a satirical comedy that explores themes of greed, deception, and corruption in Venetian society.

(A) The Tempest - Written by William Shakespeare, it is believed to be one of his last plays and was likely composed around **1610-1611.** It is a complex play that combines elements of romance, comedy, and tragedy, centring around themes of power, magic, and forgiveness.

(B) All For Love - Written by John Dryden, it was first performed in 1677 and is a tragedy based on the story of Antony and Cleopatra. It explores themes of love, loyalty, and the conflict between personal desires and duty.

(D) The School for Scandal - Written by Richard Brinsley Sheridan, it premiered in 1777 and is a witty comedy of manners that satirizes gossip, hypocrisy, and social conventions of the time. It remains one of the most popular and enduring plays of the 18th century.

Question 52

The heroic couplet is a pair of

1. **Ten-syllable lines that rhyme**
2. Twelve-syllable lines that rhyme
3. Eight-syllable lines that do not rhyme
4. Eight-syllable lines that rhyme

Correct Explanations:

A heroic couplet is a traditional form of English poetry, commonly used in epic and narrative poetry, and **consists of rhyming lines in iambic pentameter**. The heroic couplet pioneered by Geoffrey Chaucer in the Legend of Good Women and the Canterbury Tales is generally considered to have been perfected by John Dryden and Alexander Pope in the Restoration Age early 18th century, respectively.

English heroic couplets, especially in Dryden and his followers, are sometimes varied by the **use of the occasional alexandrine, or hexameter line, and triplet**. Often these two variations are used together to heighten a climax.

- ➤ That poetic meter, iambic pentameter, distinguishes a heroic couplet from a regular couplet.
- ➤ **Each line in iambic pentameter consists of 5 iambs and totals ten syllables.**
- ➤ Each iamb has two syllables: one unstressed syllable and one stressed syllable.

Question 53

"When nature prompted and no law denied Promiscuous use of concubine and bride;
Then Israel's monarch after Heaven's own heart, His vigorous warmth did variously impart
To wives and slaves."

From which poem are these lines taken?

1. Absalom and Achitophel: A Poem
2. MacFlecknoe
3. A Song for St. Cecilia's Day
4. Alexander's Feast

Explanations:
Ans: Absalom and Achitophel: A Poem

These lines are taken from the **poem "Absalom and Achitophel" by John Dryden.**

"Absalom and Achitophel" is a satirical poem written by John Dryden in 1681.

The lines in question describe King David, a Biblical figure who was known for his many wives and concubines. The poem presents David as a stand-in for King Charles II of England, and the reference to David's "promiscuous use of concubine and bride" is meant to criticize Charles's own sexual promiscuity.

The lines also suggest that David was "after Heaven's own heart," which is a reference to a passage in the Bible where God describes David as a man after his own heart (1 Samuel 13:14). Dryden uses this description ironically since the poem portrays David/Charles as a flawed ruler who has failed to live up to his responsibilities.

Other Explanations:
"MacFlecknoe," "A Song for St. Cecilia's Day," and "Alexander's Feast" are all poems written by the English poet John Dryden.

"MacFlecknoe" is a **satirical poem** in which Dryden **mocks a rival poet named Thomas Shadwell, portraying him as a talentless hack who is unworthy of being his successor.** The poem is notable for its use of elaborate and vivid language to create a comic and absurd vision of Shadwell's poetic world.

"A Song for St. Cecilia's Day" is an ode written to **celebrate the feast day of St. Cecilia, the patron saint of music.** The poem is notable for its celebration of the power of music to move and inspire the human spirit and for its vivid and imaginative descriptions of the sounds and effects of music.

"Alexander's Feast" is another **ode** written by Dryden, this time **celebrating the power of music to stir the emotions and passions of the human soul.** The poem tells the story of a banquet held by Alexander the Great, during which a musician named **Timotheus performs a song that moves Alexander to tears.** The poem is notable for its vivid and descriptive language, as well as its celebration of the power of art, to move and transform its audience.

Question 54

Which of the following poems are written by Alexander Pope?

    A.   The Dunciad

    B.   Moral Essays
    C.   Grongar Hill
    D.   Cooper's Hill
    E.   Absalom and Achitophel

Choose the correct answer from the options given below:

1. A and C only.
2. B and E only.
3. **A and B only.**
4. C and D only.

Explantions:
The Dunciad is a mock-heroic poem written by Alexander Pope in the 18th century. It satirizes the literary and intellectual incompetence of the "dunces" of his time.

Moral Essays is a collection of four poems by Alexander Pope, published between 1731 and 1735. The poems deal with ethical and philosophical themes and are considered one of the most important works of English moral literature.

Grongar Hill is a poem written by John Dyer in 1726. It describes the beauty of the landscape around the Grongar Hill in Wales.

Cooper's Hill is a poem written by John Denham in 1642. It describes the beauty of the landscape around the River Thames and is considered one of the first examples of topographical poetry in English literature.

Absalom and Achitophel is a satirical poem written by John Dryden in 1681. It critiques the political situation of his time by using the story of King David and his son Absalom as an allegory.

Question 55

Choose the correct chronological sequence in which the following texts were published.

    A.   The Tower
    B.   The Hind and the Panther

C. The Wild Swans at Coole
D. Mac Flecknoe
E. The Whitsun Weddings

Choose the correct answer from the options given below:

1. ABDEC
2. BCAED
3. BACDE
4. **DBCAE**

Explanations:
The correct chronological sequence of publication for the listed texts is as follows:

1. *Mac Flecknoe by John Dryden (1682)*
2. *The Hind and the Panther by John Dryden (1687)*
3. *The Tower by W. B. Yeats (1928)*
4. *The Wild Swans at Coole by W. B. Yeats (1919)*
5. *The Whitsun Weddings by Philip Larkin (1964)*

Question 56

Find the chronological order of the writers in terms of the period they belonged to:

A. Richard Steele
B. Charles Lamb
C. John Dryden
D. Francis Bacon
E. Matthew Arnold

Choose the correct answer from the options given below:

1. ABCDE
2. BDECA
3. CBDAE
4. **DCABE**

Explanations:

1. Francis Bacon (1561-1626)
2. John Dryden (1631-1700)
3. Richard Steele (1672-1729)
4. Charles Lamb (1775-1834)
5. Matthew Arnold (1822-1888)

Question 57

Which among the following is true about Religio Laici?

A. John Dryden wrote Religio Laici.
B. Religio Laici strongly criticised the Anglican Church.
C. Religio Laci means A Layman's Faith
D. Religio Laci was published in 1690.
E. Religio Laci was a philosophical-religious prose treatise.

Choose the correct answer from the options given below:

1, A, B and C
2. A and C
3. A and D
4. D and E

Explanations
Answer: 2. A and C

***Religio Laici, Or A Layman's Faith (1682)* is a poem written in heroic couplets by John Dryden.** It was written in response to the publication of an English translation of the Histoire critique du vieux testament by the French cleric Father Richard Simon. Simon's book applied detailed criticism to the textual history of the Bible and argued that, given the compromised nature of much of the Bible, Christians would do better to base their faith on the history and traditions of the Roman Catholic Church.

His earlier *Religio Laici (1682)* had argued in eloquent couplets for the consolations of Anglicanism and against unbelievers, Protestant dissenters, and Roman Catholics.

Other Explanations:

In his longest poem, the beast fable *The Hind and the Panther (1687)*, he argued the case for his adopted church **against the Church of England and the sects.**

Arrange the correct chronological sequence of the publication of the following texts:

> A. Essay of Dramatic Poesy
> B. A Room of One's Own
> C. Culture and Anarchy
> D. The Lives of the Poets
> E. "Preface to the Lyrical Ballads"

Choose the correct answer from the options given below:

> 1. A, D, E, C, B
> 2. D, A, E, B, C
> 3. A, C, D, E, B
> 4. E, D, C, A, B

Explanations
Answer: 1. A, D, E, C, B

A. John Dryden's *Essay of Dramatick Poesy* was likely written in 1666 during the Great Plague of London and published in 1668. In this essay, Dryden argues that poetic drama with English and Spanish influence is a justifiable art form when compared to traditional French poetry.

D. *Lives of the Most Eminent English Poets* (1779–81), alternatively known as Lives of the Poets, is a work by Samuel Johnson that includes short biographies and critical appraisals of 52 poets who lived during the eighteenth century. The poets are arranged roughly by the date of death.

E. *The Preface to Lyrical Ballads* is an essay by William Wordsworth, first published in the second edition of the poetry collection Lyrical Ballads in 1800 and later expanded in the third edition of 1802. It is considered a de facto manifesto of the Romantic movement, with four guidelines: using ordinary life as the best subject for poetry, employing everyday language, prioritising the expression of feelings over action or plot, and defining poetry as the spontaneous overflow of powerful emotions.

C. *Culture and Anarchy: An Essay in Political and Social Criticism* is a series of periodical essays by Matthew Arnold, first published in Cornhill Magazine from 1867 to 1868 and later collected as a book in 1869. The preface was added in 1869. The essays address political and social issues and offer Arnold's views on culture and society.

B. *A Room of One's Own* is an essay by Virginia Woolf, published in 1929, based on two lectures she gave in 1928 at Newnham College and Girton College, the first two colleges for women at Cambridge. In the essay, Woolf discusses the status of women, particularly women artists, and argues that financial independence and a dedicated space are essential for women to pursue their creative endeavours.

Question 59

The character who discusses the relative merits of French drama and English drama in Essay of Dramatic Poesy is

1. Neander
2. Lisideius
3. Crites
4. Eugenius

Explanations:
Answer: 2. Lisideius

In 1668, Dryden published *Of Dramatick Poesie, an Essay,* a leisurely discussion between four contemporary writers of whom Dryden (as Neander) is one. This work is a defence of English drama against the champions of both ancient Classical drama and the Neoclassical French theatre; it is also an attempt to discover general principles of dramatic criticism. By deploying his disputants so as to break down the conventional oppositions of ancient and modern, French and English, Elizabethan and Restoration, Dryden deepens and complicates the discussion. This is the first substantial piece of modern dramatic criticism; it is sensible, judicious, and exploratory and combines general principles and analysis in a gracefully informal style. Dryden's approach in this and all his best criticism is characteristically speculative and shows the influence of detached scientific inquiry. The prefaces to his plays and translations over the next three decades were to constitute a substantial body of critical writing and reflection.

The four men debate a series of three topics:
1. The relative merit of classical drama (upheld by Crites) vs. modern drama (championed by Eugenius);
2. Whether French drama, as Lisideius maintains, is better than English drama (supported by Neander, who famously calls Shakespeare "the greatest soul, ancient or modern");
3. Whether plays in rhyme are an improvement upon blank verse drama—a proposition that Neander, despite having defended the Elizabethans, now advances against the sceptical Crites (who also switches from his original position and defends the blank verse tradition of Elizabethan drama).

Question 60

Who among the following was NOT one of the original members of Johnson's Literary Club?

1. Oliver Goldsmith
2. John Dryden
3. Edmund Burke
4. John Hawkins

Explanations:
Answer: 2. John Dryden

The Club, also known as the Literary Club, is a renowned dining club in London that was established in February 1764. Its founders were artist Joshua Reynolds, essayist **Samuel Johnson, and philosopher-politician Edmund Burke.** The original nine members included prominent figures such as Reynolds, Johnson, Burke, Christopher Nugent, Topham Beauclerk, Bennet Langton, **Oliver Goldsmith,** Anthony Chamier, and **John Hawkins.** The Club served as a gathering place for intellectuals, writers, and artists, fostering lively discussions and camaraderie among its esteemed members.

Question 61

Who does Achitophel represent in John Dryden's allegorical poem Absalom and Achitophel?

1. First Earl of Shaftesbury
2. First Duke of Monmouth
3. First Duke of Buckingham
4. First Duke of York

Explanations:
Answer: 1. First Earl of Shaftesbury

Absalom and Achitophel is a verse satire written by John Dryden and published in 1681. The poem explores the Exclusion crisis, a contemporary event centred around the efforts to prevent James, Duke of York, a Roman Catholic convert, from succeeding to the throne. Dryden draws inspiration from the biblical story of Absalom and Achitophel, using biblical names to represent key figures in the crisis. For instance, Monmouth represents Absalom, **Shaftesbury represents Achitophel, and Charles II represents David.** Despite the prevailing anti-Catholic sentiments of the time, Dryden's skillful analysis of the motives behind the political intrigues helps defend the Duke of York's position. A second part of the poem, featuring contributions from Nahum Tate and containing lines by Dryden aimed at his literary rivals, was published in 1682.

RESTORATION COMEDY

- ➢ **Restoration comedy**: English comedy from **1660–1710**.
- ➢ **Comedy of manners** is a synonym for **Restoration comedy**.
- ➢ **Public stage performances banned** for 18 years by Puritans.
- ➢ **Theatres reopened in 1660**, marking a **drama renaissance**.
- ➢ **Sexually explicit language** encouraged by **King Charles II** and his court.
- ➢ **Socially diverse audiences**: aristocrats, servants, and middle class.
- ➢ Attracted by **topical writing**, busy plots, and **first professional actresses**.
- ➢ Rise of **celebrity actors** during this period.
- ➢ **Aphra Behn**: first professional **female playwright**.

War of the theatres, 1695–1700

- ➢ The company owners wrote the young **United Company employee Colley Cibber**:

"had made a monopoly of the stage, and consequently presum'd they might impose what conditions they pleased upon their people. [They] did not consider that they were all this while endeavouring to enslave a set of actors whom the public were inclined to support."

- ➢ Performers like the legendary **Thomas Betterton,**
- ➢ The tragedienne **Elizabeth Barry**
  The rising young comedian **Anne Bracegirdle**
- ➢ They had he audience on their side, and confident of this walked out.
- ➢ **Actors gained Royal license**, bypassing Rich's original patents.
- ➢ **Cooperative company** formed with detailed rules and shares.
- ➢ Opened with **William Congreve's Love For Love**, huge success.
- ➢ **London had two competing companies**, revitalizing Restoration drama.
- ➢ **Rich's company offered attractions** like jugglers, dancers, animals.
- ➢ **Cooperative actors appealed to snobbery**, claiming legitimacy.
- ➢ Used **prologues by boys and epilogues by ladies on horseback.**

List of Restoration Comedies:

- ➢ *George Etherege – The Comical Revenge (1664),* ***She Would If She Could (1668), The Man of Mode (1676)***
- ➢ *John Dryden – An Evening's Love (1668), Marriage a la Mode (1672)*
- ➢ *Charles Sedley – The Mulberry-Garden (1668), Bellamira: or, The Mistress (1687)*
- ➢ *George Villiers, 2nd Duke of Buckingham – The Rehearsal (1671)*
- ➢ *William Wycherley – Love in a Wood (1671), The Country Wife (1675), The Plain Dealer (1676)*
- ➢ ***Thomas Shadwell*** *– Epsom Wells (1672), The Virtuoso (1676), A True Widow (1678), The Woman Captain (1679), The Squire of Alsatia (1688), Bury Fair (1689), The Volunteers (1692)*
- ➢ *Edward Ravenscroft – The Careless Lovers (1673) The London Cuckolds (1681), Dame Dobson (1683), The Canterbury Guests (1694)*
- ➢ *John Crowne – The Country Wit (1676), City Politiques (1683), Sir Courtly Nice (1685), The English Friar (1690), The Married Beau (1694)*
- ➢ *Thomas Rawlins – Tom Essence (1676), Tunbridge Wells (1678)*

- ➢ ***Aphra Behn – The Counterfeit Bridegroom (1677), The Rover (1677), The Roundheads (1681), The Revenge (1680), The City Heiress (1682), The Lucky Chance (1686)***
- ➢ *Thomas D'Urfey – A Fond Husband (1677), Squire Oldsapp (1678), The Virtuous Wife (1679), Sir Barnaby Whigg (1681), The Royalist (1682) A Commonwealth of Women (1685), A Fool's Preferment (1688), Love for Money (1691), The Marriage-Hater Matched (1692), The Campaigners (1698)*
- ➢ *Thomas Otway – Friendship in Fashion (1678)*
- ➢ *Thomas Southerne – Sir Anthony Love (1690), The Wives Excuse (1691), The Maid's Last Prayer (1693)*
- ➢ ***William Congreve – The Old Bachelor (1693), Love For Love (1695), The Way of the World (1700)***
- ➢ ***John Vanbrugh – The Relapse (1696), The Provoked Wife (1697)***
- ➢ ***George Farquhar – Love and a Bottle (1698), The Constant Couple (1699), Sir Harry Wildair (1701), The Recruiting Officer (1706), The Beaux' Stratagem (1707)***
- ➢ *Susanna Centlivre – The Perjured Husband (1700), The Basset-Table, (1705), The Busie Body (1709*

William Wycherley (1641-1716)

- ➢ The productive period of Wycherley's life was brief but fruitful.
- ➢ He produced **four plays in five years:**
- ➢ **(Code: Love in a wood, the gentleman dance with the country wife and the plain dealer)**
- ➢ *Love in a Wood (1672),*
  - o His **debut play was first staged at the Theatre Royal**, Drury Lane, by the King's Company.
- ➢ *The Gentleman Dancing Master (1673),*
- ➢ *The Country Wife (1675),*
  - o **First performed in 1675,** during the tolerant Restoration period.
  - o Reflected **aristocratic, anti-Puritan ideology**, controversial for explicitness.
  - o **Title contains lewd pun** on the word "country."
  - o Based on **Molière's plays** but with colloquial prose and fast plot.
  - o **Plot centers on a rake** pretending impotence for affairs.
  - o **Young country wife discovers London life**, especially its men.

- o Rake **Horner claims impotence**, contracted in France from "common women."
- o **Horner's supposed cure** was a drastic surgical reduction.
- o 1. **Horner's Impotence Trick and Seduction Plan**
  - Horner's **impotence trick drives the Play's action**.
  - Based on Terence's **classic comedy *Eunuchus* strategy**.
  - **Horner spreads rumors of impotence**, deceiving husbands.
  - His ruse **leads to successful seduction** of aristocratic wives.
- o 2. **Near-Discoveries and Final Trick**
  - Horner **narrowly avoids exposure** throughout the Play.
  - Margery Pinchwife **almost reveals Horner's secret**.
  - Horner and his lovers **trick Pinchwife** into believing the lie.
  - Horner **continues his deception past the last act**.
- o 3. **Margery and Pinchwife's Marriage**
  - **Pinchwife marries naïve Margery**, hoping to avoid cuckoldry.
  - **Margery learns from Horner** about upper-class seduction.
  - **Margery's innocence contrasts** with London's sexual culture.
  - **Pinchwife's jealousy unintentionally informs** Margery about town life.
- o 4. **Harcourt and Alithea's Love Story**
  - **Harcourt pursues Alithea**, despite her engagement to Sparkish.
  - **Alithea remains loyal** to Sparkish, despite his flaws.
  - **Sparkish doubts Alithea's virtue** after a compromising situation.
  - Alithea **admits her love for Harcourt** after Sparkish's betrayal.

- ➢ *The Plain Dealer (1677).*
  - o First performed on 11 December **1676**.
  - o The Play is based on **Molière's Le Misanthrope**
  - o Generally considered Wycherley's finest work, along with The Country Wife.
  - o The Play was highly **praised by John Dryden and John Dennis,**

- o There were many equally condemned for its obscenity.
- o The title character is **Captain Manly**, a sailor.
- o He doubts the motives of everyone he meets **except for his sweetheart, Olivia, and his friend, Varnish.**
- o When **Olivia jilts him and marries Varnish,** he attempts to gain revenge by sending a **pageboy (unknown to him, a girl in disguise, and is in love with him) to seduce Olivia.**
- o When the **truth of the page's identity** is discovered, **Manly marries her** instead.
- ➢ Attempted to reconcile a personal conflict between deep-seated puritanism and an ardent physical nature in his plays.
- ➢ As a satirist, his age admired him: **William Congreve regarded Wycherley as one appointed "*to lash this crying age.*"**

William Congreve (1670–1729)

- ➢ English dramatist who shaped the English comedy of manners
- ➢ His brilliant comic dialogue, satirical **portrayal of the sexes' war,** and ironic scrutiny of the affectations of his age.
- ➢ His plays were produced **between 1693 and 1700.**
- ➢ The **last play was not successful,** and repeated attacks were forthcoming upon his defects, so **he wrote no more.**
- ➢ He reportedly was particularly stung by a critique by **Jeremy Collier (*A Short View of the Immorality and Profaneness of the English Stage*).**
- ➢ He wrote a long reply, ***"Amendments to Mr. Collier's False and Imperfect Citations."***
- ➢ In 1697 he produced one tragedy, *The Mourning Bride*, which had no success.
- ➢ The plots are full of scandalous notions delicately adumbrated.
- ➢ The style is as keen and deadly as a sharp sword.
- ➢ One of Congreve's favorite **actresses was Mrs. Anne Bracegirdle**, who performed many female lead roles in his plays.
- ➢ His first play, ***The Old Bachelor***, written to amuse himself while convalescing, was produced at the **Theatre Royal, Drury Lane, in 1693.**
- ➢ Congreve's mentor **John Dryden gave the production rave reviews** and proclaimed it a brilliant first piece.
- ➢ He was also a member of the **Whig Kit-Kat Club.**
- ➢ His significant plays were:
    - o ***The Old Bachelour (1693),***
    - o ***The Double-Dealer (1693),***

- o *Love for Love (1695),*
- o *The Mourning Bride (1697)*
- o *The Way of the World (1700).*

The following is a passage from ***The Way of the World.*** Two gentlemen are backbiting an acquaintance.

Fainall. He comes to town in order to equip himself for travel.
Mirabell. For travel! Why the man that I mean is above forty.
Fainall. No matter for that; 'tis for the honour of England, that all Europe should know that we have blockheads of all ages.
Mirabell. I wonder there is not an act of parliament to save the credit of the nation, and prohibit the exportation of fools.
Fainall. By no means, 'tis better as 'tis; 'tis better to trade with a little loss, than to be quite eaten up with being overstocked.
Mirabell. Pray, are the follies of this knight-errant, and those of the squire his brother, anything related?
Fainall. Not at all; Witwoud grows by the knight, like a medlar grafted on a crab. One will melt in your mouth, and t'other set your teeth on edge; one is all pulp, and the other all core.
Mirabell. So one will be rotten before he be ripe, and the other will be rotten without ever being ripe at all.

The Way of The World (1700)

- ➤ Premiered in March 1700 at Lincoln's Inn Fields, London.
- ➤ Considered one of the best **Restoration comedies** performed occasionally.
- ➤ Initially, the play was criticized for **continuing immorality.**
- ➤ Plot centers on **lovers Mirabell and Millamant's marriage struggle**.
- ➤ Mirabell must get **Lady Wishfort's blessing** to marry Millamant.
- ➤ Lady Wishfort despises Mirabell and **prefers nephew Sir Wilfull.**
- ➤ Lady Wishfort, a widow, seeks **marriage with Sir Rowland.**
- ➤ **Fainall secretly has an affair with Mrs. Marwood.**
- ➤ Mrs. Fainall, Lady Wishfort's daughter, **once had an affair** with Mirabell.
- ➤ **Waitwell, Mirabell's servant, marries Foible, Lady Wishfort's servant.**
- ➤ Waitwell pretends to be **Sir Rowland to trick Lady Wishfort.**

Summary of the Play:

Act 1:

- Set in a **chocolate house after card game**.
- Mirabell's servants **Waitwell and Foible married**.
- **Mirabell loves Millamant**, seeks Fainall's advice.
- Witwoud informs Mirabell of potential **inheritance loss.**
- **Mirabell needs Lady Wishfort's consent for marriage.**

Act 2:

- **Set in St. James' Park**, discussing hatred of men.
- Fainall accuses Mrs. Marwood of loving Mirabell.
- Mrs. Fainall hates husband, plots with Mirabell.
- Millamant upset, expresses displeasure at Mirabell's plan.
- Mirabell reminds servants of their roles.

Acts 3, 4, 5:

- **All are set in the home of Lady Wishfort.**
- **Lady Wishfort is tricked into marrying Sir Rowland.**
- **Sir Rowland is actually Waitwell in disguise.**
- Mirabell plans to rescue Lady Wishfort from bigamy.
- Mrs. Marwood overhears plot, informs Fainall.
- Fainall plans to take wife's money, leave.
- **Mirabell and Millamant discuss marriage terms ("proviso scene").**
- Mirabell proposes, Millamant accepts with Mrs. Fainall's encouragement.
- Lady Wishfort wants Millamant to marry Sir Wilfull.
- Lady Wishfort learns of Sir Rowland's plot.

Act 5:

- Fainall blackmails Lady Wishfort with Mrs. Fainall's affair.
- Lady Wishfort offers consent to Mirabell's marriage.
- **Mirabell produces contract saving Lady Wishfort's fortune.**
- **Mirabell restores Mrs. Fainall's property, marries Millamant.**

George Etherege (1635-1691)

- ➤ Not much is known regarding the life of Etheredge.
- ➤ He appears to have been a courtier, and to have served abroad.
- ➤ Etherege probably accompanied his father to France in the 1640s.
- ➤ If all stories about him are true, he had an ample share of the popular vices.
- ➤ He is said to have been **killed by tumbling downstairs while drunk.**
- ➤ His three plays are:
  - o ***The Comical Revenge, or Love in a Tub (1664)***,
    - ■ Etherege's first comedy,
  - o ***She Would if She Could (1668)***,
    - ■ **Second comedy (1668) failed because of poor acting.**
  - o ***The Man of Mode (1676).***
    - ■ His last and wittiest comedy
- ➤ They are more uneven than Wycherley's, and at their worst are grosser;
- ➤ They are clever, and can be lively and amusing.

George Farquhar (1678-1707)

- ➤ Irish playwright of real comic power
- ➤ Wrote for the English stage at the beginning of the 18th century.
- ➤ The son of a clergyman, Farquhar entered Trinity College, Dublin, as a sizar.
- ➤ He preferred working as an unsuccessful actor at the Smock Alley Theatre in Dublin.
- ➤ During a performance of **John Dryden's *Indian Emperour,*** he failed to distinguish between a **tipped foil and a deadly rapier, gravely wounding a fellow actor.**
- ➤ After this incident, he abandoned acting.
- ➤ His first play, ***Love and a Bottle*** was well received at London's Drury Lane Theatre in 1699.
- ➤ Followed in the same year by ***The Constant Couple.***
- ➤ A sequel to the latter, ***Sir Harry Wildair,*** appeared in 1701.
- ➤ Between 1702 and 1704, he wrote:
  - o ***The Inconstant*** (adapted from **John Fletcher's *Wild-Goose Chase***).
  - o ***The Twin-Rivals***

- o *The Stage-Coach*, a farce translated from French.
- ➤ He wrote seven plays, the best of which are the last two:
  - o *The Recruiting Officer (1706)*
  - o *The Beaux' Stratagem (1707).*

Sir John Vanbrugh (1664-1726)

- ➤ English architect, dramatist and herald.
- ➤ Best known as the designer of Blenheim Palace and Castle Howard.
- ➤ He was knighted in 1714.
- ➤ As a young man and a committed Whig.
- ➤ He was part of the scheme to overthrow James II and put William III on the throne.
- ➤ The French imprisoned him as a political prisoner.
- ➤ He was attacked on both counts
- ➤ He was one of the prime targets of **Jeremy Collier's *Short View of the Immorality and Profaneness of the English Stage.***
- ➤ His best three comedies are:
  - o *The Relapse (1697),*
    - ■ The play is a sequel to **Colley Cibber's *Love's Last Shift, or, The Fool in Fashion.***
  - o *The Provoked Wife (1698),*
    - ■ **The second original comedy.**
    - ■ It made its first appearance in **Lincoln's Inn Fields in 1697.**
    - ■ Lady Brute provoked by sour husband Sir John.
    - ■ Marriage built on money and sexual desire fails.
    - ■ Sir John goes on a drunken night out.
    - ■ Disguised as a woman, Sir John faces magistrate.
    - ■ Lady Brute and Belinda plan secret affair.
    - ■ They disguise as doxies to meet suitors.
    - ■ Lady Fanciful spies on them, jealous of Heartfree.
    - ■ Belinda wins Heartfree despite Lady Fanciful's interference.
    - ■ Sir John attempts to rape his own wife.
    - ■ Brute accepts defeat after gallants are discovered.
  - o *The Confederacy (1705).*

Colley Cibber (1671-1757)

> - English actor-manager, playwright, and Poet Laureate.
> - His colorful memoir ***Apology for the Life of Colley Cibber (1740)***
>   - Describes his life in a personal, anecdotal, and even rambling style.
> - He wrote **25 plays for his own company at Drury Lane**
>   - Half of which were adapted from various sources.
>   - Led Robert Lowe and Alexander Pope, among others, to criticize his ***"miserable mutilation" of "crucified Molière [and] hapless Shakespeare."***
> - He wrote ***Love's Last Shift*** to provide himself with a role.
> - The play established his reputation both as an actor and as a playwright.
> - The playwright **Sir John Vanbrugh honored it with a sequel,** *The Relapse: or Virtue in Danger (1696)*,
>   - In which **Cibber's character Sir Novelty Fashion has become Lord Foppington, a role created by Cibber.**
> - In 1700 Cibber produced his famous adaptation of **Shakespeare's *Richard III*.**
> - Cibber also wrote other comedies of manners, including:
>   - *She Wou'd, She Wou'd Not (1702)*,
>   - *The Careless Husband (1704)*.

Jeremy Collier's Attack

Short View of the Immorality and Profaneness of the English Stage (1698)

> - In March 1698, Jeremy Collier published his anti-theatre pamphlet
> - In the pamphlet, Collier attacked several playwrights:
>   - **William Wycherley,**
>   - **John Dryden,**
>   - **William Congreve,**
>   - **John Vanbrugh,**
>   - **Thomas D'Urfey.**
> - Collier attacks rather recent, rather popular comedies from the London stage.
> - He accuses the playwrights of profanity, blasphemy, indecency, and undermining public morality through the sympathetic depiction of vice.

- ➤ **Collier begins his pamphlet with this conclusion:**
  - ○ *"[N]othing has gone farther in Debauching the Age than the Stage Poets, and Play-House" (Collier A2).*
- ➤ Collier blames **Restoration comedy** for lacking **poetic justice**.
- ➤ He condemns **characters** as **impious** and **wicked**, using thorough readings.
- ➤ Collier criticizes **playwrights** for not punishing their **wicked favorites**.
- ➤ He accuses playwrights of **profaneness**, quoting plays like *The Provoked Wife*.
- ➤ **Blasphemy** wasn't on stage due to **censorship** at the time.
- ➤ Collier's strategy was **innovative** for anti-theatre **pamphlets**.
- ➤ A **pamphlet war** ensued, lasting until **1726**.
- ➤ **John Dennis** and **Vanbrugh** responded to Collier's accusations in **1698**.
- ➤ **Congreve** refuted Collier's claims in his **Amendments** pamphlet.
- ➤ **Thomas D'Urfey** replied through **satirical plays** like *Campaigners*.
- ➤ **Collier's pamphlet** stirred **public opposition** to indecent plays.
- ➤ He argued, "The business of plays is to recommend **Virtue**."
- ➤ **Congreve** countered, saying comedy should *"It is the business of a comic poet to paint the vices and follies of humankind"*.
- ➤ Collier followed **Neoclassical decorum** like **Thomas Rymer**.
- ➤ Collier's work coincided with **public discontent** with **Restoration comedy**.
- ➤ External factors like the **Glorious Revolution** ended **Restoration theatre**.
- ➤ **William III** granted **nolle prosequi** to Collier for his pamphlet.

RESTORATION TRAGEDY

Thomas Otway (1651–85).

- ➤ As was so often the case with the dramatists of the time,
- ➤ Otway had a varied and troubled career,
- ➤ closed with a miserable death.
- ➤ His first play, Alcibiades, was produced about 1675;
- ➤ Then followed Don Carlos (1676), The Orphan (1680),
- ➤ And his masterpiece, **Venice Preserved (1682)**.
- ➤ **"Soldier's Fortune"** is also a play, written by Thomas Otway

Nathaniel Lee (1653–92).

- ➤ Lee's life is the usual tale of mishaps, miseries, and drunkenness,
- ➤ With a taint of madness as an additional calamity.
- ➤ He wrote many tragedies, some of which are:
  - o ***Nero (1673),***
  - o ***Sophonisba (1676),***
  - o ***The Rival Queens (1677),***
  - o ***Mithridates (1678).***
- ➤ He also collaborated with Dryden in the production of two plays.

Elkanah Settle (1648–1724).

- ➤ Dryden has given him prominence by attacking him in his satires.
- ➤ In his day he obtained some popularity with a heroic play:
  - o ***The Empress of Morocco (1673).***

John Crowne (1640–1703).

- ➤ Crowne attacked Dryden and who were in turn assailed by the bigger man.
- ➤ Crowne's best-known works are the tragedies of:
  - o ***Caligula (1698),*** a heroic play,
  - o ***Thyestes***, in blank verse, and
  - o Sir Courtly Nice (1685) a comedy.

Nicholas Rowe (1674–1718).

- ➤ During his lifetime Rowe was a person of some importance.
- ➤ He was made Poet Laureate in 1714.
- ➤ His best-known plays are:
  - o *Tamerlane (1702),*
  - o *The Fair Penitent (1703),*
  - o *Jane Shore (1714).*
- ➤ Johnson says of him, "*His reputation comes from the reasonableness of some of his scenes, the elegance of his diction, and the suavity of his verse.*"

RESTORATION PROSE

- ➤ **Restoration prose** was dominated by **Christian religious writing**.

- ➢ **Fiction** and **journalism** began during the Restoration period.
- ➢ **Religious writing** intertwined with **political** and **economic** concerns.
- ➢ **Philosophical writing** thrived with Neo-classicism and empirical science.
- ➢ **Thomas Sprat** published *History of the Royal Society* in **1667**.
- ➢ **William Temple** praised **retirement** and **nature** in his prose works.
- ➢ Temple introduced the **Ancients and Moderns quarrel** with his *Reflections*.
- ➢ **John Locke** wrote **Two Treatises of Government**, inspiring **American Revolution** thinkers.
- ➢ **Radical religious writing** persisted despite the Restoration moderation.
- ➢ **John Milton** and other Puritan authors retired or adapted.
- ➢ **Bunyan's The Pilgrim's Progress** allegorizes **personal salvation** and Christian life.
- ➢ **Izaak Walton's The Compleat Angler** is also an **introspective** work.
- ➢ **Robert Boyle** wrote popular **Meditations on God** beyond the Restoration.
- ➢ **Broadsheet publications** were the common way of spreading news.
- ➢ **Professional journalism** emerged in **England** after **1689**.
- ➢ **Fictional biographies** and **long fiction** began in the Restoration period.
- ➢ **French and Spanish Romance** fiction was popular in **England**.
- ➢ **Aphra Behn** was significant in the rise of the **English novel**.

John Bunyan (1628-1688)

(**Code**: *Bunyan Grace Pilgrim's Gospel Mr. Badman's Holy War or BB GG PP War*)

- ➢ **John Bunyan's life** is known through **Grace Abounding (1666)**.
- ➢ **Grace Abounding** is a **religious autobiography** of Bunyan's life.
- ➢ **Bunyan depicted** his youth as **depraved and sinful**.
- ➢ **Religious converts** often exaggerate their former **wickedness**.
- ➢ **Bunyan served** as a soldier in the **Civil War**.
- ➢ His **religious conversion** came in **1656**, saving him.
- ➢ **Bunyan became a preacher** and was **arrested unlicensed**.
- ➢ He spent **12 years** in **Bedford jail (1660-1672)**.
- ➢ **Released**, Bunyan's license was canceled, **imprisoned again**.
- ➢ His famous works: *The Pilgrim's Progress (1677)*, among others.
- ➢ **Bunyan's works** are primarily **allegorical in nature**.
- ➢ **Allegorical personages** like *Mr. Worldly Wiseman* are interesting.
- ➢ **Bunyan's allegories** are **clear, forceful, and engaging**.

- ➤ The plot maintains **variety and avoids monotony.**
- ➤ **Bunyan's prose style** is **based on Biblical models.**
- ➤ His **prose** is **homely, strong, and balanced.**
- ➤ **Bunyan's writing** is **humorous, never vulgar or sentimental.**
- ➤ His style remains a **masterpiece of English language.**
- ➤ In John Bunyan's day, successful English writers were nearly synonymous with wealth.
- ➤ Men like Richard Baxter and John Milton could afford to write because they didn't need to earn a living.
- ➤ But Bunyan, a traveling tinker like his father, was nearly penniless before becoming England's most famous author.
- ➤ His wife was also destitute, bringing only two Puritan books as a dowry.
- ➤ *"We came together as poor as poor might be,"* Bunyan wrote, *"not having so much household-stuff as a dish or spoon betwixt us both."*

Major Works: Between 1656, when he published his first work,
- ➤ *Some Gospel Truths Opened*
  - ○ (a tract against the Ranters and Quakers, who were somewhat indistinguishable),
- ➤ **Bunyan published 42 titles.**
- ➤ A further two works, including **his *Last Sermon***, were published the following year by George Larkin.
- ➤ **Charles Doe**, a friend of Bunyan, published **Bunyan's works** in **1692.**
- ➤ The collection included **12 unpublished titles**, mostly **sermons.**
- ➤ In **1765**, Bunyan's **Relation of My Imprisonment** was published.
- ➤ The allegory ***The Pilgrim's Progress***, written during Bunyan's twelve-year imprisonment, although not published until 1678
- ➤ ***The Life and Death of Mr. Badman (1680),***
  Pilgrim's Progress Part II and The Holy War (1682).
- ➤ ***Grace Abounding to the Chief of Sinners***, a spiritual autobiography, was published in **1666** when he was still in jail.

The Pilgrim's Progress (1678, 1684)

- ➤ A religious allegory published in 1678 and 1684.
- ➤ The work is a symbolic vision of the good man's pilgrimage through life.
- ➤ At one time, second only to the Bible in popularity.
- ➤ Bunyan started his work in **Bedfordshire prison** for violating Conventicle **Act 1664.**

- ➤ The **Conventicle Act 1664** banned religious services outside **Church of England**.
- ➤ The English text has **108,260 words** divided into **two parts**.
- ➤ The **first part** was completed and registered on **22 December 1677**.
- ➤ **First publication** is dated **18 February 1678**, per **Term Catalogue**.

Plot Summary:
- ➤ **Christian** begins journey from **City of Destruction** to **Celestial City**.
- ➤ He carries a **burden of sins** after reading **the Bible**.
- ➤ **Evangelist** directs Christian towards the **wicket-gate**.
- ➤ Christian falls into the **Slough of Despond**, saved by **Help**.
- ➤ **Mr. Worldly Wiseman** misleads Christian toward **Mr. Legality**.
- ➤ Christian's burden worsens; **Evangelist** redirects him to **wicket-gate**.
- ➤ **Good-will** lets Christian through and sends him to **Interpreter's house**.
- ➤ At the **cross and sepulcher**, Christian's burden falls off.
- ➤ **Three Shining Ones** give him a scroll for the **Celestial Gate**.
- ➤ Christian climbs **Hill Difficulty**, loses scroll, retrieves it from the **arbor**.
- ➤ He meets **Discretion, Prudence, Piety**, and **Charity** at **palace Beautiful**.
- ➤ Christian battles **Apollyon** in the **Valley of Humiliation**.
- ➤ He passes through the **Valley of the Shadow of Death**.
- ➤ Christian and **Faithful** reach **Vanity Fair**, causing a commotion.
- ➤ **Faithful** is executed and taken to the **Celestial City**.
- ➤ Christian escapes prison with **Hopeful**, crossing the **plain of Ease**.
- ➤ They avoid **By-path Meadow** but are imprisoned by **Giant Despair**.
- ➤ Christian uses the key **Promise** to escape **Doubting Castle**.
- ➤ They reach the **Delectable Mountains**, misled by **Flatterer**.
- ➤ **Christian and Hopeful** cross a river and enter the **Celestial City**.

Second Part:
- ➤ **Christiana**, her sons, and **Mercy** begin their pilgrimage.
- ➤ They visit **Christian's stopping places**, adding **Gaius' Inn**.
- ➤ **Greatheart**, their guide, kills **four giants** and **monster Legion**.
- ➤ **Mr. Feeble-Mind** joins the group, encouraged by **Greatheart**.
- ➤ They defeat **Giant Despair, Giantess Diffidence**, and demolish **Doubting Castle**.
- ➤ They free **Mr. Despondency** and **Much-Afraid's daughter** from the dungeons.
- ➤ In the **Land of Beulah**, they cross the **River of Death**.

> ➤ **Christian's sons** stay behind to support the **church**.

The following extract gives us an idea of Bunyan's narrative and descriptive power, and is a fair specimen of his masculine prose:

"I saw them in my dream, so far as this valley reached, there was, on the right hand, a very deep ditch; that ditch it is into which the blind have led the blind in all ages, and have both there miserably perished. Again, behold, on the left hand, there was a very dangerous quag, into which even if a good man falls, he finds no bottom for his feet to stand on: into that quag King David once did fall, and had no doubt therein been smothered, had not He that is able plucked him out. The pathway was here also exceeding narrow, and therefore good Christian was the more put to it: for when he sought, in the dark, to shun the ditch on the one hand, he was ready to tip over into the mire on the other; also, when he sought to escape the mire, without great carefulness he would be ready to fall into the ditch. Thus he went on, and I heard him here sigh bitterly; for besides the danger mentioned above, the pathway here was so dark, that oft-times when he lifted up his foot to set forward, he knew not where, or upon what, he should set it next. About the midst of the valley I perceived the mouth of Hell to be; and it stood also hard by the way-side. And ever and anon the flame and smoke would come out in such abundance, with sparks and hideous noises, that he was forced to put up his sword, and betake himself to another weapon, called All-prayer. So he cried, in my hearing, "O Lord, I beseech thee, deliver my soul." Thus he went on a great while, yet still the flames would be reaching towards him. Also he heard doleful voices, and rushings to and fro; so that sometimes he thought he should be torn to pieces or trodden down like mire in the streets." **The Pilgrim's Progress**

Diary-writers

> ➤ Two famous **diary-writers** worked simultaneously during this period.
> ➤ Their diaries show **advantages and drawbacks** of the diary format.
> ➤ The diaries are **private documents**, lacking formal literary excellence.
> ➤ **Ragged, incoherent style** can lead to flatness and monotony.
> ➤ Diaries are **intimate, informative**, covering public and personal affairs.
> ➤ They offer **insightful comments** on people and incidents.

Samuel Pepys (1633-1703)

> ➤ An **English diarist** and naval administrator.

- He served as administrator of the navy of England.
- He was a **Member of Parliament**.
- Most famous for the **Diary he kept for a decade while still a young man**.
- **He was** Chief Secretary to the Admiralty under **King Charles II** and **King James II**.
- He rose to the position through **patronage, diligence,** and leadership talent.
- Pepys' influence led to **significant reforms** in the Admiralty.
- His efforts contributed to the early **professionalization** of the Royal Navy.
- Pepys' **diary**, written in **cipher**, was meant to be personal.
- Reading it feels like **peeping** into his life uninvited.
- The diary reveals Pepys as **mean, lustful, vain,** and **trivial**.
- He is also **ambitious** but lacks the resolution to follow through.
- Pepys is **intensely human**, full of curiosity and **magpie alertness**.
- His writing inspires readers with **vivid curiosity** despite his flaws.

Diary:

- Pepys's detailed private Diary **from 1660 until 1669.**
- It was first published in the **19th century**.
- Most important primary sources for the English Restoration period.
- **Personal revelations** with eyewitness accounts of **significant events** such as:
    - **The Great Plague of London,**
    - **The Second Dutch War,**
    - **The Great Fire of London.**
- Pepys had a journalist's gift for capturing scenes or people **in few brilliant, arresting words**.
- He makes us see what he **sees in a flash:**
- His Aunt James,
  "a poor, religious, well-meaning, good soul, talking of nothing but God Almighty, and that with so much innocence that mightily pleased me";
- His sister Pall"
  "a pretty, good-bodied woman and not over thick, as I thought she would have been, but full of freckles and not handsome in the face."
- He could describe an incredible scene with extraordinary vividness: for example.
- **The day General George Monck's soldiers unexpectedly marched into a sullen City and proclaimed there should be a free**

Parliament—

"And Bow bells and all the bells in all the churches as we went home were a-ringing; it was past imagination, both the greatness and suddenness of it."

> **He described, too, the Restoration and coronation:**
> **The horrors of the Plague**

"But, Lord! how sad a sight it is to see the streets empty of people, and very few upon the 'Change. Jealous of every door that one sees shut up, lest it should be the plague; and about us two shops in three, if not more, generally shut up."

> **The Fire of London, writing down his account—so intense was the artist in him—even as his home and its treasures were being threatened with destruction:**

*"I down to the water-side, and there got a boat and through bridge, and there saw a **lamentable fire**. Poor Michell's house, as far as the Old Swan, already burned that way, and the fire running further, that in a very little time it got as far as the Steeleyard, while I was there. Everybody endeavouring to remove their goods, and flinging into the river or bringing them into lighters that layoff; poor people staying in their houses as long as till the very fire touched them, and then running into boats, or clambering from one pair of stairs by the water-side to another. And among other things, the poor pigeons, I perceive, were loth to leave their houses, but hovered about the windows and balconys till they were, some of them burned, their wings, and fell down. Having staid, and in an hour's time seen the fire: rage every way, and nobody, to my sight, endeavouring to quench it, but to remove their goods, and leave all to the fire, and having seen it get as far as the Steele-yard, and the wind mighty high and driving it into the City; and every thing, after so long a drought, proving combustible, even the very stones of churches, and among other things the poor steeple by which pretty Mrs.——— lives, and whereof my old school-fellow Elborough is parson, taken fire in the very top, and there burned till it fell down..."*

"Sir W. Pen and I to Tower-streete, and there met the fire burning three or four doors beyond Mr. Howell's, whose goods, poor man, his trayes,

and dishes, shovells, &c., were flung all along Tower-street in the kennels, and people working therewith from one end to the other; the fire coming on in that narrow streete, on both sides, with infinite fury. **Sir W. Batten not knowing how to remove his wine, did dig a pit in the garden, and laid it in there; and I took the opportunity of laying all the papers of my office that I could not otherwise dispose of.** *And in the evening Sir W. Pen and I did dig another, and put our wine in it; and I my Parmazan cheese, as well as my wine and some other things."*

- ➤ The diarist **Samuel Pepys is the one who, after watching the performance of William Shakespeare's play, A Midsummer Night's Dream, observed that** *"it is the most insipid, ridiculous play that I ever saw in my life."* Pepys recorded his thoughts on the play in his diary on **September 29, 1662,** after seeing a performance at the theatre in **London's Lincoln's Inn Fields.**

John Evelyn, (1620-1706):

- ➤ English gentleman wrote 30 books on arts, forestry, religion.
- ➤ His **Diary** is key to 17th-century English **life** insights.
- ➤ **Kept a diary from 1640 until his death.**
- ➤ His diary is more polished, possibly for public view.
- ➤ The style lacks freshness, unlike Pepys'.
- ➤ It contains accurate and detailed information throughout.
- ➤ During moving events like the **Great Fire**, it becomes eloquent.
- ➤ **The Diary of John Evelyn**, first published in 1818 (2nd edition, 1819)
- ➤ Under the title Memoirs Illustrative of the Life and Writings of John Evelyn, in an edition by William Bray.
- ➤ Bray was assisted by William Upcott, who had access to the Evelyn family archives.
- ➤ Evelyn's Diary has entries **running from 1640**, when the author was a student at the **Middle Temple, to 1706.**
- ➤ Its claim as a memoir to be a diary is not strict; **up to around 1683**
- ➤ His travels are described, buildings or pictures may be related anachronistically, revealing the later use of other sources.

Other Diarists:

Ralph Josselin (1617-1683): An English clergyman who kept a diary from **1641 to 1683.** Josselin's diary provides valuable insight into the lives of **rural communities in 17th-century England,** as well as his personal struggles with faith and family.

John Aubrey (1626-1697): An English antiquary and writer who is best known for his Brief Lives, a collection of biographical sketches of his contemporaries. Aubrey's own diary, which he kept from 1645 until his death, is a valuable source of information on 17th-century science, politics, and society.

Thomas Turner (1729-1793): An English shopkeeper who kept a diary from 1754 until his death. Turner's diary provides a fascinating glimpse into the daily life of a working-class person in 18th-century England, as well as his observations on politics, religion, and culture.

Aphra Behn (1640-1689)

- English playwright, poet, translator from the Restoration era.
- First English woman to earn living by writing.
- Noticed by **Charles II**, employed as a spy.
- After returning, began writing plays for the stage.
- Part of a coterie with **John Wilmot** and **Lord Rochester**.
- Wrote under pastoral pseudonym **Astrea**.
- Political writings during **Exclusion Crisis** caused legal trouble.
- Shifted focus to prose genres and translations.
- Declined writing for **King William III**, a Stuart supporter.
- Best-known for **Oroonoko** and the play **The Rover**.
- **She is remembered in Virginia Woolf's A Room of One's Own**: *"All women together ought to let flowers fall upon the tomb of Aphra Behn which is, most scandalously but rather appropriately, in Westminster Abbey, for it was she who earned them the right to speak their minds."*

Literary Career:
- Behn's early works were tragicomedies in verse.
  - *The Forc'd Marriage (1670),*
  - *The Amorous Prince followed (1671),*
  - *Abdelazer (1676).*

- **The Rover (two parts, produced in 1677 and 1681)**:
    - It was commercially successful.
    - Depicts the adventures of English Cavaliers in Madrid and Naples.
    - The exile of the future Charles II.
- ***The Emperor of the Moon (1687)***:
    - It was first performed in 1687
    - Presaged the harlequinade, a form of comic theatre.
    - Evolved into the English pantomime.
- ***Oroonoko (1688)***
- ***Love-Letters Between a Nobleman and His Sister (1684–87),***
- ***The Fair Jilt (1688).***
- ***Poems upon Several Occasions, with A Voyage to the Island of Love (1684),***
- ***Lycidus; or, The Lover in Fashion (1688).***

Oroonoko: or the Royal Slave (1688)

- Published **in 1688 by William Canning** with two other fictions later that year.
- It was **also adapted into a play**.
- **Oroonoko**, a noble-born general from **Coromantee**, is famous for valor.
- He falls in love with **Imoinda**, a beautiful young woman.
- **Imoinda** is desired by **Oroonoko**'s grandfather, the king of Coramantien.
- Though **Imoinda** returns **Oroonoko**'s love, she rejects the king.
- The couple secretly meets, but the king discovers their affair.
- Furious, the king banishes **Imoinda** to a distant colony.
- **Oroonoko** believes **Imoinda** to be dead after her banishment.
- **Oroonoko** is tricked into slavery by an English captain.
- He is taken to **Surinam** and given the slave name **Caesar**.
- **Imoinda**, renamed **Clemene**, has also been enslaved in Surinam.
- **Oroonoko** and **Imoinda** are reunited in the same colony.
- They live together as husband and wife in relative freedom.
- **Imoinda** becomes pregnant, and **Oroonoko** seeks their freedom.
- He is told to wait until the governor arrives to decide.
- Frustrated, **Oroonoko** leads a rebellion against their masters.
- **Oroonoko** fights valiantly in the rebellion but is ultimately defeated.
- **Imoinda** stands by **Oroonoko**, sharing in his struggles and fate.

- ➤ The story ends in tragedy with **Oroonoko**'s ultimate loss and death.
- ➤ The narrator admires **Oroonoko**'s heroism, valor, and nobility.
- ➤ She hopes her account immortalizes **Oroonoko** and **Imoinda**'s love.

Eliza Haywood (1693-1756)

- ➤ Elizabeth Fowler, was an English writer, actress, and publisher.
- ➤ An increased recognition of Haywood's literary works began **in the 1980s.**
- ➤ Described as "prolific even by the standards of a prolific age,"
- ➤ Haywood wrote and published over 70 works in her lifetime.
- ➤ She wrote fiction, drama, translations, poetry, literature, and periodicals.
- ➤ Haywood today is studied primarily as one of the **18th-century founders of the novel in English.**
- ➤ Haywood mentions her marriage in her writings, though little is known about it.
- ➤ She supported herself by writing, acting, and adapting works for the theatre.
- ➤ Among such works are Memoirs of a
  - o *Certain Island Adjacent to the Kingdom of Utopia (1725)*
  - o *The Secret History of the Present Intrigues of the Court of Caramania (1727).*
- ➤ **Alexander Pope attacked her with coarse brutality in his poem The Dunciad (1728),**
- ➤ **Jonathan Swift called her a "stupid, infamous woman."**
- ➤ She subsequently wrote the experimental novel
  - o *The Adventures of Eovaai, Princess of Ijaveo (1736)*
- ➤ Attacked Samuel Richardson's landmark *Pamela (1740)* **with her satirical novel *Anti-Pamela (1741).***
- ➤ Later she achieved success with *The Female Spectator (1744–46)*
  - o The first periodical to be written by a woman,
- ➤ Her realistic novels
  - o ***The History of Miss Betsy Thoughtless (1751)***
  - o ***The History of Jemmy and Jenny Jessamy (1753).***

The Female Spectator (1644-46)

- ➤ Considered the first periodical written by women for women.

- ➤ It was loosely modeled on *The Spectator* by **Joseph Addison and Richard Steele**.
- ➤ **Female Spectator** spoke exclusively from a female viewpoint.
- ➤ It featured four characters: the narrator and three assistants.
  - o **Euphrosine** is a beautiful, unmarried daughter of a merchant.
  - o **Mira** is sophisticated and happily married.
  - o **Widow of Quality** represents an experienced, older woman.
- ➤ Each journal issue covered a single topic in essay form.
- ➤ Essays focused on love, marriage, and moral attitudes.
- ➤ Essays followed a straightforward structure with few digressions.
- ➤ Language was forceful, clear, and leisurely balanced.
- ➤ Essays included cautionary anecdotes with female viewpoints.
- ➤ Anecdotes showed consequences of behaviors in various situations.
- ➤ Stories featured women disguising as men for love.
- ➤ Other tales involved elopements or affairs with consequences.
- ➤ Some stories were detailed enough to resemble "miniature novels."
- ➤ **Haywood** omitted current affairs, saying newspapers covered them.
- ➤ She advocated women's education through her journal.
- ➤ She discussed **Baconian empiricism** and the natural world.
- ➤ **Haywood** encouraged women's interest in scientific studies, like microscopes.

John Locke (1632-1704)

- ➤ British philosopher, Oxford academic, and medical researcher.
- ➤ His works shaped **modern philosophical empiricism and liberalism**.
- ➤ He inspired the **European Enlightenment and U.S. Constitution.**
- ➤ Philosophical views aligned with **Boyle, Newton, Royal Society.**
- ➤ His political thought emphasized **social contract, religious toleration**.
- ➤ Ideas were accepted after **England's Glorious Revolution.**
- ➤ Locke's ideas **influenced U.S. independence in 1776.**
- ➤ Locke's theory shaped modern identity and self-conception.
- ➤ He influenced philosophers like **Rousseau, Hume, and Kant.**
- ➤ Locke defined self through continuity of consciousness.
- ➤ **He postulated the mind as a blank slate.**
- ➤ His work fostered the rise of political liberalism.
- ➤ Emphasized the importance of **individual rights and governance**.
- ➤ Advocated tolerance, especially **in matters of religion.**
- ➤ His ideas laid the **foundation for modern empiricism.**

- ➢ Locke's monumental ***An Essay Concerning Human Understanding (1689)***
  - o The first great defenses of modern empiricism
  - o Concerns determining the limits of human understanding.
  - o It thus tells us in some detail what one can legitimately claim to know and what one cannot.
  - o **He describes the mind at birth as a blank slate (tabula rasa) filled later through experience.**
  - o Influenced many enlightenment philosophers, such as **David Hume and George Berkeley.**
  - o **Book I of the Essay is Locke's attempt to refute the rationalist notion of innate ideas.**
  - o **Book II: Locke's theory of ideas is presented in Book II.**
    - ▪ Simple ideas are passively acquired, like **"red", "sweet," "round".**
    - ▪ Complex ideas are actively built, **such as numbers.**
    - ▪ **Locke distinguishes primary and secondary qualities.**
    - ▪ **Primary qualities include shape and motion.**
    - ▪ **Secondary qualities are sensations like "red."**
    - ▪ **Secondary qualities depend on primary qualities.**
    - ▪ **Locke proposes a psychological theory of identity.**
  - o **Book III focuses on language analysis.**
  - o **Language plays a key role in communication.**
  - o **Book III is concerned with language.**
  - o **Book IV with knowledge, including intuition, mathematics, moral philosophy, natural philosophy ("science"), faith, and opinion.**
- ➢ Locke's connection with Anthony Ashley Cooper influenced his career.
- ➢ He became a government official, economic writer, and political activist.
- ➢ Locke supported the Glorious Revolution, leading to its success in 1688.
- ➢ Among Locke's political works ***The Second Treatise of Government.***
  - o He argues that sovereignty resides in the people and explains the nature of legitimate government in terms of natural rights and the social contract.
- ➢ Locke advocated separation of Church and State in ***Letter Concerning Toleration.***
- ➢ He opposed authoritarianism on both individual and institutional levels.
- ➢ Locke encouraged individuals to seek truth through reason, not authority.

- ➤ He emphasized distinguishing legitimate from illegitimate functions of institutions.
- ➤ **Thoughts on Education is a treatise on education written by John Locke**
- ➤ Locke believed reason and natural law optimize human and societal flourishing.
  - ○ *"A Letter Concerning Toleration"*
  - ○ *"An Essay Concerning Human Understanding"*
  - ○ *"Essays on the Law of Nature"*
  - ○ *"Some Thoughts Concerning Education"*
  - ○ *"The Reasonableness of Christianity"*
  - ○ *"Two Tracts on Government"*
  - ○ *"Two Treatises of Government"*
    - ▪ *Full: Two Treatises of Government: In the Former, The False Principles, and Foundation of Sir Robert Filmer, and His Followers, Are Detected and Overthrown. The Latter Is an Essay Concerning The True Original, Extent, and End of Civil Government)*
- ➤ Leviathan had a profound impact on subsequent philosophers who embraced the social-contract framework, including **renowned thinkers like John Locke, Jean-Jacques Rousseau, and Immanuel Kant.**
- ➤ Hume is celebrated for his **empirical approach** to human knowledge, standing alongside other empiricists like **Francis Bacon, Thomas Hobbes, John Locke, and George Berkeley.**

(**Code**: *Locke Law of Human Nature Understanding Educatiion of two tracts and treatises on Government*)

Sir William Temple (1628-1699)

- ➤ English diplomat, statesman, and essayist.
- ➤ Recalled in 1679, he briefly advised Charles II.
- ➤ Retired to the country, focused on gardening and writing.
- ➤ Remembered for writing about Chinese garden designs.
- ➤ Never saw a Chinese garden, praised irregularity.
- ➤ Employed Jonathan Swift as his secretary.
- ➤ Early influence on English landscape garden style.
- ➤ Temple began his diplomatic career in 1665 under Henry Bennet.
- ➤ Awarded a baronetcy in 1666 and negotiated the Triple Alliance.

> ➢ Negotiated the treaty ending the Dutch War in 1674.
> ➢ Helped arrange Princess Mary's marriage to William of Orange.
> ➢ Reorganized the Privy Council but retired from politics by 1681.
> ➢ *Observations upon the United Provinces* pioneered cross-cultural understanding.
> ➢ Jonathan Swift collected and published Temple's essays after his retirement.
> ➢ Temple's writing style influenced Jonathan Swift's literary works.
> ➢ **Swift's *"Battle of the Books"*** defended Temple's essay *"**Upon Ancient and Modern Learning**."*.

Questions:

Question 62

Which of the following are the major themes in William Congreve's The Way of the World?

1. jealousy and revenge
2. love and intrigue
3. intrigue and death
4. love and loyalty

Explanations:

Answer: 2. love and intrigue

Love and intrigue are two of the major themes in William Congreve's The Way of the World. The play explores the complexities of courtship and love in a Restoration society, where wealth and social status are often more important than true love. The character of Millamant is a strong-willed and independent woman who refuses to marry for anything other than love. She is courted by Mirabell, who is equally determined to win her affection. However, they both face opposition from Lady Wishfort, who wants Millamant to marry her own nephew, Sir Wilfull Witwoud, in order to secure her own social standing.

Question 63

In which Act of William Congreve's The Way of The world does the Proviso scene between Miirabell and Millamant take place?

1. Act I
2. Act III
3. Act II
4. Act IV

Explanations:
Answer: 4. Act IV

The Proviso scene between Mirabell and Millamant in William Congreve's play "The Way of the World" takes place in Act IV. This scene is a crucial moment in the play where Mirabell and Millamant engage in a witty and clever dialogue while discussing the conditions of their impending marriage. The Proviso scene showcases the complex dynamics of their relationship and their negotiation of power and independence within the constraints of societal expectations.

Extra Perk:
In William Congreve's play "The Way of the World," the settings vary throughout the acts. Here is a breakdown of the settings act by act:

Act I: The play opens in a chocolate house in London. Mirabell and Fainall discuss their plans while interacting with other characters, including Waitwell and Foible.

Act II: This act takes place in Lady Wishfort's house in London. The setting includes Lady Wishfort's dressing room and other rooms where characters gather and interact, such as Mrs. Marwood and Millamant.

Act III: The action shifts to St. James's Park in London, where Mirabell and Millamant have a private conversation.

Act IV: Act IV primarily takes place in Lady Wishfort's house. The Proviso scene between Mirabell and Millamant occurs in Millamant's dressing room.

Act V: The final act returns to Lady Wishfort's house, where the resolution of the play's various conflicts and plotlines takes place. The setting includes Lady Wishfort's chamber and a gallery.

Question 64

Arrange the following characters in their chronological sequence of appearance:

A. Mirabell
B. Shylock

C. Jimmy Porter
D. Sir Epicure Mammon

Choose the correct answer from the options given below
1. D, B, A, C
2. **B, D, A, C**
3. D, B, C, A
4. B, D, C, A

Correct Explanations:
➢ Shylock is a fictional character in William Shakespeare's play The Merchant of Venice (c. **1600**).
➢ Sir Epicure Mammon is a theatrical character in the play The Alchemist (**1610**).
➢ Mirabell is a character in the The Way of the World (**1700**) by the English playwright William Congreve.
➢ Jimmy Porter, the lead character in John Osborne's **1956** play Look Back in Anger.

Question 65

Which of the playwrights have been correctly matched with their works?

A. William Wycherly - The Rivals
B. Ben Jonson - Volpone, or the Fox
C. William Congreve - The Country Wife
D. Aphra Behn - The Dutch Lover
E. Richard Sheridan - A School for Scandal

Choose the correct answer from the options given below:

1. C, D and E
2. B, C and D
3. A, C and E
4. B, D and E

Explanations:
Ans: B, D and E

Volpone, or the Fox is a comedy written by Ben Jonson and first performed in 1605. The play is set in Venice and revolves around the wealthy and cunning Volpone, who pretends to be dying in order to receive gifts from his wealthy acquaintances. The play is a biting satire of greed and materialism, and explores themes of deception, corruption, and the corrupting influence of wealth.

The Dutch Lover is a Restoration comedy written by Aphra Behn and first performed in 1673. The play is set in Holland and revolves around the romantic entanglements of the wealthy merchant Jeronimo and his love interest, the beautiful and headstrong Lucinda.

A School for Scandal is a comedy of manners written by Richard Brinsley Sheridan and first performed in 1777. The play is set in London and revolves around the scandalous behavior of a group of wealthy aristocrats, who engage in gossip, deceit, and manipulation.

Extra Perk:

The Rivals is a comedy of manners written by Richard Brinsley Sheridan and first performed in 1775. The play is set in Bath, England, and revolves around the romantic pursuits of the wealthy Captain Jack Absolute, who is in love with the beautiful Lydia Languish. The play is known for its witty dialogue, intricate plot, and memorable characters, including the eccentric Mrs. Malaprop.

The Country Wife is a Restoration comedy written by William Wycherley and first performed in 1675. The play is set in London and follows the exploits of the philandering Horner, who feigns impotence in order to gain access to the wives of wealthy men. The play is known for its frank sexual content and bawdy humor, and is considered a classic of English Restoration theatre.

Question 66

Arrange the works in the chronological order of the staging/ publication of the following plays:

A. A Woman Killed with Kindness
B. John Bull's Other Island

C. The Double Dealer
D. The Shoemaker's Holiday
E. The Conscious Lovers

Choose the correct answers from the options given below:
1. B, D, C, A and E
2. D, A, C, E and B
3. C ,D, A,B and E
4. E, B, D, C and A

Explanations:
Ans: D, A, C, E and B

The chronological order of the staging of the plays is:

➢ *The Shoemaker's Holiday (1600)*
➢ *The Double Dealer (1693)*
➢ *A Woman Killed with Kindness (1603)*
➢ *The Conscious Lovers (1722)*
➢ *John Bull's Other Island (1904)*

Question 67

John Bunyan authored the following:

A. The Pilgrim's Progress
B. Grace Abounding
C. Short View
D. The Holy War
E. Thoughts on Education

Choose the correct answer from the options given below:

1. A, B and C
2. A, C and D
3. A, D and E
4. A, B and D

Explanations:
Ans: A, B and D

The Pilgrim's Progress: The Pilgrim's Progress is a Christian allegory written by John Bunyan and published in 1678. It tells the story of a man named Christian who journeys from the City of Destruction to the Celestial City, facing many trials and tribulations along the way.

Grace Abounding: Grace Abounding is an autobiographical work by John Bunyan, published in 1666. It describes his spiritual journey and the struggles he faced in his faith, including his imprisonment for preaching without a license.

The Holy War: The Holy War is an allegorical work by John Bunyan, published in 1682. It tells the story of a battle for the city of Mansoul between the forces of good and evil.

Question 68

Find the chronological order of publication of the given works:

- A. Boswell's Life of Johnson
- B. Hobbes's Leviathan
- C. Pepys's Diary
- D. Bunyan's Pilgrim's Progress
- E. Locke's Human Understanding

Choose the correct answer from the options given below:

1. **BCDEA**
2. ACDEB
3. CDABE
4. DEACB

Explanations:
1. Bunyan's Pilgrim's Progress, published in 1678
2. Hobbes's Leviathan, published in 1651
3. Locke's Human Understanding, published in 1689
4. Pepys's Diary, published in 1825 (though written in the 1660s and 1670s)
5. Boswell's Life of Johnson, published in 1791.

Question 69

Which two of the following events are described in Samuels Pepys's Diary?

- A. The Plague in London
- B. The Great Fire of London
- C. The War of Spanish Succession
- D. Essex Rebellion

Choose the correct answer from the options given below:

1. A and B only
2. A and C only
3. B and C only
4. B and D only

Explanations:
Answer: 1. A and B only

Samuel Pepys's diary, which he kept from 1660 to 1669, provides a detailed and fascinating glimpse into the daily life and events of 17th century England. Some of the events that are described in Pepys's diary include:

The Restoration of the monarchy: Pepys witnessed the return of Charles II to England in 1660 and the restoration of the monarchy after the Puritan Commonwealth period.

The Great Plague: Pepys documented the spread of the bubonic plague in London in 1665, including the rising death toll and the measures taken by the government to try to contain the disease.

The Great Fire of London: Pepys was in London during the devastating fire of 1666, and his diary provides a detailed account of the fire's progression and the efforts to extinguish it.

Naval and military affairs: Pepys was a naval administrator and his diary provides insight into naval and military affairs during this time period, including the Anglo-Dutch Wars and the Second Anglo-Dutch War.

Social and cultural events: Pepys recorded his attendance at various social and cultural events, including plays, operas, and meetings of the Royal Society.

Question 70

Who among the following is exclusively associated with diary writing in English?

1. **Samuel Pepys**
2. Samuel Johnson
3. Ben Jonson
4. Samuel Richardson

Explanations:

Samuel Pepys (1633-1703) was an English diarist and naval administrator. He served as administrator of the Royal Navy and Member of Parliament and **is most famous for the diary he kept for a decade.** Pepys had no maritime experience, but he rose to be the Chief Secretary to the Admiralty under both King Charles II and King James II through patronage, diligence, and his talent for administration. His influence and reforms at the Admiralty were important in the early professionalisation of the Royal Navy.

The detailed private diary that Pepys kept from 1660 until 1669 was first published in the 19th century and is one of the most important primary sources for the English Restoration period. It provides a combination of personal revelation and eyewitness accounts of great events, such as the **Great Plague of London, the Second Dutch War, and the Great Fire of London.**

Question 71

Who among the following, after watching the performance of William Shakespeare's play, A Midsummer Night's Dream, observed that "it is the most insipid, ridiculous play that I ever saw in my life"

1. John Evelyn
2. Samuel Pepys
3. John Dryden
4. Robert Greene

Explanations:

Ans: Samuel Pepys.

The diarist **Samuel Pepys is the one who, after watching the performance of William Shakespeare's play, A Midsummer Night's Dream, observed that** "it is the most insipid, ridiculous play that I ever saw in my life." Pepys recorded his thoughts on the play in his diary on **September 29, 1662,** after seeing a performance at the theatre in **London's Lincoln's Inn Fields.**

Question 72

Samuel Pepys' claim to fame rests on his

1. Biography
2. Autobiography
3. Diary
4. Speculative Fiction

Explanations:

Ans: Diary

Samuel Pepys (1633-1703) was an English administrator and Member of Parliament, who is **best known for his detailed diary that he kept for nearly a decade, between 1660 and 1669.** The diary provides a vivid and personal account of the major events of his time, including the **Restoration of the Monarchy, the Great Plague, and the Great Fire of London.** In addition to his diary, Pepys was also a significant figure in the development of the British Navy and served as Secretary to the Admiralty. He was a notable collector of books, manuscripts, and other cultural artifacts, and his library was one of the most extensive and valuable private collections of his time.

Question 73

Who among the following was a famous diarist?

1. John Evelyn
2. John Bunyan
3. Earl of Rochester
4. Robert Walker

Explanations:

Answer: 1. John Evelyn

John Evelyn, (1620-1706), English country gentleman, author of some 30 books on the fine arts, forestry, and religious topics. His Diary, kept all his life, is considered an invaluable source of information on the social, cultural, religious, and political life of 17th-century England.

Question 74

Which two works in the following list are written by Aphra Behn?

- A.   Rover
- B.   Oroonoko
- C.   Soldier's Fortune
- D.   The Princess of Cleve

Choose the correct answer from the options given below:

1.   **A and B only**
2.   B and C only
3.   B and D only
4.   A and C only

Correct Explanations:
"Oroonoko" is a novella or a short novel by Aphra Behn, and it was published in 1688. It is often considered one of the first English novels due to its innovative use of narrative perspective, character development, and themes.

"Rover" is a play by Aphra Behn, first performed in 1677. It is a Restoration comedy that centres around the adventures of a group of English cavaliers in Naples.

"Soldier's Fortune" is also a play, written by Thomas Otway and first performed in 1681. It is a tragicomedy that explores the themes of love, betrayal, and social class in the context of the English Restoration period.

"The Princess of Cleve" is a novel by Madame de La Fayette, a French writer, published in 1678. It is considered one of the earliest examples of the modern psychological novel. The novel explores the inner life and emotions of the protagonist, Mademoiselle de Chartres, as she navigates the complex social and political landscape of the French court.

Question 75

Which of the playwrights have been correctly matched with their works?

- A. William Wycherly - The Rivals
- B. Ben Jonson - Volpone, or the Fox
- C. William Congreve - The Country Wife
- D. Aphra Behn - The Dutch Lover
- E. Richard Sheridan - A School for Scandal

Choose the correct answer from the options given below:

1. C, D and E
2. B, C and D
3. A, C and E
4. B, D and E

Explanations:
Ans: B, D and E

Volpone, or the Fox is a comedy written by Ben Jonson and first performed in 1605. The play is set in Venice and revolves around the wealthy and cunning Volpone, who pretends to be dying in order to receive gifts from his wealthy acquaintances. The play is a biting satire of greed and materialism, and explores themes of deception, corruption, and the corrupting influence of wealth.

The Dutch Lover is a Restoration comedy written by Aphra Behn and first performed in 1673. The play is set in Holland and revolves around the romantic entanglements of the wealthy merchant Jeronimo and his love interest, the beautiful and headstrong Lucinda.

A School for Scandal is a comedy of manners written by Richard Brinsley Sheridan and first performed in 1777. The play is set in London and revolves around the scandalous behavior of a group of wealthy aristocrats, who engage in gossip, deceit, and manipulation.

Prose romances preceded the emergence of novel as a popular literary genre. Which texts among the following fall under the category of Prose Romance?

1. The Pilgrim's Progress and The Spectator
2. Oroonoko and The Fair Jilt
3. Pamela and Clarissa
4. Amelia and Ferdinand, Count Fathom

Explanations:
Answer: 2. Oroonoko and The Fair Jilt

The correct answer is 2. Oroonoko and The Fair Jilt, as these texts are notable examples of prose romance, a genre that precedes the novel in English literature.

Oroonoko **by Aphra Behn, published in 1688**, is an early example of the philosophical novel that explores themes of morality, virtue, and the supposed superiority of "primitive" societies over European ones, reflecting early abolitionist sentiments. The story, drawn from Behn's experiences in Surinam, revolves around the enslaved African prince, Oroonoko, highlighting the cruelty and moral bankruptcy of "civilized" white Christians. The narrative combines adventure, **romance**, and a critical examination of slavery, marking a significant contribution to the development of the English novel.

The Fair Jilt, also by Aphra Behn and published in 1688, presents a sensationalized story inspired by rumors of Prince Francisco de Tarquini. This novella delves into **the themes of love, desire, deceit, and the extremities to which these emotions drive individuals.** Through the character of Miranda, Behn explores the amatory fiction genre, focusing on the destructive aspects of love and passion, which results in a tale filled with deception and murder attempts.

Who proposed the idea that the mind at the time of birth is like a blank slate or tabula rasa?

1. John Locke

2. J S Mill
3. Bertrand Russell
4. Francis Bacon

Explanations
Answer: 1. John Locke

An Essay Concerning Human Understanding is a work by **John Locke** concerning the foundation of human knowledge and understanding. It first appeared in 1689 with the printed title An Essay Concerning Human Understanding. **He describes the mind at birth as a blank slate (tabula rasa, although he did not use those actual words) filled later through experience.** The essay was one of the principal sources of empiricism in modern philosophy and influenced many Enlightenment philosophers, such as David Hume and George Berkeley.

CHAPTER 3

AUGUSTAN POETRY, PROSE, FICTION, DRAMA (1702-1784)

THE AGE OF POPE (1700-1750)

THE HISTORICAL BACKGROUND (1700–50)

> - **Augustan literature**: British style during Queen Anne, George I, II.
> - First half of the 18th century; ended in the 1740s.
> - **Pope** (1744) and **Swift** (1745) deaths marked the end.
> - Featured **novel** development and **satire** explosion.
> - Drama changed from political satire to melodrama.
> - Poetry evolved into a personal **exploration** focus.
> - **Augustan Age** also refers to a "classical" literary period.
> - Applied mainly to **18th century England**, sometimes **17th century France**.
> - Some limit it to **Queen Anne's reign** (1702–14).
> - **Pope, Addison, Steele, Gay, Prior** flourished in this era.
> - Others extend it to **Dryden** and forward to **Johnson**.
> - **Philosophy** emphasized **empiricism**, evolving **mercantilism** and **capitalism**.
> - **Era's boundaries** are vague, rooted in **18th-century criticism**.
> - **Satire** characterized by irony, calm, hiding sharp critiques.
> - **Regulated literary forms** but foreshadowed **Romantic era concerns**.
> - Literature shifted towards **modern sensibility** and away from courtly focus.
> - **Anne (1665–1714)**: Queen of England from 1702.
> - Became **Queen of Great Britain** after 1707.
> - England won a **long war with France**.
> - **Scotland joined** the new United Kingdom.
> - She was the last Stuart ruler.
> - **Anne's children** died, prompting the **Act of Settlement** in 1701.

- ➢ **Hanoverian succession** took effect in 1714, despite **Tory opposition**.
- ➢ The year **1714** influenced writers like **Addison, Steele, Swift**.
- ➢ **Whig** and **Tory** terms emerged during **Charles II's reign**.
- ➢ By 1700, politics split into two opposing **groups**.
- ➢ **Whigs** valued **personal freedom**; **Tories** favored **royal divine right**.
- ➢ **Whigs** supported **Hanoverian succession**; **Tories** were **Jacobites**.
- ➢ **Tories** objected to the **foreign war** due to taxes; **Whigs** saw war as profitable.
- ➢ In religion, **Whigs** were **Low Churchmen**, **Tories** were **High Churchmen**.
- ➢ The **War of Spanish Succession** was led by **Marlborough**, a **Tory**.
- ➢ **Tories** ended the war in 1713 with the **Treaty of Utrecht**.

The Hanoverian Period (1714-1837)

- ➢ **Hanoverians** came to power under unstable conditions.
- ➢ **George I** was 52nd in line, nearest **Protestant** heir.
- ➢ **Jacobites** supported two Stuart descendants in 1715, 1745.
- ➢ **Hanoverian period** was remarkably **stable** with long-reigning kings.
- ➢ **Six monarchs** ruled from 1714 to 1901; **George III** longest-reigning king.
- ➢ **Political stability** led to the growth of a **constitutional monarchy**.
- ➢ **Whigs** dominated 18th-century politics; **Tories** in the early 19th century.
- ➢ **Robert Walpole**, Britain's first **Prime Minister**, emerged.
- ➢ **Income tax** introduced; **Great Reform Act** expanded the electorate.
- ➢ Britain gained a vast **empire** despite losing the **American colonies**.
- ➢ By the end, the **British Empire** covered a third of the globe.

THE ENLIGHTENMENT

- ➢ **Enlightenment**: Intellectual movement emphasizing **reason** over superstition.
- ➢ **Thinkers** like **Locke, Newton, Voltaire** spread new ideas.
- ➢ Promoted **openness, investigation, religious tolerance** across Europe and America.
- ➢ Seen as a key turning point in **Western civilization**.
- ➢ **Key Ideas**:
  - ○ **Rationalism**: Humans can gain knowledge through **reason**.

- o **Empiricism**: Knowledge comes from **experience** and observation.
- o **Progressivism**: Belief in **unlimited progress** through reason.
- o **Cosmopolitanism**: Thinkers saw themselves as **citizens of the world**.

Neoclassicism:

- ➤ Opposed the **frivolous Rococo** style; inspired by **Nicolas Poussin**.
- ➤ Believed solid **drawing** was rational and **morally superior**.
- ➤ **Jacques-Louis David** emphasized precise drawing and smooth surfaces.
- ➤ Art should reflect **rationality and seriousness**.
- ➤ Neoclassicism reflected **Enlightenment values** of moderation and rational thinking.
- ➤ Featured **clarity of form, sober colors, shallow space**, and classical subjects.

Development of Literary Forms:

THE AGE OF PROSE

- ➤ **Pope's age** intensified the post-Restoration movement.
- ➤ **Poetical passion** drifted further away.
- ➤ Focused on **wit, common sense**, and **neatness** in poetry.
- ➤ **Lyrical note** was almost absent in this period.
- ➤ Desire for **perspicuity, edge, and correctness** in poetry.
- ➤ Devotion to **heroic couplet** became almost obsessive.
- ➤ **Pope** was the **supreme master** of this style.
- ➤ **Pope's work**: "rhymed prose...differing from prose...only in the form of expression."
- ➤ **Prose predominance** noted in **Swift, Addison, Steele, Defoe**.
- ➤ **Poetry's spirit** ebbs and flows throughout literary history.
- ➤ **Poetry soared** in **Elizabethan age**, fluttered in **Dryden's era**.
- ➤ In **Pope's lifetime**, poetry was "like veiled lightnings asleep."
- ➤ **Prose dominated** the period's literary scene.

Political Writing

- ➢ **Political Writing**: Authors gained importance, influencing **Whig** and **Tory** politics.
- ➢ Writers were bribed with **places, pensions**, and political influence.
- ➢ **Swift**, a **Tory**; **Addison**, a **tepid Whig**; **Steele**, shifted sides.
- ➢ Era of **political pamphleteering** flourished for both factions.

Clubs and Coffee-houses:

- ➢ **Political clubs** and **coffee-houses** became centers of social and political life.
- ➢ **The Tatler**'s activities were based on the clubs.
- ➢ Literary associations like **Scriblerus** and **Kit-Cat Clubs** emerged.
- ➢ In the first number of *The Tatler* Steele announces as a matter of course that the activities of his new journal will be based upon the clubs.

"All accounts of Gallantry, Pleasure and Entertainment shall be under the article of White's Chocolate-House; Poetry under that of Will's Coffee-House; Learning under the title of Grecian; Foreign and Domestic News you will have from Saint James' Coffee-House."

Periodical Writing:

- ➢ **Political struggle** led to numerous journals like **Examiners** and **Guardians**.
- ➢ **Prose-writers** became key in this political discourse.

New Publishing Houses:

- ➢ Rise in **political interest** and decline of drama grew the reading public.
- ➢ Publishers like **Curll, Tonson**, and **Dunton** employed many writers.
- ➢ **Hack-writers** lived in **Grub Street**, symbolizing **literary drudgery**.

New Morality:

- ➢ **Restoration immorality** declined with **William III** and **Queen Anne**.
- ➢ **Addison** aimed to mix **wit with morality** in writing.

> ➤ **Respect for women** increased, though **satirical coarseness** remained.

Poetry: Classicism triumphs fully in poetry.

(a) Lyric:

> ➤ **Lyric almost disappears**, remaining light and artificial.
> ➤ Best found in **Prior**, **Gay**, and **Ramsay**'s works.

(b) Ode:

> ➤ **Pindaric form** survives weakly.
> ➤ **Pope's odes** were unsuccessful; **Lady Winchilsea** also mediocre.

(c) Satiric:

> ➤ **Satire** was **common** and of **high quality**, best in **Pope's Dunciad**.
> ➤ Lighter, brighter, and more **cynical** satire spread to other forms.
> ➤ **Pope** favored the **epistolary satire** in later years.

(d) Narrative Poetry:

> ➤ **Pope's Homer translation** stands out; **Blackmore's epics** are weaker.
> ➤ Slight **ballad revival** in **Gay** and **Prior**, though imitations are lifeless.

(e) Pastoral:

> ➤ **Artificial pastoral** popular for its rustic, elegant, and easy style.
> ➤ **Pope** and **Philips** were examples of pastoral poets.

Drama:

> ➤ **Restoration comedy** withered; few notable works.
> ➤ **Addison's Cato**: the only passable tragedy.
> ➤ **Steele's comedies** are a cleaned-up survival of Restoration.
> ➤ **The Beggar's Opera** stands out with its vitality and songs.

Prose:

- Distinct **advance in prose** with rise of **periodical literature**.

The Rise of the Periodical Press

- **First periodical: Gazetta (1536)** in Venice.
- Manuscript newspaper provided **war news** in Venice.
- **News-sheets** in England under Elizabeth appeared irregularly.
- **The Weekly Newes (1622)** by **Nathaniel Butter** was England's first regular paper.
- Contained **foreign news**, no editorials or literary content.
- During the **Civil War**, both **Royalists** and **Roundheads** published newspapers.
- **Royalist paper: Mercurius Anglicus.**
- **Roundhead papers: Mercurius Pragmaticus** and **Mercurius Politicus.**
- After the **Restoration**, newspapers became popular but troublesome.
- **Government suspended private papers** in 1662, creating **The Public Intelligencer.**
- **The Oxford Gazette (1665)** became **The London Gazette (1666).**
- The **Gazetteer** became an official post, held by **Steele.**
- **Freedom of the Press** restored in 1682.
- Many **Mercuries** and other periodicals flourished.
- **Advertisements** began appearing in papers like **The Jockey's Intelligencer (1683).**
- **The Daily Courant (1702):** First daily newspaper, lasted until 1735.
- **Whigs vs. Tories** sparked Press expansion in the early 18th century.
- **Defoe's Review (1704)** was a **Whig paper.**
- **The Examiner** was a **Tory paper**, contributors included **Swift** and **Prior.**
- These papers were mostly **political** but had **satirical merit.**
- **Steele's Tatler (1709)** started as a news-paper.
- **Addison** and **Steele** made **literary essays** the focus of **The Tatler.**
- **The Spectator (1711)** enhanced the literary journal format.
- **Daily essay** became the main attraction of **The Spectator.**
- **Steele's Plebeian (1718)** was an early **political periodical.**

The Rise of the Essay

- **Johnson's essay definition**: A short, unmethodical, personal piece.
- Essays should be **literary, easy, and elegant** in style.
- **English essay roots** in Elizabethan **Lodge, Lyly, Greene**.
- **Sidney's Apologie for Poetrie (1580)**: Early essay form.
- **Francis Bacon (1561–1626)**: First real English essayist.
- **Bacon's essays**: Miscellaneous themes, brief, but not personal.
- Bacon influenced by **Montaigne's essays** (1580).
- **Bacon's essays** are philosophical musings, lacking intimacy.
- **Abraham Cowley (1618–67)**: Linked **Addison** and **Bacon**.
- Cowley's essays: **Discursive**, familiar themes like "Myself."
- **Character writers** like Hall, Earle, Overbury gave character-sketches.
- **Overbury** wrote short, pithy sketches like "The Tinker."
- **Dryden's Essay of Dramatic Poesie (1666)**: Not an essay proper.
- **Locke's Essay concerning Human Understanding (1690)**: A treatise.
- **Temple's Essay on Poetry (1685)**: Long but closer to the essay form.
- **Periodical press** advanced the short essay form.
- **Addison and Steele** developed the essay in **Tatler** and **Spectator**.
- **Swift** contributed essays to periodicals.
- **Pope** also wrote for the periodicals.
- **Defoe** had a wide range of miscellaneous work.
- **Essays gained character** with periodical development.
- **Early essayists** lacked the personal, literary style of later ones.
- **Bacon's later editions** (1612, 1625) expanded on his earlier essays.
- Bacon's essays are **disconnected** and lack personal insight.
- **Cowley** introduced a more **pleasant style**, less distant.
- **Character-writers** offered humor and acute people observations.
- **Locke and Dryden's works** fall into the treatise category.
- **Essay format** grew under the rise of journalism.
- **Addison and Steele's** work set the foundation for future essays.
- Essays **evolved with periodicals** into varied, flexible forms.

Prose Narrative:

- **Allegory** still common in works like **Gulliver's Travels**.
- **Swift** advanced narrative by adding satire and story.
- **Fiction** gained prominence in **Defoe's** novels like **Robinson Crusoe**.

- ➢ **Swift's allegory** subordinates to the satire in his method.
- ➢ Moving towards the **proper novel**, discussed in the next chapter.

Miscellaneous Prose:

- ➢ Large body of **religious, political, philosophical work**.
- ➢ Much of this prose is **satirical**.
- ➢ **Swift** dominated **political prose** with works like **Drapier's Letters**.
- ➢ **Swift's Tale of a Tub** is important in **religious prose**.
- ➢ **Bolingbroke's Spirit of Patriotism** is political prose.
- ➢ **Berkeley's Alciphron** (philosophical) and **Steele's The Christian Hero** (religious).

French Influence

Theism:

- ➢ **Theism**: Belief in a **supreme being** or deities.
- ➢ Commonly describes **monotheism** (classical theism) or **polytheism**.
- ➢ Unlike **Deism**, it accepts **revelation** as divine knowledge.
- ➢ **Atheism** rejects or doesn't accept **belief in God** or gods.
- ➢ **Agnosticism**: Belief that the existence of deities is **unknown or unknowable**.

Deism:

- ➢ **Deism**: Belief in **God** based on **reason**, not revelation.
- ➢ Rejects religious texts and relies on **natural theology**.
- ➢ Popular during the **17th century** and **Enlightenment**.
- ➢ **Deists** believe in God through **empirical observation** of nature.
- ➢ **Deism declined** by the late 18th century but revived in the **19th century**.
- ➢ Influenced movements like **Unitarianism** and has modern-day **advocates**.

Denis Diderot (1713-1784)

- ➢ **Denis Diderot (1713-1784)**: French **philosopher, art critic**, and **writer**.

- ➤ Best known as co-founder and editor of the **Encyclopédie**.
- ➤ Studied **philosophy**, briefly **law**, considered clergy work.
- ➤ Became a **writer** in 1734; disowned by father.
- ➤ Lived a **bohemian life** before writing **The Indiscreet Jewels** (1748).

Four Phases of Diderot's Life:

- ➤ **Struggled in the 1730s-40s** to establish himself in **Old Regime Paris** as a writer.
- ➤ **Intellectual ascent** after 1749, gaining fame through the **Encyclopédie** project.
- ➤ **Intellectual celebrity** after 1765, producing important but often unpublished work.
- ➤ **Twilight period** after 1773, supported by **Catherine the Great**, adding political radicalism to his philosophy.

Voltaire (1694-1778)

- ➤ French writer and public activist, key figure in the **Enlightenment**.
- ➤ Voltaire redefined **philosophy** but wasn't a philosopher in the modern sense.
- ➤ Wrote **plays, stories, and poems** with philosophical themes.
- ➤ Criticized philosophers like **Leibniz**, **Malebranche**, and **Descartes**.
- ➤ Defended **natural science** against **philosophical pretensions**.
- ➤ Fought against **fanaticism** and **superstition**, influencing modern philosophy.
- ➤ **Life and career** shaped his contributions to European philosophy.
- ➤ His views reinforced the **distinction between science and philosophy**.
- ➤ Wrote in nearly every literary form, producing **20,000 letters** and **2,000 books/pamphlets**.
- ➤ Known for **satirizing intolerance**, religious dogma, and French institutions.
- ➤ Renowned internationally and fought against **censorship laws**.

Candide (1759):

- ➤ **Voltaire's best-known work, a satirical novella** criticizing **metaphysical optimism**.

- ➤ Influenced by events like the **Lisbon earthquake** (1755) and the **Seven Years' War**.
- ➤ Criticized **Leibniz's optimism** and principle of **sufficient reason**.
- ➤ Thirty episodic chapters in two schemes:
  - ○ Two-part scheme: first half as **rising action**, second half as **resolution**.
  - ○ Three-part scheme:
    - ■ **I-X** set in **Europe**.
    - ■ **XI-XX** in the **Americas**.
    - ■ **XXI-XXX** back in **Europe and Ottoman Empire**.

Jean-Jacques Rousseau (1712-1778)

- ➤ Genevan **philosopher, writer, composer**.
- ➤ Influenced **Enlightenment, French Revolution**, and **modern thought**.
- ➤ Least academic but **highly influential** philosopher.
- ➤ Marked the **end of Enlightenment**, moving politics and ethics forward.
- ➤ **Revolutionized taste** in music and arts.
- ➤ Encouraged **new child education** and emotional expression.
- ➤ Promoted **religious sentiment** over dogma.
- ➤ Opened eyes to **nature's beauty** and **liberty**.
- ➤ **Discourse on Inequality** and **The Social Contract** key political works.
- ➤ **Julie** helped develop **pre-romanticism** and **romanticism**.
- ➤ **Emile** is a cornerstone of **educational philosophy**.
- ➤ **Confessions** and **Reveries** emphasized **subjectivity and introspection**.
- ➤ **Befriended Diderot** and wrote about him in **Confessions**.
- ➤ Popular with **Jacobins** during the **French Revolution**.
- ➤ Interred as a **national hero** in the **Panthéon** in 1794.
- ➤ **Emile** is Rousseau's most important work on **education**.
- ➤ **Banned** and burned for the **"Savoyard Vicar"** section.
- ➤ Inspired the **French Revolution's educational reforms**.
- ➤ **Five books** in Emile: **child, adolescent, female counterpart, civic life**.
- ➤ Emile is educated as a **natural child** removed from society.
- ➤ **Natural education** shapes Emile to be **moral, rational, social**.

- Emile learns through **tutor's knowledge**, gradually integrating social elements.
- Aim is to balance **natural upbringing** with **social adaptation**.
- **Education** is designed for a **well-rounded individual**, not specific roles.
- **Emile** teaches a child to be a man, not tied to **priest, soldier, lawyer**.
- **Rousseau's philosophy** impacted **parenting, education**, and **social roles**.
- His **emotional and naturalist** approach was revolutionary.
- His works, particularly **Emile**, laid the groundwork for **modern education**.
- **Rousseau's legacy** continues through his emphasis on **nature and liberty**.

Notable Works:
- *"A Discourse Upon the Origin and Foundation of the Inequality Among Mankind"*
- *"A Discourse on the Sciences and the Arts"*
- ***"Confessions"***
- ***"Emile: or, On Education,"***
- ***"Julie; or, The New Eloise"***
- *"Letter to Monsieur d'Alembert on the Theatre."*
- *"Letters Written from the Mountain"*
- *"Rousseau juge de Jean-Jacques"*
- *"The Cunning-Man"*
- *"The Profession of Faith of a Savoyard Vicar"*
- *"The Reveries of a Solitary Walker"*
- ***"The Social Contract"***

Questions

The Advancement of Learning (full title: Of the Proficience and Advancement of Learning, Divine and Human) is a 1605 book by Francis Bacon. It inspired the taxonomic structure of the highly influential Encyclopédie by Jean le Rond d'Alembert and Denis Diderot, and is credited by Bacon's biographer-essayist Catherine Drinker Bowen with being a pioneering essay in support of empirical philosophy.

Coined by Theodor Adorno and Max Horkheimer, this term, embedded in the chapter "The Culture Industry: Enlightenment as Mass Deception" from 'Dialectic of Enlightenment,' unveils a powerful narrative.

"An Essay on Man" is a poem published by Alexander Pope in 1733–1734. It was dedicated to Henry St John, 1st Viscount Bolingbroke (pronounced 'Bull-en-brook'), hence **the opening line: "Awake, my St John...".** It is an effort to rationalize or rather "**vindicate the ways of God to man**" (l.16), a variation of John Milton's claim in the opening lines of Paradise Lost, that he will "justifie the wayes of God to men" (1.26). It is concerned with the natural order God has decreed for man. Because man cannot know God's purposes, he cannot complain about his position in the great chain of being (ll.33–34) and must accept that "**Whatever is, is right" (l.292)**, a theme that was satirized by Voltaire in Candide (1759). More than any other work, it popularized optimistic philosophy throughout England and the rest of Europe.

Question 78

What is the correct sequence of various periods of Englah Literature

    A. Caroline Age
    C. Restoration Age
    B, Jacobean, Age
    D. Commonwealth Period
    E. Augustan Age

Choose the correct answer from the options given below :

    (1) D, B, A, E, C
    (2) A, B, B, C, D
    (3) B, A, D, C, B
    (4) B, C, A, D, B

Explanations:
Answer: (3) B, A, D, C, A

B. (1603-1625) The Jacobean era was a period in English history that lasted from 1603 to 1625, during the reign of King James I

A. (1625 to 1649) The Caroline era is the period in English and Scottish history that corresponds to the reign of King Charles I, which lasted from 1625 to 1649. The term comes from the Latin word Carolus, which means Charles.

D. (1649-1660) The Commonwealth was the political structure during the period from 1649 to 1660 when England and Wales, later along with Ireland and Scotland, were governed as a republic after the end of the Second English Civil War and the trial and execution of Charles I.

C. (1660 to 1688) Restoration literature refers to English literature written during the period of the English Restoration, which lasted from roughly 1660 to 1688. This period was marked by the return of Charles II to the throne after the rule of republican governments following the execution of Charles I.

E. (1700–1745) The Augustan Age in English literature was a period from roughly 1700 to 1750, named after the Roman Emperor Augustus. It was a time when English writers were influenced by the Latin poets of Augustus's reign, and their work was characterized by order, balance, and clarity.

Question 79

Arrange the chronological sequence in which the following works were published:

> A. Reflections on the Revolution in France
> B. Preface to Shakespeare
> C. The Social Contract
> D. Treatise on Human Nature
> E. Enquiry Concerning Human Understanding

Choose the correct answer from the following options:

> 1. A, B, C. D. E
> 2. C. A, B, E. D
> 3. D. E. C. B. A
> 4. B. C, A. D. E

Explanations:
Answer: 3. D. E. C. B. A

A Treatise of Human Nature: An Experimental Approach to Moral Subjects (1739–40) is a renowned work by Scottish philosopher David Hume, highly regarded for its influence in the field of philosophy. The Treatise promotes philosophical empiricism, scepticism, and naturalism, introducing an empirical investigation into human nature inspired by Isaac Newton's scientific achievements.

An Enquiry Concerning Human Understanding (1748) is an updated version of David Hume's earlier work, A Treatise of Human Nature (1739–40). Disappointed with the initial reception of the Treatise, Hume revised and condensed his ideas in this more concise and argumentative book to disseminate his philosophical concepts to a wider audience.

The Social Contract, also known as On the Social Contract; or, Principles of Political Right (1762), is a French-language book by Jean-Jacques Rousseau, addressing the establishment of a political community in response to the challenges posed by commercial society as discussed in his previous work, Discourse on Inequality (1755).

The Plays of William Shakespeare, edited by Samuel Johnson and George Steevens, is an 18th-century edition of Shakespeare's dramatic works. Johnson's comprehensive edition, published in 1765, aimed to determine the original language of the plays and included explanatory notes to aid readers in understanding the texts.

Reflections on the Revolution in France (1790) is a political pamphlet by Edmund Burke, an Irish statesman. It contrasts the French Revolution with the unwritten British Constitution and critiques British supporters and interpreters of the events in France, presenting a thought-provoking analysis.

Augustan Poetry

- ➢ **Augustan poetry** in Latin literature flourished under **Caesar Augustus** with **Virgil, Horace, and Ovid**.
- ➢ In **English literature**, Augustan poetry refers to **18th-century poetry**.
- ➢ The term came from **George I**, who saw himself as an **Augustus**.

- ➤ **18th-century English poetry** was **political**, **satirical**, and focused on the individual vs. society.
- ➤ It embraced **wit**, **urbanity**, and **classical Roman forms**.
- ➤ Named after the **Roman Augustan period**, modeled after **Virgil, Horace, Propertius**.
- ➤ Period began after the **Restoration** and ended with **Pope's death** in 1744.
- ➤ **Romanticism** eventually overshadowed the **Augustans**.
- ➤ Notable poets include: **Pope, Dryden, Gay, Swift, Johnson.**
- ➤ Augustans wrote **long verse narratives** or **mock epics**, often satirical.
- ➤ Examples: **The Rape of the Lock** (Pope) and **MacFlecknoe** (Dryden).
- ➤ Used **heroic couplets**, introduced by **Geoffrey Chaucer**.
- ➤ Read **Dryden's An Essay of Dramatic Poesy** and **Pope's An Essay on Criticism** for more insight into their aesthetics.

ALEXANDER POPE (1688-1744)

His Life:
- ➤ **Pope** was born in **London**, only child of a tradesman.
- ➤ Two key influences: **poor health** and **Catholic faith**.
- ➤ His infirmity led to **private education**.
- ➤ His knowledge was broad but prone to **errors**.
- ➤ Being **Catholic** blocked **professional and political careers**.
- ➤ Turned to **writing** as his only path to **fame**.
- ➤ Passionate about being an **author** from a young age.
- ➤ Spent his youth at **Binfield**, near **Windsor Forest**.
- ➤ At 20, he met **Wycherley** and other key figures like **Addison** and **Swift**.
- ➤ Early verses gained **recognition**.
- ➤ His **Homer translation** brought **wealth**.
- ➤ Became the **dominant poet** of his time.
- ➤ Moved to **Twickenham** in 1718, admired and mocked by literary society.
- ➤ Lived at Twickenham until his death in 1744.
- ➤ **John Spence** described Pope as a child of "lovely temper."
- ➤ Nicknamed the **"Little Nightingale"** for his melodious voice.
- ➤ As a child, he was unlike the **outspoken moralist** of his later years.
- ➤ Barred from public school due to his **religion**.

- ➤ **Self-educated**, teaching himself **French, Italian, Latin, Greek**.
- ➤ Discovered **Homer** at age six.

Career:
- ➤ **Pope's "Ode to Solitude"** marked his earliest work.
- ➤ His illness was likely **Pott's disease** (tuberculosis).
- ➤ **Pope's height** never exceeded **four and a half feet**.
- ➤ His appearance made him a target for enemies.
- ➤ **"Pastorals"** published in **1710**, gained recognition.
- ➤ **Essay on Criticism** established the **heroic couplet**.
- ➤ Formed the **Scriblerus Club** with **Swift and Gay**.
- ➤ **"The Rape of the Lock"** secured **Pope's fame**.
- ➤ Translated **Homer's Iliad** using a **subscription model**.
- ➤ **Pope moved** to Twickenham after his father's death.
- ➤ Built a **famous grotto** at Twickenham estate.
- ➤ Translated **Odyssey**, used **subscription model** again.
- ➤ His **Shakespeare edition** faced heavy criticism.
- ➤ **Theobald's criticism** of Pope led to **Dunciad**.
- ➤ **"The Dunciad"** satirized **witless critics and scholars**.
- ➤ Pope carried **loaded pistols** after **Dunciad** publication.
- ➤ "His littleness is his protection" - **Broome** on Pope.
- ➤ Published **Essay on Man** in **1734**.
- ➤ Secretly edited letters, delivered to **Curll**.
- ➤ Scandal over **sanitized edition** of Pope's letters.
- ➤ **Pope's health** deteriorated after **1738**.
- ➤ Revised **Dunciad**, made **Colley Cibber** chief dunce.
- ➤ Began and abandoned **Brutus**, an epic in **blank verse**.
- ➤ **Pope died** at Twickenham on **May 30, 1744**.
- ➤ **Romantic poets** criticized Pope's **artifice** and satire.
- ➤ His reputation revived in the **1930s**.
- ➤ Now considered the **dominant poetic voice** of the century.
- ➤ Known for **prosodic elegance** and **biting wit**.
- ➤ **Demanding moral force** in Pope's satire.
- ➤ **Pope's legacy** endures as a model of **poetic craft**.

His Charactor:
- ➤ **Pope's character** is essential to understand his writings.
- ➤ His **vices and virtues** are clearly reflected in his work.
- ➤ By 30, Pope was wealthy but **unhappy**.
- ➤ Easily stung by criticism, he often **retaliated viciously**.
- ➤ His life was marked by **conflicts** with friends and foes.

- ➤ **Flaws in his disposition** made him highly sensitive.
- ➤ **Stingy**, despite being rich, became a common saying.
- ➤ **Snobbishness** led him to fawn over lords and attack fellow poets.
- ➤ **Extremely vain**, he couldn't handle criticism.
- ➤ Engaged in **deceptive** actions, perplexing his biographers.
- ➤ His **publication methods** displayed duplicity and bad faith.
- ➤ Despite flaws, friends recognized his **curious generosity**.
- ➤ If friends tolerated his weaknesses, he was **loyal**.
- ➤ His core nature wasn't unkind but affected by **vanity** and insecurity.
- ➤ Above all, **Pope was an artist**, driven by his craft.
- ➤ **Lived for his art**, seeking **perfection** in his writing.
- ➤ His work reflected the **joy of creation**.
- ➤ **Artistic perfection** and permanency were his goals.
- ➤ Pope's legacy lies in his **dedication to art**.
- ➤ Ultimately, he will be judged as an **artist** above all.

Major Works:

- ➤ *1709: Pastorals*
  - o Claimed to have written at sixteen.
  - o Published in Jacob Tonson's Poetical Miscellanies of 1710.
  - o Brought him recognition.
  - o **They appeared in 1709, when he was twenty-one.**
  - o They contain the usual trumpery of:
    - ▪ **"sylvan strains,"**
    - ▪ **"warbling Philomel,"**
    - ▪ Other expressions that are **the bane of the artificial pastoral.**

- ➤ *1711: An Essay on Criticism*
  - o Published in 1711.
  - o **"To err is human; to forgive, divine",**
  - o **"A little learning is a dang'rous thing"**
  - o "Fools rush in where angels fear to tread".
  - o Part II of An Essay on Criticism includes a famous couplet:
  - o ***A little Learning is a dangerous thing;***
  - o ***Drink deep, or taste not the Pierian Spring:***—lines 215–216
    - ▪ Spring in the Pierian Mountains in Macedonia,
    - ▪ A sacred to the Muses.
  - o **The Essay also gives this famous line (towards the end of Part II):**
    - ▪ ***To Err is Human; to Forgive, Divine.***—line 525

- The phrase "fools rush in where angels fear to tread" from Part III (line 625)
- Forebears **Horace's Ars Poetica and Lucretius' De rerum natura.**
- Begins with standard rules that govern poetry, by which a critic passes judgment.
- Pope comments on the classical authors.
- He discusses the laws to which a critic should adhere while analyzing poetry.
- The **final** section of *An Essay on Criticism* discusses the moral qualities and virtues inherent in an ideal critic, who Pope claims is also the ideal man.
- Pope refers such as Virgil, Homer, Aristotle, Horace, and Longinus.
- This is a testament to his belief that the "Imitation of the ancients.
- Pope also says,
  - *"True Ease in Writing comes from Art, not Chance,*
  - *As those move easiest who have learn'd to dance"*
    (362–363),
  - meaning poets are made, not born.
- Essay concludes concerning Pope himself.
- William Walsh, the last of the critics mentioned, was a mentor and friend of the Pope who had died in 1708.
- **Attacked by John Dennis,** who was mockingly mentioned in work.
- **Dennis also appears in Pope's later satire, *The Dunciad*.**
- **Thomas Rymer** and **Jonathan Swift were among other critics.**
- Rymer, who had the strongest critique, said, *"till of late years England was as free from critics as it is from wolves...they who are least acquainted with the game are aptest to bark at everything that comes in their way.";*
- Swift's statement concentrated on critics who were damned *"as barbarous as a judge who should take up a resolution to hang all men that came before him upon trial."*

➤ *1712: Messiah (from the Book of Isaiah, and later translated into Latin by Samuel Johnson)*
➤ *1712: The Rape of the Lock (enlarged in 1714)*
  - First published in **1712**, revised in **1714**.
  - **Mock-epic** satirizing a **high-society quarrel**.

- o Arabella Fermor (**Belinda**) and Lord Petre involved.
- o Petre **snipped a lock of hair** without permission.
- o Satirical yet shows **interest in 18th-century society**.
- o Revised version focuses on **acquisitive individualism**.
- o **Purchased artifacts** dominate over human actions.
- o The poem compares **trivial incidents** to the **epic world**.
- o Based on an event told by **John Caryll**.
- o Arabella and Petre from **Catholic aristocratic families**.
- o Catholics faced legal **restrictions** under **Test Act**.
- o **Petre's lock-cutting** caused a breach between families.
- o The title refers to **"to snatch, to grab, to carry off"**.
- o Refers to the **theft of a lock of hair**.
- o In the age's view, the act **brought dishonor**.
- o **Non-consensual invasion** seen as a serious violation.
- o **Summary of the Poem:**
    - **Pope opens** by declaring a "dire offense."
    - A lord assaults a "gentle belle," causing rejection.
    - Belinda is more attached to **Shock, her lapdog,** than to any of the "beaux" who court her.
    - **Story begins** with Belinda still asleep.
    - **Sylph Ariel** warns her of a "dread event."
    - **Belinda awakes** and prepares for the day.
    - Unseen **Sylphs** help with her grooming.
    - **Baron admires** Belinda's locks and plots to steal one.
    - **Baron builds an altar** with love trophies.
    - He prays to **"obtain and long possess"** the lock.
    - **Ariel summons Sylphs** to protect Belinda.
    - Belinda arrives at **Hampton Court** and plays ombre.
    - **Baron attempts** to cut the lock with scissors.
    - **Sylphs prevent** him three times from cutting.
    - **Baron succeeds** in stealing the lock.
    - A Sylph is cut, but "airy substance unites again."
    - **Belinda throws a tantrum** over the lost lock.
    - **Gnome Umbriel** visits the Cave of Spleen.
    - Receives a bag of **"sighs, sobs, and passions."**
    - Also receives a vial of **"fears, sorrows, griefs, tears."**
    - Umbriel pours these contents on **Belinda** and **Thalestris.**
    - **Many people** demand the return of the lock.

- **Baron refuses** to return the lock.
- **Clarissa advises** keeping good humor, but is ignored.
- **Battle ensues** using glares, songs, and wits.
- **Belinda fights** with the Baron.
- She throws **snuff up his nose** to subdue him.
- She demands the return of the **lock**.
- **The lock is missing** and can't be found.
- **Lock becomes a constellation**, outlasting them all.
- **Lock's immortality** in the stars ends the conflict.

- *1713: Windsor Forest*
  - Another pastoral in the familiar meter.
  - **Artificial Pastoral**.
  - Shows a broader treatment, and a still stronger grip of the stopped couplet.
- *1715: The Temple of Fame: A Vision*
- *1715–1720: Translation of the Iliad*
  - Pope **knew little Latin and less Greek**, and that the translation was no translation at all.
  - Similarly Ben Jonson who commented that **Shakespeare knew little Latin and less Greek.**
  - **Bentley, remarked to the chagrined author, "A pretty poem, Mr. Pope, but you must not call it Homer."**
- *1717: Eloisa to Abelard*
- *1717: Three Hours After Marriage, with others*
  - A restoration comedy written in 1717.
  - **Premiered on 16 January 1717 at the Theatre Royal, Drury Lane.**
  - **John Gay, in collaboration with Alexander Pope and John Arbuthnot.**
  - The play, which falls under the genre of **satirical farce**.
  - Satirises various targets, including **Richard Blackmore**.
  - The story revolves around **Doctor Fossil, an arrogant and ageing scientist.**
  - **Doctor Fossil marries a much younger woman named Mrs. Townley.**
  - Subplot the presence of **Phoebe Clinket, a female poet, and Sir Tremendous, a literary critic.**
- *1717: Elegy to the Memory of an Unfortunate Lady*
- *1723–1725: The Works of Shakespear, in Six Volumes*

- ➤ *1725–1726: Translation of the Odyssey*
- ➤ *1727: Peri Bathous, Or the Art of Sinking in Poetry*
- ➤ *1728: The Dunciad*
  - o **Mock-heroic, narrative poem** published in 3 versions from 1728 to 1743.
  - o Celebrates a goddess Dullness.
  - o The progress of her chosen agents as they bring **decay, imbecility, and tastelessness** to the Kingdom of Great Britain.
  - o After Pope **had edited the works of William Shakespeare**
    - ▪ **Lewis Theobald attacked him in** *Shakespeare Restored* **(1726)**.
  - o Pope responded in 1728 with the **first version of his Dunciad**.
  - o **Theobald appears as Tibbald, the favorite son of the Goddess of Dullness** (Dulness).
  - o A suitable hero for what Pope considered the reign of pedantry.
  - o A year later, Pope published *The Dunciad Variorum*.
  - o Pope did not formally acknowledge his authorship of the Dunciad until **1735.**
  - o In 1742 Pope published *The New Dunciad*.
    - ▪ In it the empire of the **Goddess of Dullness has become universal.**
    - ▪ The poet laureate **Colley Cibber savaged Pope in print.**
    - ▪ Pope responded by revising the Dunciad to replace **Theobald with Cibber as the work's dubious hero**
- ➤ *1731–1735: Moral Essays*
  - o Written with an eye on the public.
  - o Addressed chiefly to Swift and Gay.
  - o Consist of pompous essays upon abstract subjects.
  - o **Epistle to Cobham** (1734, addressed to Sir Richard Temple, Lord Cobham), "Of the Knowledge and Characters of Men"
  - o **Epistle to a Lady** (1735, addressed to Martha Blount), "Of the Characters of Women"
  - o **Epistle to Bathurst** (1733, addressed to Allen, Lord Bathurst), "Of the Use of Riches"
  - o **Epistle to Burlington** (1731, addressed to Richard Boyle, Earl of Burlington), "Of False Taste"
- ➤ *1733–1734: Essay on Man*
  - o Owes much to the **suggestions of Bolingbroke.**

- o   At the beginning Pope says *"The proper study of mankind is man,"*
- o   The verse has all its author's care and lucidity.
- o   The style is cut to the very bone, as it is in the well-known line, *"Man never is but always to be blessed."*
- o   A poem published in 1733–1734.
- o   Dedicated to Henry St John, 1st Viscount Bolingbroke
- o   The opening line: **"Awake, St John…"**.
- o   **"vindicate the ways of God to man"** (l.16),
- o   a variation of John Milton's claim in the opening lines of Paradise Lost, that he will "justifie the wayes of God to men" (1.26).
- o   **"Whatever is, is right" (l.292)**, a theme that was satirized by Voltaire in Candide (1759).
- o   Known as Moral Epistles,Ethic Epistles and Moral Essays.
- o   Voltaire called it *"the most beautiful, useful, and sublime didactic poem ever written in any language."*
- o   In 1756 Rousseau wrote to Voltaire admiring the poem and saying that it *"softens my ills and brings me patience."*
- o   Rousseau also critiqued the work, questioning *"Pope's uncritical assumption that there must be an unbroken chain of being from inanimate matter to God."*

➢   ***1735: The Prologue to the Satires (Epistle to Dr. Arbuthnot and Who breaks a butterfly upon a wheel?)***
- o   Addressed to his friend **John Arbuthnot,** a physician.
- o   First published in 1735 and composed in 1734.
- o   Pope learned that Arbuthnot was dying.
- o   Pope described it **as a memorial of their friendship**.
- o   It has been called Pope's *"most directly autobiographical work,"*.
- o   He defends his practice in the genre of satire and attacks those who had been his opponents and rivals throughout his career.
- o   **John Arbuthnot was a member of the Martinus Scriblerus Club, Pope, Jonathan Swift, and John Gay.**
- o   He was formerly the physician of Queen Anne.
- o   Canonical form is **composed of 419 lines of heroic couplets**. The Epistle to Dr. Arbuthnot is notable as the source of the phrase *"damn with faint praise,"*
- o   Another of its memorable lines is **"Who breaks a butterfly upon a wheel?"**

- o The poem includes character sketches **of "Atticus" (Joseph Addison) and "Sporus" (John Hervey).**
- o *Addison is presented as having great talent that is diminished by fear and jealousy.*
- o **Hervey is sexually perverse, malicious, absurd, and dangerous.**
- o Pope marks the virulence of the **"Sporus"** attack by having Arbuthnot exclaim, ***"Who breaks a butterfly upon a wheel?"***
- o By emphasizing friendship, Pope counters his image as *"an envious and malicious monster"* whose *"satire springs from a being devoid of all natural affections and lacking a heart."*
- o It was an *"efficient and authoritative revenge."*
- o Although rejected by a critic contemporary with ***Pope as a "mere lampoon,"***
- o **Contains the famous satirical portrait of Addison, with whom Pope had quarreled:**

> *Peace to all such; but were there one whose fires*
> *True genius kindles, and fair fame inspires;*
> *Blest with each talent and each art to please,*
> *And born to write, converse, and live with ease:*
> *Should such a man, too fond to rule alone,*
> ***Bear, like the Turk, no brother near the throne,***
> *View him with scornful, yet with jealous eyes,*
> *And hate for arts that caused himself to rise;*
> ***Damn with faint praise,*** *assent with civil leer,*
> *And without sneering, teach the rest to sneer;*
> ***Willing to wound, and yet afraid to strike,*** **(antithesis)**
> *Just hint a fault, and hesitate dislike;*
> *Alike reserved to blame, or to commend,*
> *A timorous foe, and a suspicious friend;*
> *Dreading even fools, by flatterers besieged,*
> *And so obliging, that he ne'er obliged;*
> ***Like Cato,*** *give his little senate laws,*
> *And sit attentive to his own applause;*
> *While wits and templars every sentence raise,*
> *And wonder with a foolish face of praise:—*
> *Who but must laugh, if such a man there be?*
> ***Who would not weep, if Atticus were he?***

(Code: *Mr. PP is a critic and messiah locked in the windsor forest near the temple of Iliad where unfortunate lady Eloisa married the Odyssey of Peri Bath.*

Doomed Moral Man Dr. Arbuthnot)

Other Poets:

Matthew Prior (1664–1721):
- His first long work is ***The Town Mouse and the Country Mouse (1687)***
  - Written in collaboration with Charles Montagu,
  - Ridiculing ***The Hind and the Panther***.
  - Other longer works are ***Alma (1716)*** *and* ***Solomon (1718)***.

John Gay (1685–1732):
- His chief works are **Rural Sports (1713)**, modelled on Pope's Pastorals
- *What d'Ye Call it?* (1715), a pastoral farce.
- ***Trivia, or The Art of Walking the Streets of London*** (1715)
- *Acis and Galatea*
- ***The Beggar's Opera (1728)***.
- His ballad *Black-eyed Susan* is still popular.

Edward Young (1683–1765):
  - The Last Day (1713)
  - The Force of Religion (1714)
  - The Love of Fame (1724)
  - The Complaint, or Night Thoughts (1742).

Sir Samuel Garth (1661–1719):
- ***The Dispensary***, published in 1699, is the one work which gives him his place.

Richard Savage (1697–1743):
- His early **friendship with Johnson**
- His two chief poems are ***The Bastard (1728)*** and ***The Wanderer (1729)***.

Lady Winchilsea (1661–1720):
- She became acquainted with Pope and other literary notables.
- Some of her poems, which were of importance in their day, are
  - ***The Spleen (1701), a Pindaric ode;***
  - *The Prodigy (1706);*
  - *Miscellany Poems (1714)*, containing the Nocturnal Reverie.
- Wordsworth says, *"It is remarkable that, excepting the Nocturnal Reverie and a passage or two in Windsor Forest of Pope, the poetry of the period intervening between the publication of Paradise Lost and The Seasons does not contain a single new image of nature."*

Ambrose Philips (1675–1749):
- A friend of Pope, and wrote Pastorals (1709), which Pope damned with faint praise.
- The two poets quarreled, and Pope gave the other immortality in ***The Dunciad***.
- *The Distressed Mother (1712).*
- His poetry was called ***"namby-pamby,"***

Sir Richard Blackmore (1650–1729):
- *Prince Arthur (1695),*
- *Job (1700),*
- *The Creation (1712).*
- They are written in tolerable heroic couplets.

Thomas Parnell (1679–1718):
- The best of his work is contained in ***The Hermit (1710)***

Allan Ramsay (1686–1758):

- He started a **bookseller's shop in the city,**
- Became a kind of local unofficial ***Poet Laureate***.
- *Lochaber No More*
- ***Gentle Shepherd (1725)***, a pastoral drama.

Questions

Arrange the following authors in the chronological order of their birth:

- A. Oscar Wilde
- B. William Langland
- C. Geoffrey Chaucer
- D. John Dryden
- E. Alexander Pope

Choose the correct answer from the options given below:

1. B, C, D, E, A
2. A, B, C, E, D
3. B, C, D, A, E
4. C, B, A, D, E

Explanations:
Answer: 1. B, C, D, E, A

Oscar Wilde (1854- 1900)
- ➢ *The Picture of Dorian Gray*
- ➢ *The Importance of Being Earnest*
- ➢ *Lady Windermere's Fan*
- ➢ *An Ideal Husband*

William Langland (1332- 1386)
- ➢ *Piers Plowman*

Geoffrey Chaucer (1343- 1400)
- ➢ *The Canterbury Tales*
- ➢ *Troilus and Criseyde*

John Dryden (1631- 1700)
- ➢ *Absalom and Achitophel*
- ➢ *Mac Flecknoe*
- ➢ *All for Love*
- ➢ *The Conquest of Granada*

Alexander Pope (1688-1744)
- ➢ *The Rape of the Lock*
- ➢ *An Essay on Criticism*
- ➢ *An Essay on Man*

> *The Dunciad*

Which two poems in the following list are Odes Written in the Horatian manner?

> (A) Ben Jonson, "To the Immortal Memory and Friendship of that Noble Pair, Sir Lucius Cary and Sir H. Morison"
> (B) Andrew Marwell, "Upon Cromwell's Return from Ireland"
> (C) Alexander Pope, "Ode on Solitude"
> (D) Alfred Tennyson, "Ode on the Death of the Duke of Wellington"

Choose the correct answer from the options given below:

1. (A) and (B) Only
2. (B) and (D) Only
3. (B) and (C) Only
4. (A) and (D) Only

Explanations:
Answer: 3. (B) and (C) Only

The two poems in the given list that are Odes written in the Horatian manner are option (B) Andrew Marvell's "Upon Cromwell's Return from Ireland" and option (C) Alexander Pope's "Ode on Solitude."

The reason for this categorization is that Odes written in the Horatian manner follow the style and structure of the Roman poet Horace. They typically contain a measured and balanced form, focusing on subjects like nature, morality, or philosophical contemplation. Marvell's poem "Upon Cromwell's Return from Ireland" and Pope's poem "Ode on Solitude" both conform to this style, utilizing Horatian elements in their composition.

Ben Jonson's poem "To the Immortal Memory and Friendship of that Noble Pair, Sir Lucius Cary and Sir H. Morison" is not categorized as an Ode in the Horatian manner, and Alfred Tennyson's "Ode on the Death of the Duke of Wellington" is not included in the list as an option.

Which two among the following condemned transporting 50000 slaves into England in 1771?

A. Samuel Johnson

    B.   Alexander Pope
    C.   Horace Walpole
    D.   Thomas Gray

Choose the correct answer from the options given below:
    1. **A and B only**
    2. B and D only
    3. B and C only
    4. A and C only

Correct Explanations:
It is true that both Samuel Johnson and Alexander Pope were outspoken critics of the slave trade, and condemned the transportation of slaves to England.

It is worth noting that the transatlantic slave trade was at its height in the 18th century, with millions of enslaved Africans being forcibly transported to the Americas to work on plantations and in other industries. Many people, including Johnson and Pope, spoke out against the trade and the inhumane treatment of slaves.

Johnson, in particular, was a well-known abolitionist who wrote a number of essays and pamphlets condemning the slave trade. He was also a member of the Literary Club, a group of writers and intellectuals who were active in promoting social and political reform. Pope, too, was critical of the slave trade, and used his poetry to raise awareness of the issue.

Question 83

Which of the following statements hold true with respect to Alexander Pope's "Essay on Criticism"?

    A.   It is "an inquiry into the nature and value of poetry",
    B.   It presents "a series of generalizations about good taste",
    C.   It explores the challenges of impartial and just criticism.
    D.   It underlines the traits of "the good critic",
    E.   It critically reflects on Plato's rejection of poetry.

Choose the correct answer from the options given below;
    1.   A and B only

2. B and C only
3. A, B, C and E only
4. **B, C and D only**

Correct Explanations:

A. "An inquiry into the nature and value of poetry" is a fair description of the essay's subject matter but its not entirely true. The essay explores the characteristics that make poetry effective, as well as the role of the poet and the audience in the creation and reception of poetry.

B. "A series of generalizations about good taste" is also a reasonable description of the essay. **Pope offers a number of guidelines for good poetry and good criticism, based on his own understanding of classical literature and his observations of contemporary English poetry.**

C. "It explores the challenges of impartial and just criticism" is another accurate statement. **Pope discusses the difficulties of being a good critic, including the need to balance personal taste and critical judgment,** and the importance of recognizing the limitations of one's own perspective.

D. "It underlines the traits of the good critic" is also true. **Pope suggests that the ideal critic should be knowledgeable, insightful, and fair-minded, with a deep appreciation of the art of poetry.**

E. However, "It critically reflects on Plato's rejection of poetry" is not accurate. While Pope was certainly familiar with Plato's views on poetry, he does not explicitly address them in "Essay on Criticism."

Question 84

In An Essay on Criticism, Pope

A. analyses the causes of faulty criticism and praises the great critics of the past.
B. analyses the causes of faulty criticism and characterises the good criti.

C. analyses the structure of a good essay and praises the great critics of the past.
D. analyses the structure of a good essay and suggest how such an essay could be converted into good criticism.
E. analyses the merits of the poetry of Wordsworth and praises the great critics of the past.

Which of the above statements are correct?

1. A and B
2. A, B, and C
3. C, D and E
4. A and D

Explanations:
Ans: A and B

The correct option is "analyses the causes of faulty criticism and characterises the good critic". In An Essay on Criticism, Alexander Pope analyses the causes of faulty criticism and characterises the good critic. He also provides guidelines for the critic to follow and argues that the critic should be guided by nature and the ancients, rather than by personal preference or the contemporary taste.

In "An Essay on Criticism," Alexander Pope analyses the causes of faulty criticism and characterises the good critic. The poem was published in 1711 and is written in heroic couplets, with each line consisting of ten syllables. In it, Pope discusses the qualities that make a **good critic, such as good taste, knowledge of the subject, and a sense of balance and proportion.** He also criticises the flaws of bad critics, such as their narrow-mindedness and lack of originality.

Question 85

Which of the following poems are written by Alexander Pope?

A. The Dunciad
B. Moral Essays
C. Grongar Hill
D. Cooper's Hill

E.   Absalom and Achitophel

Choose the correct answer from the options given below:

1.   A and C only.
2.   B and E only.
3.   **A and B only.**
4.   C and D only.

Explanations:
The Dunciad is a mock-heroic poem written by Alexander Pope in the 18th century. It satirizes the literary and intellectual incompetence of the "dunces" of his time.

Moral Essays is a collection of four poems by Alexander Pope, published between 1731 and 1735. The poems deal with ethical and philosophical themes and are considered one of the most important works of English moral literature.

Grongar Hill is a poem written by John Dyer in 1726. It describes the beauty of the landscape around the Grongar Hill in Wales.

Cooper's Hill is a poem written by John Denham in 1642. It describes the beauty of the landscape around the River Thames and is considered one of the first examples of topographical poetry in English literature.

Absalom and Achitophel is a satirical poem written by John Dryden in 1681. It critiques the political situation of his time by using the story of King David and his son Absalom as an allegory.

Question 86

Which of the following playwrights have collaborated in writing the satire *Three Hours after Marriage?*

A. John Gay
B. John Dryden
C. Alexander Pope
D. William Congreve
E. John Arbuthnot

Choose the correct answer from the options given below:

1. A, B and D
2. A, C and E
3. A, B and E
4. A, D and E

Explanations
Answer: 2. A, C and E

Three Hours After Marriage is a restoration comedy written in 1717, primarily by **John Gay, in collaboration with Alexander Pope and John Arbuthnot.** The play, which falls under the genre of satirical farce, satirises various targets, including Richard Blackmore.

The story revolves around **Doctor Fossil,** an arrogant and ageing scientist who marries a much younger woman named Mrs. Townley. Shortly after their marriage, Mrs. Townley becomes the object of affection for two rival suitors. The wife and suitors go to great lengths to hide their intentions from Dr. Fossil, leading to comical situations. The plot is further complicated by the presence of Phoebe Clinket, a female poet, and Sir Tremendous, a literary critic.

Three Hours After Marriage premiered on 16 January 1717 at the Theatre Royal, Drury Lane. The cast included notable actors such as Benjamin Johnson as Doctor Fossil, Anne Oldfield as Mrs. Townley, Margaret Bicknell as Phoebe Clinket, and Colley Cibber as Plotwell. Other cast members included William Penkethman, Henry Norris, Elizabeth Willis, Thomas Walker, James Quin, and John Bowman.

Question 87

"A little learning is a dangerous thing, Drink deep, or taste not the Pierian spring."

Which literary critic has expressed the above given thought?

1. De Quincey
2. Alexander Pope

    3. William Shakespeare
    4. Samuel Johnson

Explanations:
Answer: 2. Alexander Pope

An Essay on Criticism is one of the first major poems written by the English writer Alexander Pope (1688–1744), published in 1711. It is the source of the famous quotations **"To err is human; to forgive, divine", "A little learning is a dang'rous thing" (**frequently misquoted as "A little knowledge is a dang'rous thing"), and "Fools rush in where angels fear to tread".

Part II of An Essay on Criticism includes a famous couplet:

A little Learning is a dangerous thing;
Drink deep, or taste not the Pierian Spring:—lines 215–216

This is in reference to the spring in the Pierian Mountains in Macedonia, sacred to the Muses. The first line of this couplet is often misquoted as "a little knowledge is a dangerous thing".

The Essay also gives this famous line (towards the end of Part II):

To Err is Human; to Forgive, Divine.—line 525

The phrase "fools rush in where angels fear to tread" from Part III (line 625[9]) has become part of the popular lexicon, and has been used for and in various works.

"An Essay on Man" is a poem published by Alexander Pope in 1733–1734. It was dedicated to Henry St John, 1st Viscount Bolingbroke (pronounced 'Bull-en-brook'), hence **the opening line: "Awake, my St John..."**. It is an effort to rationalize or rather **"vindicate the ways of God to man"** (1.16), a variation of John Milton's claim in the opening lines of Paradise Lost, that he will "justifie the wayes of God to men" (1.26). It is concerned with the natural order God has decreed for man. Because man cannot know God's purposes, he cannot complain about his position in the great chain of being (ll.33–34) and must accept that **"Whatever is, is right" (1.292)**, a theme that was satirized by Voltaire in Candide (1759). More than any other work, it popularized optimistic philosophy throughout England and the rest of Europe.

Chronologically arrange the following works on literary criticism in order of their publication:

    A. An Apologie for Poetrie
    B. The Art of Rhetorique
    C. Preface to Lyrical Ballads
    D. An Essays in Criticism
    E. The Metaphysical Poets

Choose the correct answer from the options given below:

1.   E,A,B,C,D
2.   B,A,C,D,E
3.   C,D,B,A, E
4.   ACE D.B

Explanations:
Answer: 2. B,A,C,D,E **Corrected (B,A,D,C,E)**

Thomas Wilson (1524–1581), an esteemed English diplomat and judge, notably served as a privy councillor and Secretary of State to Queen Elizabeth I from 1577 to 1581. Renowned for his contributions to **English literature, his works "The Art of Logique" (1551) and "The Arte of Rhetorique" (1553)** stand as pioneering comprehensive studies on logic and rhetoric in English. Additionally, Wilson authored "A Discourse upon Usury" (1572) and became the first to translate Demosthenes into English, marking significant literary achievements of his time.

Sir Philip Sidney began his journey as a poet in 1578, with a relatively brief but impactful literary career spanning 7 to 8 years. His seminal work, **"The Defence of Poesy," also known under the titles "The Defence of Poesie" and "An Apologie for Poetrie,"** stands as a powerful testament to the value of poetry, penned by someone deeply versed in both the practice and the classical understanding of the art.

***An Essay on Criticism* is one of the first major poems written by the English writer Alexander Pope (1688–1744), published in 1711**. It is the source of the famous quotations "To err is human; to forgive, divine", "A little learning is a dang'rous thing" (frequently misquoted as "A little knowledge is a dang'rous thing"), and "Fools rush in where angels fear to tread".

The Preface to Lyrical Ballads is an essay, composed by William Wordsworth, for the second edition published in **1800** of the poetry collection Lyrical Ballads, and then greatly expanded in the third edition of 1802. It came to be seen as a de facto manifesto of the Romantic movement.

***The Metaphysical Poets* by T.S. Eliot First published in the Times Literary Supplement, 20 October 1921**. By collecting these poems from the work of a generation more often named than read, and more often read than profitably studied, Professor Grierson has rendered a service of some importance.

AUGUSTAN PROSE, FICTION, DRAMA (1702-1784)

Licensing Act of 1737

- ➤ **Licensing Act of 1737** controlled censorship in British theatre.
- ➤ Aimed to regulate **criticism of government** through plays.
- ➤ Modified by **Theatres Act of 1843** and **1968**.
- ➤ **Lord Chamberlain** acted as the official theatre censor.
- ➤ **Examiner of Plays** assisted in reviewing and licensing performances.
- ➤ **Censorship applied** to political and religious content.
- ➤ Power originally with **Master of the Revels** during **Elizabeth I's reign**.
- ➤ **Edmund Tylney** exercised censorship until 1610.
- ➤ Censorship paused during **English Civil War** in 1642.
- ➤ **Stage plays returned** with the **Restoration in 1660**.
- ➤ **Robert Walpole** oversaw censorship during the **Licensing Act**.
- ➤ Act remained in effect until **Theatres Act of 1968**.

Clubs and Coffeehouses

- ➤ **Coffeehouses** were hubs for men to discuss current issues.
- ➤ Many became famous due to **poets and writers**.
- ➤ **Lloyd's of London** was an example of such coffeehouses.

- **Will's Coffeehouse** gained fame from **John Dryden**.
- Conversations were not always serious, often **rowdy**.
- Alcohol contributed to **chaotic coffeehouse environments**.
- **Alexander Pope** was influenced by **Coffeehouse culture**.
- **Rape of the Lock** was inspired by **coffeehouse gossip**.

Scriblerus Club

- **The Scriblerus Club** was an informal group of London authors.
- Key figures were **Swift**, **Pope**, and other Augustan writers.
- Members included **John Gay**, **Arbuthnot**, **St. John**, and **Parnell**.
- Founded in **1714**, the club ended in **1745**.
- **Pope and Swift** had the most lasting influence from the club.
- They created the satirical persona **Martinus Scriblerus**.
- Most of their work was unpublished until the **1740s**.
- **Robert Harley** and **Henry St. John** occasionally joined meetings.
- The club aimed to **satirize the abuses of learning**.
- Their work inspired **The Memoirs of Martinus Scriblerus**.
- **Pope's Dunciad** second edition included Scriblerus material.
- **Richard Owen Cambridge** wrote **The Scribleriad**, a mock-epic.
- **Martinus Scriblerus** is the hero of **The Scribleriad**.
- **Henry Fielding's Welsh Opera** was a tribute to the **Scriblerians**.
- Fielding used the pen name **"Scriblerus Secundus."**

Kit-Cat Club

- The **Kit-Cat Club** was an early 18th-century **English club** in London.
- It had strong **political and literary associations**.
- Members were **committed Whigs**.
- They met at the **Trumpet Tavern** and **Water Oakley** in Berkshire.
- Initial meetings held at a **tavern in Shire Lane** run by **Christopher Catt**.
- The club's name came from Catt's **"Kit Cats"** (mutton pies).
- Later moved to the **Fountain Tavern** on **The Strand**.
- The club eventually met at **Barn Elms**, Jacob Tonson's home.
- In summer, meetings were held at the **Upper Flask** in **Hampstead Heath**.
- Members included:
  - **William Congreve,**
  - **John Locke,**

- o **Joseph Addison**.
  - o **Sir John Vanbrugh**
- ➤ Politicians members were:
  - o **Duke of Somerset,**
  - o the Earl of Burlington,
  - o Duke of Newcastle-upon-Tyne,
  - o The Earl of Stanhope,
  - o Viscount Cobham,
  - o Abraham Stanyan
  - o **Sir Robert Walpole.**

SIR RICHARD STEELE (1672–1729)

- ➤ **Sir Richard Steele** was born in 1672 in **Dublin**.
- ➤ He was an **essayist, dramatist, journalist, and politician**.
- ➤ Best known as principal author of **The Tatler** and **The Spectator**.
- ➤ Collaborated with **Joseph Addison** on **The Spectator**.
- ➤ Steele had a varied career due to his **ardent disposition**.
- ➤ Educated at **Charterhouse** and **Oxford**, but left without a degree.
- ➤ Joined the **army** as a cadet, then entered **politics**.
- ➤ Became a **Whig MP**, but was expelled from **Parliament**.
- ➤ Later became a **Tory** and quarreled with **Addison**.
- ➤ Published several **periodicals** and died ten years after Addison.
- ➤ Launched **The Tatler** in April 1709, publishing three times a week.
- ➤ Wrote under the pseudonym **Isaac Bickerstaff** in **The Tatler**.
- ➤ Aimed to expose "false arts of life" in **The Tatler**.
  "to expose the false arts of life, to pull off the disguises of cunning, vanity, and affectation, and to recommend a general simplicity in our dress, discourse, and our behavior."
- ➤ Steele wrote **most essays** for **The Tatler** (188 out of 271).
- ➤ **Addison** contributed 42 essays to **The Tatler**.
- ➤ Steele wrote 36 with Addison.
- ➤ **The Tatler** was closed due to **Whig-Tory conflicts**.
- ➤ Steele and Addison founded **The Spectator** in **1711**.
- ➤ In **1713**, they also started **The Guardian**.
- ➤ Steele was known for his focus on **simplicity and behavior**.
- ➤ Steele's work on **The Tatler** remains widely regarded.
- ➤ Steele wrote some prose comedies, the best of which are:
  - o *The Funeral (1701),*

- *The Lying Lover (1703),*
    - *The Tender Husband (1705),*
    - *The Conscious Lovers (1722).*
- ➤ He started *The Tatler in 1709,*
- ➤ *The Spectator in 1711,*
- ➤ Several other short-lived periodicals, such as
    - *The Guardian (1713),*
    - *The Reader (1714),*
    - *The Englishman (1715),*
    - *The Plebeian (1718).*

The Trumpet Club by Richard Steele

Context:

- ➤ **Isaac Bickerstaff**, narrator of **The Tatler**, was popularized by **Swift**.
- ➤ Bickerstaff is a **humorous astrologer** who jokes about himself.
- ➤ **Mr. Spectator** narrates **The Spectator**, observing **human nature**.
- ➤ Mr. Spectator excels at storytelling through **keen observation**.
- ➤ **Nestor Ironside** narrates **The Guardian**, advising the **Lizard family**.
- ➤ **The Tatler** and **The Spectator** were created by **Steele and Addison**.
- ➤ **Steele** signed both periodicals' final issues alone.
- ➤ **The Guardian** is considered **inferior** to the earlier works.
- ➤ Steele contributed **wit and imagination** to all three works.
- ➤ He satirized **fashion** and urged **benevolence** in response to suffering.

Summary:

- ➤ The author relaxes through conversation before sleep.
- ➤ He spends time with contemporaries preparing for slumber.
- ➤ He views himself as taking a nap before bed.
- ➤ "I should think myself unjust to posterity..."
- ➤ He mentions the club originally had **fifteen members**.
- ➤ The author believes his wit is better than the others.
- ➤ He introduces the first member, **Sir Jeffery Notch**.
- ➤ Sir Jeffery has owned the **right-hand chair** for decades.
- ➤ Sir Jeffery considers himself an **honest, deserving gentleman**.
- ➤ The second member is **Major Matchlock**, who recounts battles.
- ➤ Major Matchlock tells stories of being knocked off his horse.
- ➤ The third member, **Honest old Dick Reptile**, laughs but speaks little.
- ➤ Another member, a bencher, has **extraordinary wit** next to the narrator.

- The bencher recalls **Jack Ogle** stories and **Hudibras** quotes.
- The narrator is respected for his **learning**, called the **Philosopher**.
- "What does the scholar say to it?" says Sir Jeffery.
- The club meets at **six in the evening**, the narrator arrives late.
- Sir Jeffery offers the narrator a pipe as a gesture of goodwill.
- The narrator asks Sir Jeffery to recount the story of **Old Gauntlett**.
- **Gauntlett**, a game cock, won and lost large sums in youth.
- **Old Reptile** listens intently and winks at his nephew to remember.
- Narrator feels melancholy when young men start long-winded stories.
- Conversations often become **Canterbury tales** lasting hours.
- The narrator suggests **laying up knowledge** for useful old age.
- A man's mind becomes a **magazine of wit or folly** with age.
- In old age, they consider their talk **worth hearing**.
- The narrator compares their discourse to **Nestor's** for sweetness.
- The narrator fears being thought **guilty of excess** in talking.
- He reflects on **Milton** referencing Homer's eloquent spirit.
- Milton's passage suggests the spirit's "tongue-dropped manna."

JOSEPH ADDISON (1672–1718)

- **Addison** was educated at **Charterhouse** and **Oxford**.
- He became a **Fellow of Magdalen College** at Oxford.
- Recognized by **Whig leaders** as a future literary supporter.
- Received a **travel scholarship** and toured Europe.
- **Whig misfortunes** in 1703 left him in **poverty**.
- Wrote *The Campaign* in 1704, praising the **Whigs' war policy**.
- The poem brought him **fame and fortune**.
- Addison received various **official appointments** and pensions.
- Married a **dowager countess** in **1716**.
- Became **Secretary of State** in **1717**.
- **Died in 1719** at the age of forty-seven.
- Addison gained early fame for his **Latin verses**.
- *The Campaign (1704)* solidified his reputation as a major poet.
- The poem, in **heroic couplets**, is considered a "rhymed gazette."
- The poem's **style is mediocre**, glorifying **Marlborough**.
- The famous passage compares Marlborough to an **angel riding a storm**.

- ➢ **Whig Lord Treasurer Godolphin** appointed Addison **Commissioner of Appeals** after reading the poem.

  "Twas then great Marlbro's mighty soul was prov'd,
  That, in the shock of charging hosts unmov'd,
  Amidst confusion, horror, and despair,
  Examin'd all the dreadful scenes of war;
  In peaceful thought the field of death survey'd,
  To fainting squadrons sent the timely aid,
  Inspir'd repuls'd battalions to engage,
  And taught the doubtful battle where to rage.
  So when an angel by divine command
  With rising tempests shakes a guilty land,
  Such as of late o'er pale Britannia past,
  Calm and serene he drives the furious blast;
  And pleas'd th' Almighty's orders to perform,
  Rides in the whirlwind, and directs the storm."

- ➢ **Addison's play Cato** (1713) was his greatest dramatic effort.
- ➢ Part of **Cato** was written as early as **1703**.
- ➢ The play lacks merit, showing **Addison wasn't a dramatist**.
- ➢ Written in **laborious blank verse** with dull speeches.
- ➢ **Cato** resonated with political parties of the time.
- ➢ The play ran for **thirty-five nights** and was later revived.
- ➢ His opera **Rosamond** (1706) and **The Drummer** (1715) were failures.
- ➢ **Steele published** the first issue of **The Tatler** on **April 12, 1709**.
- ➢ **Addison**, Steele's friend, offered to contribute to **The Tatler**.
- ➢ Addison's first contribution was in **No. 18**, semi-political.
- ➢ Addison wrote **42 numbers** of **The Tatler**; Steele wrote **188**.
- ➢ **The Tatler** ended in **January 1711**.
- ➢ Steele started **The Spectator** in **March 1711**.
- ➢ **The Spectator** ran daily until **December 1712**.
- ➢ **The Spectator** sold **10,000 copies** per issue at its peak.
- ➢ Addison wrote **274 essays** for **The Spectator** out of 555.
- ➢ Steele contributed **236 essays** to **The Spectator**.
- ➢ **The Guardian** started in **March 1713**, with Addison contributing **53 essays**.
- ➢ **The Guardian** ended after **175 numbers**.
- ➢ Addison's essays **mildly censored morals** of the time.
- ➢ Topics covered **fashions, jokes, conversation**, and light politics.

- ➤ Deeper themes included **immorality, jealousy, prayer, and death.**
- ➤ Addison used **allegory** to express ideas, e.g., **Vision of Mirza.**
- ➤ **Literary criticism** had a mild presence in the essays.
- ➤ Steele first hit on the idea of **Sir Roger de Coverley,** an imaginary eccentric old country knight who **frequented the Spectator Club in London**
- ➤ The **Spectator Club series** became famous in **The Spectator.**
  - ○ **Will Honeycomb, a middle-aged beau;**
  - ○ **Sir Andrew Freeport, a city merchant;**
  - ○ **Captain Sentry, a soldier;**
  - ○ **Mr. Spectator, a shy, reticent person, who bears a resemblance to Addison himself.**
- ➤ The **Coverley papers** could have been the first English novel.
- ➤ **No strong plot**, but essay-series nears the **eighteenth-century novel**.
- ➤ Addison only **referenced** Sir Roger's love for a widow.
- ➤ Introducing **female characters** could have made it a full novel.
- ➤ The series brought readers **close to the first novel** in English.
- ➤ **Swift criticized** the tone of **The Spectator** as effeminate.
- ➤ Swift said, "I will not meddle with **The Spectator.**"
- ➤ Swift felt **The Spectator** was too soft, focused on the **"fair sex."**

Let's have a look at an extract to illustrate both his humor and his style.

"As I was yesterday morning walking with Sir Roger before his house, a country fellow brought him a huge fish, which, he told him, Mr William Wimble had caught that very morning; and that he presented it with his service to him, and intended to come and dine with him. At the same time he delivered a letter, which my friend read to me as soon as the messenger left him." —"Sir Roger,

"I desire you to accept of a jack, which is the best I have caught this season. I intend to come and stay with you a week, and see how the perch bite in the Black river. I observed with some concern, the last time I saw you upon the bowling-green, that your whip wanted a lash to it; I will bring half a dozen with me that I twisted last week, which I hope will serve you all the time you are in the country. I have not been out of the saddle for six days last past, having been at Eton with Sir John's eldest son. He takes to his learning hugely."

"I am, Sir, your humble servant, "Will Wimble"

"This extraordinary letter, and message that accompanied it, made me very curious to know the character and quality of the gentleman who sent them; which I found to be as follow:—Will Wimble is younger brother to a baronet, and descended of the ancient family of the Wimbles. He is now between forty and fifty; but being bred to no business and born to no estate, he generally lives with his eldest brother as superintendent of his game. He hunts a pack of dogs better than any man in the country, and is very famous for finding out a hare. He is extremely well versed in all the little handicrafts of an idle man. He makes a May-fly to a miracle; and furnishes the whole country with angle-rods. As he is a good-natured, officious fellow, and very much esteemed on account of his family, he is a welcome guest at every house, and keeps up a good correspondence among all the gentlemen about him. He carries a tulip root in his pocket from one to another, or exchanges a puppy between a couple of friends, that live perhaps in the opposite sides of the country. He now and then presents a pair of garters of his own knitting to their mothers or sisters; and raises a great deal of mirth among them, by inquiring as often as he meets them, how they wear? These gentleman-like manufactures and obliging little humours make Will the darling of the country." **The Spectator**

Notable Works:
- ➤ *"A Letter from Italy"*
- ➤ *"A Poem to his Majesty"*
- ➤ *"An Epistle to Dr. Arbuthnot"*
- ➤ *"Remarks on Several Parts of Italy"*

The Tatler (1709) by Richard Steele

- ➤ **The Tatler** was a **British literary journal** started by **Richard Steele** in 1709.
- ➤ Published for **two years**, featuring essays on **contemporary manners.**
- ➤ Influenced **The Spectator, Johnson's Rambler**, and **Goldsmith's Citizen of the World.**
- ➤ Influenced later essayists like **Charles Lamb** and **William Hazlitt.**
- ➤ **Steele and Addison** liquidated The Tatler for a fresh start with **The Spectator.**

- The collected issues of **The Tatler** are often published with **The Spectator**.
- Steele used the pseudonym **"Isaac Bickerstaff, Esquire"**.
- The first **consistently adopted journalistic persona** in the first person.
- Inspired by the **17th-century "characters" genre** established by **Overbury** and **Shaftesbury**.
- **The Tatler** featured **gossip and news** from London's coffeehouses.
- Steele mixed **real gossip** with **invented stories**.
- Avoided politics, focusing on **middle-class manners** and Whiggish views.
- Steele placed "reporters" in **London's four main coffeehouses**.
- Each issue was subdivided by content from **White's, Will's, Grecian, and St. James's**.
- Published **three times a week**.
- Steele involved **Jonathan Swift** and **Joseph Addison** as contributors.
- Both Swift and Addison wrote under **Isaac Bickerstaff**.
- The **Tatler** ran from **12 April 1709** to **2 January 1711**.
- The collected edition was titled **The Lucubrations of Isaac Bickerstaff, Esq.**.
- The Tatler's authorship was revealed only in the collected volume.
- The journal's original persona was **liquidated** in 1711.
- Steele and Addison then co-founded **The Spectator**.
- **The Spectator** used a new persona, different from Bickerstaff.
- **The Tatler** set a pattern for future **literary journals**.
- Steele's innovation laid the groundwork for modern **journalistic styles**.

The Spectator (1711-1712) Addison and Steele

- **The Spectator** was a daily publication by **Addison and Steele** (1711-1712).
- Each issue was around **2,500 words** and had **555 numbers**.
- The papers were collected into **seven volumes**.
- It was revived in **1714** without Steele, forming an **eighth volume**.
- **Eustace Budgell** and **John Hughes** also contributed.
- In Number 10, **Mr. Spectator** aimed "to enliven morality with wit."
- The journal reached **thousands of middle-class readers** daily.
- Addison aimed to bring **philosophy to clubs, assemblies, and coffee-houses**.

- ➢ Women were a target audience to elevate their **life and conversation.**
- ➢ Steele stated, "this paper will be more useful...to the female world."
- ➢ He recommended the paper as part of the **"tea-equipage."**
- ➢ The Spectator provided topics for **polite social discussions.**
- ➢ It promoted **family, marriage, and courtesy**, reflecting **Enlightenment values.**

The Rambler (1750-1752) By Johnson

- ➢ **The Rambler** was a periodical by **Samuel Johnson.**
- ➢ Targeted the **rising middle class** of the 18th century.
- ➢ Aimed to help integrate **middle-class into aristocratic circles.**
- ➢ Published **Tuesdays and Saturdays** from 1750 to 1752.
- ➢ Johnson's most **consistent and sustained work** in English.
- ➢ **The Rambler** totaled **208 articles.**
- ➢ Differed in **style of prose** from other periodicals.

The Idler (1758–1760) By Johnson

- ➢ **The Idler** (1758–1760) was a series of **103 essays.**
- ➢ Mostly written by **Samuel Johnson**, with some contributors.
- ➢ Published in the **Universal Chronicle** weekly.
- ➢ **Johnson wrote some essays** quickly, like casual letters.
- ➢ Popular essays were **reprinted without permission.**
- ➢ Johnson threatened to **reprint competitors' work** for charity.
- ➢ **The Vulture** essay was omitted due to **anti-war satire.**
- ➢ Replaced by an essay on **imprisonment of debtors.**

Questions

Question 89

Arrange the following 19th Century magazines the chronological order of publication:

(A) The London Magazine
(B) Quarterly Review
(C) The Spectator
(D) Edinburgh Review

Choose the correct answer from the options given below:

1. (A), (D), (C), (B)
2. (D), (B), (A), (C)
3. (B), (A), (D), (C)
4. (C), (D), (B), (A)

Explanations:
Answer: 1. (A), (D), (C), (B)

The London Magazine: The London Magazine has a long history, with its first publication dating back to 1732. However, it experienced intermittent publication during the 19th century. The magazine features a wide range of literature, including poetry, short stories, essays, and book reviews. It has published works by renowned authors such as William Wordsworth, John Keats, and Samuel Taylor Coleridge.

The Edinburgh Review: The Edinburgh Review was first published in 1802. The magazine covers a broad range of subjects, including literature, science, philosophy, politics, and history. It has featured contributions from influential writers like Lord Byron, Thomas Carlyle, and Walter Scott.

The Quarterly Review: The Quarterly Review was first published in 1809.

The Spectator (Magazine): It was first published in 1828, which falls within the 19th century.

The Spectator (Periodical) was a daily publication founded by Joseph Addison and Richard Steele in England, lasting from 1711 to 1712. Each "paper", or "number", was approximately 2,500 words long, and the original run consisted of 555 numbers, beginning on 1 March 1711.

Question 90

Arrange the following journals in the chronological order in which they started publication.
A. The Tatler
B. The Examiner
C. The Review
D. The Spectator

Choose the correct answer from the options given below
1. A, D, C, B

2. B, A, D, C
3. C, A, B, D
4. **C, A, D, B**

Correct Explanations:

The Review was founded by Daniel Defoe in 1704 and it was a political journal. It was published weekly and it primarily supported the Whig Party, although Defoe himself was a Tory. The journal contained news, political commentary, and essays, and it had a significant influence on political opinion during its time.

The Tatler was founded by Richard Steele and Joseph Addison in 1709, and it is generally considered as the first successful English periodical. The journal was published thrice weekly and was aimed at the middle class. It contained a mix of news, gossip, social commentary, and literary criticism, and it helped to establish the essay as a popular form of writing in England.

The Spectator was founded by Joseph Addison and Richard Steele in 1711, and it was a successor to The Tatler. The journal was published daily and it contained essays, poetry, and commentary on social and political issues. The Spectator was hugely popular and influential in its time, and it is often credited with helping to shape the development of the English novel.

The Examiner was a weekly paper founded by Leigh and John Hunt in 1808. The paper was known for its radical political views and support of the Whig party. It was also notable for its literary contributions, publishing the work of writers such as Percy Shelley, John Keats, and William Hazlitt. The paper continued to be published until 1886, and its legacy as an influential publication of the Romantic period in England is still recognized today.

Question 91

Arrange the following periodicals in the chronological order in which they started publication:
A. The Spectator
B. The Tatler
C. The Rambler
D. The Critical Review

Choose the correct answer from the options given below:

1. A, B, C, D
2. **B, A, C, D**
3. B, C, D, A
4. A, D, B, C

Correct Explanations:

The Tatler was a British literary and society journal published between 1709 and 1711. The publication was written by Richard Steele and Joseph Addison, two prominent writers of the Augustan age. The Tatler is credited with inventing the modern magazine format, in which essays, criticism, satire, and reporting are mixed with illustrations, poems, and other forms of writing. The Tatler tackled a wide range of topics, including politics, literature, science, and fashion. It was especially known for its social commentary and criticism of the upper-class society of the time.

The Spectator was a British daily publication that ran from 1711 to 1712. It was also written by Richard Steele and Joseph Addison and followed a similar format to The Tatler. The Spectator was a more polished and refined publication than The Tatler and targeted a more educated and sophisticated audience. The publication was known for its literary quality, including poetry, essays, and fiction. It was also known for its social and cultural commentary, which was often delivered through the fictional persona of Mr. Spectator.

The Rambler was a British literary magazine that was published between 1750 and 1752. It was written by Samuel Johnson, one of the most prominent writers of the 18th century. The Rambler followed the same format as The Tatler and The Spectator, focusing on essays, criticism, and fiction. However, it was more serious in tone and content and dealt with weighty topics such as morality, religion, and philosophy. The Rambler was widely read and helped to establish Johnson's reputation as a writer.

The Critical Review was a British literary magazine that was published between 1756 and 1817. It was known for its critical reviews of new publications and was a rival to the more well-known publication, The Monthly Review. The Critical Review was known for its controversial opinions and harsh criticism of other publications. It was also known for its political commentary, which often reflected the views of its Tory editors.

Question 92

Arrange the works in the chronological order of the staging/ publication of the following plays:

- A.   A Woman Killed with Kindness
- B.   John Bull's Other Island
- C.   The Double Dealer
- D.   The Shoemaker's Holiday
- E.   The Conscious Lovers

Choose the correct answers from the options given below:
1.   B, D, C, A and E
2.   D, A, C, E and B
3.   C ,D, A,B and E
4.   E, B, D, C and A

Explanations:
Ans: D, A, C, E and B

The chronological order of the staging of the plays is:

- *The Shoemaker's Holiday (1600)*
- *The Double Dealer (1693)*
- *A Woman Killed with Kindness (1603)*
- *The Conscious Lovers (1722)*
- *John Bull's Other Island (1904)*

Extra Perk:

The Shoemaker's Holiday: Written by Thomas Dekker, it was first performed in 1600. The play is a romantic comedy that explores themes of social mobility and class conflict in the context of the shoemaking trade in London.

A Woman Killed with Kindness: Written by Thomas Heywood, it was first performed in 1603. The play is a tragedy that tells the story of a woman who is betrayed by her husband and ultimately dies from the kindness of a man who tries to help her.

The Double Dealer: Written by William Congreve, it was first performed in 1693. The play is a comedy of manners that satirizes the hypocrisy and corruption of the aristocracy.

The Conscious Lovers: Written by Richard Steele, it was first performed in 1722. The play is a sentimental comedy that emphasizes the importance of virtue and sincerity in romantic relationships.

John Bull's Other Island: Written by George Bernard Shaw, it was first performed in 1904. The play is a satirical comedy that explores Irish identity and culture through the experiences of an Englishman who travels to Ireland to open a business.

Question 93

Find the chronological order of the writers in terms of the period they belonged to:

A.   Richard Steele
B.   Charles Lamb
C.   John Dryden
D.   Francis Bacon
E.   Matthew Arnold

Choose the correct answer from the options given below:

1.   ABCDE
2.   BDECA
3.   CBDAE
4.   **DCABE**

Explanations:
1.   Francis Bacon (1561-1626)
2.   John Dryden (1631-1700)
3.   Richard Steele (1672-1729)
4.   Charles Lamb (1775-1834)
5.   Matthew Arnold (1822-1888)

Question 94

What is the correct chronological sequence of the following English non-fictional prose writers according to their years of birth?

    A. Joseph Addison
    B. Francis Bacon
    C. Charles Lamb
    D. Virginia Woolf
    E. Matthew Amold

Choose the correct answer from the options given below:

    1. A. D. C. B. E
    2. B. A. C. E. D
    3. C. A. D. E. B
    4. D. C. B, A, E

Explanations
Answer: 2. B. A. C. E. D

Sir Francis Bacon (1561-1626) was an influential English philosopher and statesman who held the positions of Attorney General and Lord Chancellor of England during the reign of King James I.

Joseph Addison (1672-1719) was an English essayist, poet, and dramatist. Alongside Richard Steele, he played a leading role in the creation and direction of the periodicals The Tatler and The Spectator. Addison's remarkable writing abilities earned him significant government positions during the Whig party's tenure.

Charles Lamb (1775-1834) was an English essayist and critic, renowned for his collection of essays titled Essays of Elia (1823–33). Lamb attended Christ's Hospital, where he studied until 1789. He was a contemporary of Samuel Taylor Coleridge and Leigh Hunt during his time there.

Matthew Arnold (1822-1888) was an English Victorian poet and a prominent literary and social critic. Notably, he launched scathing attacks on the contemporary tastes and manners of different social classes such as the "Barbarians" (the aristocracy), the "Philistines" (the commercial middle class), and the "Populace." Arnold championed the concept of "culture" in works like Culture and Anarchy (1869).

Virginia Woolf (1882-1941) is best known as a novelist, particularly for her works Mrs. Dalloway (1925) and To the Lighthouse (1927). However, Woolf also made significant contributions to the field of literary criticism, writing groundbreaking essays on artistic theory, literary history, women's writing, and power dynamics.

Question 95

What is the correct chronological sequence of the following texts?

> A. "The Advancement of Learning"
> B. "An Apology for Poetry"
> C. "The Uses of the Spectator"
> D. "My Relations"
> E. "How it Strikes a Contemporary**

Choose the correct answer from the options given below:

> 1. A, B, C, D, E
> 2. B, A, C, D, E
> 3. C, A, D, E, B
> 4. D, C, B, A, E

Explanations
Answer: 2. B, A, C, D, E

The Defence of Poesie, literary criticism by Sir Philip Sidney, written about 1582 and published posthumously in 1595. Another edition of the work, published the same year, is titled An Apologie for Poetrie. Considered the finest work of Elizabethan literary criticism, Sidney's elegant essay suggests that literature is a better teacher than history or philosophy, and it masterfully refutes Plato's infamous decision to ban poets from the state in his Republic.

The Advancement of Learning (full title: Of the Proficience and Advancement of Learning, Divine and Human) is a 1605 book by Francis Bacon. It inspired the taxonomic structure of the highly influential

Encyclopédie by Jean le Rond d'Alembert and Denis Diderot, and is credited by Bacon's biographer-essayist Catherine Drinker Bowen with being a pioneering essay in support of empirical philosophy.

The Spectator was a daily publication founded by Joseph Addison and Richard Steele in England, lasting from 1711 to 1712.

Essays of Elia is a collection of essays written by Charles Lamb; it was first published in book form in 1823, with a second volume, Last Essays of Elia, issued in 1833 by the publisher Edward Moxon. My Relations is an essay part of this collection.

Men and Women is a collection of fifty-one poems in two volumes by Robert Browning, first published in 1855. While now generally considered to contain some of the best of Browning's poetry, at the time, it was not received well and sold poorly. How it Strikes a Contemporary is a part of this collection.

Question 96

Joseph Addison was associated with which of the following?

> A. The London Magazine
> B. The Spectator
> C. The Gentleman's Magazine
> D. The Tater
> E. The Rambler

Choose the Correct answer from the options given below

> 1. A and D
> 2. B and D
> 3. C and E
> 4. D and E

Explanations:
Answer: 2. B and D

The Spectator was a daily publication established by Joseph Addison and Richard Steele in England, operating from 1711 to 1712. Each "paper" or "number" was approximately 2,500 words in length, and the original series encompassed 555 numbers, commencing on 1 March 1711. These papers were later compiled into seven volumes. In 1714, the publication was revived independently of Steele and appeared three times a week for six months, resulting in the creation of an eighth volume. Eustace Budgell, Addison's cousin, and poet John Hughes also contributed to the periodical.

The Tatler, initiated by Richard Steele in 1709, was a British literary and society journal that remained in publication for two years. It presented a fresh approach to journalism, featuring refined essays on contemporary manners and establishing a template that would be emulated by esteemed works such as **Addison and Steele's The Spectator**, Samuel Johnson's The Rambler and The Idler, and Goldsmith's Citizen of the World. The influence of The Tatler extended to later essayists including Charles Lamb and William Hazlitt. Addison and Steele discontinued The Tatler to embark on a new venture with The Spectator, and the collected issues of The Tatler are often published alongside those of The Spectator. The journal was originally published three times a week, and **Steele eventually brought in contributions from his literary friends Jonathan Swift and Joseph Addison**, though both of them pretended to be writing as Isaac Bickerstaff and authorship was revealed only when the papers were collected in a bound volume.

Other Explanations:

The Rambler was a periodical (strictly, a series of short papers) by Samuel Johnson. The Rambler was published on Tuesdays and Saturdays from 1750 to 1752 and totals 208 articles. It was Johnson's most consistent and sustained work in the English language. Though similar in name to preceding publications such as The Spectator and The Tatler, Johnson made his periodical unique by using a style of prose which differed from that of the time period.

The Gentleman's Magazine was a monthly magazine founded in London, England, by Edward Cave in January 1731. It ran uninterrupted for almost 200 years, until 1922. It was the first to use the term magazine (from the French magazine, meaning "storehouse") for a periodical. Samuel Johnson's first regular employment as a writer was with The Gentleman's Magazine.

The London Magazine is the title of six different publications that have appeared in succession since 1732. All six have focused on the arts, literature and miscellaneous topics.

Question 97

Which among the following are the titles of the periodicals?

    A. Dickens' Household Words
    B. S.T. Coleridge' Friend
    C. Richard Steele's Guardian
    D. Franz Kafka's The Metamorphosis
    E. Leigh Hunt's Indicator

Choose the correct answer from the options given below:

    1. (A) and (B) Only
    2. (B) and (C) Only
    3. (A), (B), (C) and (E) Only
    4. (C), (D) and (E) Only

Explanations:
Answer: 3. (A), (B), (C) and (E) Only

Charles Dickens, in the 1850s, took on the role of editor for the English weekly magazine _Household Words_, named after a phrase from Shakespeare's Henry V. Throughout its conception, Dickens considered various titles such as The Robin, The Household Voice, The Comrade, The Lever, and The Highway of Life before settling on Household Words.

In 1809, Samuel Taylor Coleridge embarked on his second venture into publishing with _The Friend_, a weekly journal showcasing his broad spectrum of interests from law to literary criticism. Coleridge's disorganization and poor business acumen led to financial difficulties, necessitating loans from affluent friends to continue the publication. Despite initial support, including subscriptions from members of Parliament, The Friend faced an inevitable decline due to Coleridge's financial mismanagement.

Sir Richard Steele, in collaboration with Joseph Addison, co-founded *The Spectator*, following their initial project, ***The Tatler***. Launched on 12 April 1709, The Tatler was published three times a week under the pseudonym Isaac Bickerstaff. Steele aimed to critique societal pretenses and advocate for simplicity in life through The Tatler, which predominantly featured his writings. The magazine was discontinued in 1711 to escape political backlash, leading Steele and Addison to start The Spectator and later ***The Guardian***.

Leigh Hunt, an influential English critic and poet, co-founded ***The Examiner,*** a radical journal, becoming a nexus for the "Hunt circle" which included notable figures like William Hazlitt and Charles Lamb. Hunt played a crucial role in introducing poets like John Keats and Percy Bysshe Shelley to the public. Aside from *The Examiner,* Hunt edited ***The Reflector,*** a quarterly magazine, and ***The Indicator,*** a weekly publication that he likely filled with his literary contributions. He also briefly managed ***The Companion***, a weekly that focused on literature and the arts.

The Metamorphosis, a profound allegorical narrative by the esteemed Austrian author Franz Kafka, was first made available to the public in the German language as Die Verwandlung in the year 1915. The narrative commences with a sentence that has attained remarkable recognition within the annals of Western literature: "Upon awakening from unsettling dreams one morning, Gregor Samsa discovered that he had been metamorphosed in his bed into an enormous insect." (It is noteworthy to mention that, although Samsa is occasionally identified as a cockroach, the original German term Ungeziefer does not specify any exact species of insect.) His despotic father confines him to his sleeping quarters and subsequently, following an incident where his father propels an apple towards him, Gregor succumbs gradually to a combination of abandonment by his kin and his own remorseful desolation.

JONATHAN SWIFT (1667–1745)

- ➤ **Swift** was born in **Dublin** to English parents.
- ➤ He maintained a connection with **Ireland** throughout his life.
- ➤ Swift's father died before his birth; raised by **an uncle**.
- ➤ He was **unhappy** at both **Kilkenny school** and **Trinity College**.
- ➤ Suffered from **ear issues**, leading to **insanity** later in life.
- ➤ Left **Trinity College** in disgrace in 1686.
- ➤ Entered **Sir William Temple's household** in 1689.

- ➤ Took **holy orders** under Temple's encouragement.
- ➤ Gained secretarial and ecclesiastical positions after **Temple's death**.
- ➤ In **1710**, Swift supported the **Tories**, becoming a political star.
- ➤ Hoped for rewards, but **Queen Anne** objected to his early writings.
- ➤ Became **Dean of St. Patrick's**, Dublin, after the **Tories' fall**.
- ➤ **1704–14**: Swift focused on composing **political tracts**.
- ➤ He wrote for **The Examiner**, a **Tory journal**.
- ➤ Key works include *Remarks on the Barrier Treaty (1712) and The Public Spirit of the Whigs (1714)*.
- ➤ **Journal to Stella** was an informal **private log-book** to **Esther Johnson**.
- ➤ It shows Swift's **shrewdness and vivacity** without much scorn.
- ➤ While not as intimate as **Pepys' diary**, it reveals **Swift's inner traits**.
- ➤ Swift is portrayed as **vain, arrogant, but also generous and loyal**.
- ➤ In his **final stay in Ireland**, Swift wrote **Drapier's Letters** (1724).
- ➤ The letters supported **Ireland's revolt against Wood's halfpence**.
- ➤ Swift gained **immense popularity** for his defense of the Irish cause.
- ➤ Spent his last **thirty years** embittered and largely in **retirement**.
- ➤ Involved with **Esther Johnson (Stella)** and **Esther Vanhomrigh (Vanessa)**.
- ➤ His final years were marked by **silence, lunacy**, and his death.

Notable Works:

The Battle of the Books (1704)

- ➤ **"The Battle of the Books"** was written in **1704** as an introduction to **A Tale of a Tub**.
- ➤ It describes a **literal battle** between books in the **King's Library**.
- ➤ The authors in the library **struggle for supremacy**.
- ➤ The term represents the **feud between ancients and moderns** in literature.
- ➤ It's not just about authors but also a battle between **writers and critics**.
- ➤ The work is a **parody of heroic poetry**, similar to **Samuel Butler's Hudibras**.
- ➤ **Modern thinkers** claim to see further than the **ancients**.
- ➤ The **ancients** argue that **all knowledge** is in **Virgil, Cicero, Homer, Aristotle**.
- ➤ A literary contest in **1690** saw **Sir William Temple** defending the ancients.

> Temple argued that modern man is a **dwarf on the "shoulders of giants."**
> The satire includes an **allegory of a spider and a bee**.
> The **spider** is described as "swollen" from killing **numerous flies**.
> The spider lives on a **top shelf** in a **castle-like web**.
> A **curious bee** destroys the spider's web in passing.
> The **spider curses the bee** for ruining his superior creation.
> The **spider** sees his web as a **stately manor**, essential for his existence.
> The **bee** views himself as free to roam and live in **nature**.

"A Tale of a Tub" (1704-1710)
> **Religious allegory,** perhaps suggested by the **work of Bunyan**.
> On **three men**: Peter, Jack, and Martin.
> **Peter** stands for the **Roman Catholic Church**;
> **Jack**, who represents the extreme **Protestant sects**;
> **Martin**, the personification of the **Anglican and Lutheran Churches**.
> Each brother inherits a **coat** from their father.
> The story is written in **Digressions**.
> They alter the **coats** left to them.
> The narrative loses **clarity and coherence** as it progresses.
> Swift develops a **ferocious attack** on **Peter and Jack**.
> **Martin** escapes more lightly, showing Swift's **discrimination**.
> The **satire** is relentless and powerful.
> Swift spares nothing; **everything sacred** is criticized.
> The **Tale** alternates between **allegory** and **ironic digressions**.
> **Allegory** focuses on **Christian history**, mocking **modern scholarship**.

An Argument Against Abolishing Christianity (1712)

A Journal to Stella (1710–13)
> Collection of letters that Swift wrote for **Esther Johnson, his close friend and secret wife**.
> A kind of informal private log-book sent regularly to **Esther Johnson**.

"Cadenus and Vanessa" (1713)
> A poem about one of Swift's lovers, **Esther Vanhomrigh** (Vanessa),

Drapier's Letters" (1724-1725)

- ➢ **Drapier's Letters** were seven pamphlets written by **Jonathan Swift**.
- ➢ Written between **1724-1725** to oppose inferior copper coinage.
- ➢ Swift saw the **coin patent** granted to **William Wood** as corrupt.
- ➢ Swift argued for **Ireland's independence** from Britain in the letters.
- ➢ He used the pseudonym **M. B., Drapier** to avoid retaliation.
- ➢ Swift was honored as a **hero** by the Irish for his defiance.
- ➢ Archbishop King gave Swift the nickname **"Our Irish Copper-Farthen Dean."**

Gulliver's Travels (1726)

- ➢ *Full Title: Travels into Several Remote Nations of the World. In Four Parts. By Lemuel Gulliver, First a Surgeon, and then a Captain of Several Ships.*
- ➢ It is a **prose satire.**
- ➢ Swift claimed that he wrote Gulliver's Travels "to vex the world rather than divert it."
- ➢ The English dramatist **John Gay** remarked, "*It is universally read, from the cabinet council to the nursery.*"
- ➢ In 2015, **Robert McCrum** released his selection list of 100 best novels of all time in which *Gulliver's Travels* **is listed as "a satirical masterpiece."**
- ➢ **Gulliver** announces he published his story **under pressure.**
- ➢ He denies it is **"a mere fiction out of mine brain."**
- ➢ In the preface, he issues **corrections and clarifications**.
- ➢ Gulliver's **fussiness** extends to his assessments of cultures.
- ➢ Swift's book is a **satirical commentary** on society's obsession with **travel**.
- ➢ It critiques the **pious optimism** of **Defoe's Robinson Crusoe**.
- ➢ The novel **magnifies, twists, and inverts** human life's ordinary features.
- ➢ Swift's satire is **hilarious, scathing**, and **remarkably humane**.
- ➢ **Part I:**
    - ○ Narrated by **Lemuel Gulliver**, a **surgeon and sea captain**.
    - ○ First adventure, Gulliver **survives a shipwreck** and reaches **Lilliput**.
    - ○ He is tied up by the **6-inch tall Lilliputians** but eventually released.

- The **Lilliputians' small size** reflects their **small-mindedness**.
- **Political divisions** are based on **heel height**, symbolizing **Tories and Whigs**.
- Gulliver is asked to help in the war against **Blefuscu** over **how to break eggs**.
- He captures **Blefuscu's fleet** but refuses to help conquer them.
- After extinguishing a fire by **urinating on the palace**, Gulliver falls out of favor.
- **Sentenced to blindness and starvation**, Gulliver escapes to **Blefuscu**.
- He finds a **normal-size boat** and returns to **England**.

➢ **Part II:**
- Gulliver's second voyage leads to **Brobdingnag**.
- **Gulliver is found by a farmworker.**
- The farmer exhibits Gulliver for **money**.
- **Glumdalclitch**, the farmer's daughter, cares for him.
- The **queen buys Gulliver** from the farmer.
- Gulliver becomes a favorite at **court**.
- The **king views England** as "odious vermin."
- Gulliver offers to make **gunpowder**, but the king refuses.
- **An eagle picks up Gulliver** during his stay.
- **Gulliver is rescued** by people of his size.

➢ **Part III:**
- Gulliver is set adrift by **pirates**.
- He arrives at the **flying island of Laputa**.
- Laputans are lost in thought, needing **reminders** to focus.
- Obsessed with **mathematics and music**, but no practical use.
- Laputa is ruled by the **king of Balnibarbri** below.
- Gulliver visits **Lagado**, finding ruined farms and **squalor**.
- Scientists work on **impractical projects**, like extracting sunbeams.
- In **Glubbdubdrib**, Gulliver speaks with **historical figures**.
- He meets **immortal struldbrugs** who age and suffer miserably.
- From **Luggnagg**, Gulliver sails to **Japan**, then back to England.

- ➤ **Part IV:**
  - ○ Gulliver visits the land of the **Houyhnhnms**.
  - ○ The **Houyhnhnms** are intelligent, communal, and benevolent horses.
  - ○ **Yahoos**, a brutish humanoid race, are filthy and degenerate.
  - ○ Houyhnhnms are curious about Gulliver, a mix of **Yahoo and civilized**.
  - ○ The Houyhnhnm master concludes **England** is no better than the Yahoos.
  - ○ It is decided that **Gulliver must leave** the Houyhnhnms.
  - ○ Gulliver returns to **England disgusted** with humanity.
  - ○ He avoids his family and prefers **talking to horses**.

"A Modest Proposal" (1729)

- ➤ *Full Title: A Modest Proposal For preventing the Children of Poor People From being a Burthen to Their Parents or Country, and For making them Beneficial to the Publick.*
- ➤ **Commonly referred to as A Modest Proposal.**
- ➤ **Juvenalian satirical essay** by **Jonathan Swift**, published anonymously in **1729**.
- ➤ Suggests solving **Ireland's poverty** by selling **children as food**.
- ➤ **Satirical hyperbole** mocks heartless attitudes toward the **Irish poor**.
- ➤ Proposes butchering Irish children to feed **wealthy English landlords**.
- ➤ The essay critiques **England's exploitation** of Ireland.
- ➤ A blend of **rational tone** and **outrageous conclusion**.
- ➤ **Symbolizes** extreme solutions to solve societal problems.
- ➤ **One of the greatest examples** of sustained irony in English.
- ➤ Shock value lies in **realistic depiction** of Irish poverty.
- ➤ Swift's solution: **"A young healthy child...is a most delicious food."**
- ➤ **Financial benefits** and preparation styles are humorously listed.
- ➤ **Lampoons social engineering** and **William Petty**'s methods.
- ➤ Cites authority figures like "a knowing American" and **Psalmanazar**.

"Journal to Stella"

- ➤ A kind of informal private log-book written by him and sent regularly to **Esther Johnson**.

"The Conduct of the Allies"
"Verses on the Death of Dr. Swift"

Questions

Match List I and List II List I

List I Essayist	List II Essay
A. George Orwell	I. "On the Artificial Comedy of the Last Century"
B. Michel de Montaigne	II. 'Why I Write"
C. Charles Lamb	III. "A Modest Proposal"
E. Jonathan Swift	IV. "On the Cannibals"

Choose the correct answer from the options given below:

1. A – Ill, B – IV, C – III, D – I
2. A – II, B – IV, C – I, D – Ill
3. A – IV, B – III, C – II, D – I
4. A – II, B – III, C I, D – IV

Explanations:
Answer: 2. A–II, B – IV, C – I, D – Ill

The correct sequence of the publication dates for these essays is:

1. **Michel de Montaigne - "On the Cannibals" (1580)**
2. **Charles Lamb - "On the Artificial Comedy of the Last Century" (1822)**
3. **Jonathan Swift - "A Modest Proposal" (1729)**
4. **George Orwell - 'Why I Write" (1946)**

Michel de Montaigne's "On the Cannibals" is a classic essay from the 16th century in which Montaigne reflects on **the customs of the Tupinamba people of Brazil** and questions European assumptions of cultural superiority.

Charles Lamb's "On the Artificial Comedy of the Last Century" is a critical essay from the 19th century in which Lamb discusses the differences between comedy in his own time and the Restoration period.

Jonathan Swift's "A Modest Proposal" is a satirical essay from the 18th century in which Swift proposes a **shocking solution to the problem of poverty in Ireland**.

George Orwell's "Why I Write" is a personal essay from the 20th century in which Orwell reflects on his own motivations for writing and the political and social contexts that shaped his work.

Question 99

Arrange the following in the chronological order of publication

    (A) Modern English Usage
    (B) Proposals for Perfecting the English Language
    (C) Usage and Abusage
    (D) An American Dictionary of' the English Language

Choose the correct answer from the options given below:

    1.   (D , (B) (C) (A)
    2.   (B) (D) (A) (C)
    3.   (B) (C) (D) (A)
    4.   (D) (C) (A) (B)

Explanations:
Answer: 2. (B) (D) (A) (C)

(B) Proposals for Perfecting the English Language: This work, published in 1712 by Jonathan Swift, suggests various reforms to the English language, including spelling and grammar improvements, in order to establish a more standardized and logical system of communication.

(D) An American Dictionary of the English Language: Published in 1828 by Noah Webster, this comprehensive dictionary aimed to establish American English as a distinct form of the language. It included new American spellings and definitions and became a significant milestone in American lexicography.

(A) Modern English Usage: First published in 1926 by Henry Fowler, this influential book provides guidance on English usage, grammar, and style. It offers clear explanations and recommendations for writing effectively, making it a valuable resource for writers and language enthusiasts.

(C) Usage and Abusage: Written by Eric Partridge and first published in 1942, this book addresses common pitfalls, mistakes, and controversies in English usage. It offers insights into proper usage, word choices, and language variations, helping readers navigate the complexities of the English language.

Question 100

Match List I with List II

List I	List II
A. When I found myself on my feet, I looked about me, and must confess I never beheld a more entertaining prospect. The country round appeared like a continued garden, and the inclosed fields, which Were generally forty foot square,. resembled so many beds of flowers.	I. A Description of la City Shower
B. There is likewise another great advantage in my	II. Gulliver's Travels

scheme, that it will prevent those voluntary abortions, and that horrid practice of women murdering their bastard children, alas, too frequent among us, sacrificing the poor innocent babes, I doubt, more to avoid the expense than the shame, which would move tears and pity in the most savage and inhuman breast.	
C. Having to no purpose used all peaceable endeavors, the collected part of the semen, raised and inflamed, became adust, converted to choler, turned head upon the spinal duct, and ascended to the brain.	III. Modest Proposal
D. Sweeping from butchers' stalls, dung. guts, and blood, Drowned puppies, stinking sprats, all drenched in mud, Dead cats, and turnip tops, come tumbling down the flood	IV. A Tale of Tub

Choose the correct answer from the options given below:

1. A - IV. B - III. C - II. D - I
2. A- II. B - III. C -IV. D- I
3. A- I. B - II. C- III. D- IV
4. A- I. B - II. C- IV. D- III

Explanations:
Answer: 2. A- II. B - III. C -IV. D- I

In the quote provided from Gulliver's Travels, the protagonist, Lemuel Gulliver, describes the landscape he encounters during his travels. He expresses his amazement and delight at the picturesque view before him. The countryside is depicted as a vast garden, with fields resembling colorful flower beds. This description highlights the fantastical and imaginative nature of Jonathan Swift's satirical novel, in which Gulliver encounters extraordinary and surreal landscapes during his adventures in different lands.

A Modest Proposal" by Jonathan Swift, the speaker proposes a disturbing solution to address the issue of poverty and overpopulation in Ireland. The speaker suggests that instead of allowing infants of impoverished families to suffer and perish, they should be used as a source of food for the wealthy. The quote emphasises the speaker's cynical and satirical tone, criticising the callousness and indifference of society towards the plight of the poor. Swift's intention in writing this essay was to expose the heartless attitudes of the ruling class and provoke social and political change through irony and satire.

In the quote from "A Tale of a Tub" by Jonathan Swift, the speaker uses vivid and metaphorical language to describe the progression of a bodily process. The quote describes the transformation of semen into choler (one of the four humours in ancient medical theory) and its journey from the reproductive organs to the brain. This passage reflects the satirical and fantastical nature of the work, which uses exaggerated and absurd imagery to mock various aspects of society, religion, and human behaviour. "A Tale of a Tub" is a satirical prose work by Swift that criticises religious hypocrisy and the excesses of human nature through a series of humorous and exaggerated stories.

In the excerpt from "A Description of a City Shower" by Jonathan Swift, the speaker vividly describes a torrential rainstorm in the city. The rainwater sweeps through the streets, carrying with it various unpleasant and unsightly objects, such as animal remains, rotten fish, and vegetable waste. This depiction creates a stark contrast between the dirty, chaotic urban environment and the natural elements of rain and water. The poem satirises urban life and the filth and decay found in the city, using vivid and grotesque imagery to emphasise the squalor and unpleasantness of the urban setting.

Question 101

Which of the following are true in the context of Jonathan Swift?

    A. He was born in Dublin and studied at Kilkenny Grammar School and Trinity College, Dublin
    B. He co-authored a book with Samuel Johnson
    C. He was ordained in the Church of Ireland in 1695
    D. He was a member of Kit-Cat Club
    E. He wrote the sensational novel Lady Audley's Secret

Choose the correct answer from the options given below:

    1. A and D
    2. B and C
    3. C and D
    4. A and C

Explanations:
Answer: 4. A and C

Jonathan Swift, using the pseudonym Isaac Bickerstaff, was an **Anglo-Irish author born** on **November 30, 1667, in Dublin,** Ireland, and died on October 19, 1745, in Dublin. He is widely regarded as the foremost prose satirist in the English language, known for his works such as Gulliver's Travels (1726), A Tale of a Tub (1704), and "A Modest Proposal" (1729).

Temple was engaged in writing his memoirs and preparing some of his essays for publication, and he had Swift act as a kind of secretary. During his residence at Moor Park, Swift twice returned to Ireland, and **during the second of these visits, he took orders in the Anglican church, being ordained priest in January 1695**. Additionally, Swift formed connections with individuals like Esther Johnson (known as Stella), the daughter of Temple's housekeeper. In 1692, through Temple's assistance, Swift received an M.A. degree from the University of Oxford.

Swift maintained connections with notable figures, including Alexander Pope, with whom he was part of the Scriblerus Club. Pope remained an important contact for Swift, and their correspondence continued to link him to England.

Gower then asked a friend of Jonathan Swift to plead with Swift to use his influence at Trinity College Dublin to have a master's degree awarded to Johnson, in the hope that this could then be used to justify an MA from Oxford, but Swift refused to act on Johnson's behalf.

Samuel Johnson, in his work Lives of the Most Eminent English Poets (1779–81), provided biographies and critical evaluations of various poets, **including Swift.** However, Johnson's compilation has been criticised for its negative assessment of Swift's works, such as Lycidas by John Milton and the Metaphysical style in the life of Abraham Cowley.

The Concise Oxford Companion to English Literature instances as examples "**its strictures on Milton's Lycidas, Gray's Odes, and its evident prejudice against Swift**", as well as the hostile characterisation of the Metaphysical style in the life of Abraham Cowley.

Other Explanations:

Mary Elizabeth Braddon, her novel Lady Audley's Secret (1862) achieved great success as a sensational novel, characterised by accidental bigamy and themes that were popular in the early 1860s. It became Braddon's most well-known work, often hailed as one of the most successful sensational novels of the time.

The Kit-Cat Club, also known as the Kit Kat Club, was a prominent English club during the early 18th century. Comprised of devoted Whigs, its membership included notable writers such as **William Congreve, John Locke, Sir John Vanbrugh, and Joseph Addison, as well as influential politicians like the Duke of Somerset, the Earl of Burlington, the Duke of Newcastle-upon-Tyne, the Earl of Stanhope, Viscount Cobham, Abraham Stanyan, and Sir Robert Walpole**. The club regularly convened at the Trumpet tavern in London and occasionally at Water Oakley in Berkshire.

Other Prose Writers:

John Arbuthnot (1667–1735)

> - **Born in Scotland**, Arbuthnot studied **medicine at Oxford**.
> - He became acquainted with **Pope** and **Swift** in **London**.
> - His writings are chiefly **political**, with a witty and vivacious style.
> - Arbuthnot lacks Swift's intensity but has a similar **satirical approach**.

Notable works:

> - *Memoirs of Scriblerus* (1709)
> - *The History of John Bull* (1712 or 1713)
> - *The Art of Political Lying* (1712)

Lord Bolingbroke (1678–1751)

> - **Henry St. John**, Viscount Bolingbroke, was a major **Tory political figure**.
> - He held the position of **Secretary for War** at the age of twenty-six.
> - Exiled twice due to involvement in **Jacobite plots**, he eventually returned to England.
> - His writings reflect **Tory sentiments** and are marked by **vigorous, near-coarse rhetoric**.

Notable works:

> - *Letter to Windham* (written in 1717, published in 1753)
> - *Letters on the Spirit of Patriotism* (1749)
> - *The Idea of a Patriot King* (1749)

George Berkeley (1685–1753)

- ➤ **Born in Ireland**, Berkeley excelled in **mathematics** at **Dublin**.
- ➤ He became a **Bishop of Cloyne** and was a close associate of **Swift**.
- ➤ Known for his **philosophical works**, he combined charm with intellectual depth.
- ➤ Berkeley's writing is noted for its **clarity, gentle irony**, and **disdain for affectation**.

Notable works:

- ➤ *The Principles of Human Knowledge* (1710)
- ➤ *Dialogues of Hylas and Philonous* (1713)
- ➤ *Alciphron, or the Minute Philosopher* (1733)

Lady Mary Wortley Montagu (1689–1762)

- ➤ **Daughter of the Duke of Kingston**, she married **Edward Wortley Montagu** in 1712.
- ➤ Moved in **high literary and social circles** and corresponded regularly during her time in **Constantinople**.
- ➤ Famous for her **strong character** and **shrewd, frank letters**.
- ➤ Considered a precursor to the great **letter-writers** of the 18th century.

Notable works:

- ➤ *Letters* (written during her travels and correspondences)

Earl of Shaftesbury (1671–1713)

- ➤ **Anthony Ashley Cooper**, third Earl of Shaftesbury, was an **aristocratic writer** and **dilettante**.
- ➤ Focused more on **literature** than **politics** and traveled extensively.
- ➤ His works are **pleasant and lucid**, though not particularly profound or original.
- ➤ **Popular during his time**, he influenced **Pope's Essay on Man**.

Notable works:

> ➢ *Characteristics of Men, Manners, Opinions, and Times* (1716)

Usage Policy for NerdSchool Notes

Created by: Instructors from NerdSchool
Owned by: NERDSTABLE PVT LTD

The following notes are the intellectual property of **NERDSTABLE PVT LTD** and are made available exclusively to students who have paid for access. By using these notes, you agree to the terms and conditions outlined below:

Policy of Usage:

Personal Use Only: These notes are intended for your **personal study and exam preparation**. You are permitted to **read** and **print** them for your own reference.

No Unauthorized Distribution or Sale: You **may not sell**, **distribute**, or **replicate** these notes in any form, whether digitally or physically. This includes sharing copies with others, regardless of the medium (online platforms, printed materials, etc.).

No Plagiarism: You **may not claim** the contents of these notes as your own. Any form of direct publication or submission under your name, without proper citation, is strictly prohibited.

Non-Transferable Access: Access to these notes is restricted to the individual purchaser. **Sharing your login credentials** or any other means of access to these materials with others is a violation of this policy.

Additional Guidelines:

For Educational Use Only: These notes are designed to help students succeed in their academic exams and should be used responsibly. They are meant to supplement your learning, not to replace the guidance of instructors or textbooks.

No Commercial Use: The content in these notes cannot be used for **commercial purposes**. This includes using the material in any form of paid tutoring or educational courses that you offer without the explicit permission of NERDSTABLE PVT LTD.

Proper Attribution: If you wish to reference any part of these notes in your own academic work, proper **citation** must be made to **NerdSchool and NERDSTABLE PVT LTD.**

Legal Action: Any violation of these terms, including unauthorized distribution or commercial use, may result in **legal action**.